Helen W. Coale, MSW

The Vulnerable Therapist
Practicing Psychotherapy
in an Age of Anxiety

D0148789

*Pre-publication
REVIEWS,
COMMENTARIES,
EVALUATIONS . . .*

"*T*he Vulnerable Therapist* is a passionate, carefully documented account that will fascinate therapists everywhere who are struggling to continue to practice psychotherapy while surrounded by ethical dilemmas. Helen Coale provides detailed and poignant accounts of numerous disturbing examples of inhibitory regulatory controls and economic and legal constraints that daily challenge therapists who are attempting to survive the minefields of today's practice. All is not gloom and doom, however, as there are many suggestions for professional survival based on Coale's extensive study,

thoughtfulness, and professional experience as a child and family therapist. She gives us much to think about."

Drs. Emily and John Visher
*Stepfamily specialists,
Lafayette, CA*

"**S**ome storytellers have the gift to see the ancient story in the modern light. Helen Coale has hit the bull's-eye with her story of the 'Trojan horse' within the gates of psychotherapy. A must read for all psychotherapists who love their work."

Carrell A. Dammann, PhD
*Psychologist and Director
of Open House, Inc.,
Atlanta, GA*

The Haworth Press, Inc.

The Vulnerable Therapist
Practicing Psychotherapy in an Age of Anxiety

THE HAWORTH PRESS
Advances in Psychology and Mental Health
Frank De Piano, PhD
Senior Editor

Beyond the Therapeutic Relationship: Behavioral, Biological, and Cognitive Foundations of Psychotherapy by Frederic J. Leger

How the Brain Talks to Itself: A Clinical Primer of Psychotherapeutic Neuroscience by Jay E. Harris

Cross-Cultural Counseling: The Arab-Palestinian Case by Marwan Dwairy

The Vulnerable Therapist: Practicing Psychotherapy in an Age of Anxiety by Helen W. Coale

The Vulnerable Therapist
Practicing Psychotherapy in an Age of Anxiety

Helen W. Coale, MSW

The Haworth Press
New York • London

The Haworth Press, Inc., 10 Alice Street, Binghamton, NY 13904-1580

Quotations in Chapters 7 and 10 from *A Chorus of Stones* by Susan Griffin. Copyright © 1992 by Susan Griffin. Used by permission of Doubleday, a division of Bantam Doubleday Dell Publishing Group, Inc.

Quotations in Chapters 2, 12, and 13 from *Many Winters* by Nancy Wood. Copyright © 1974 by Nancy Wood. Illustrations © 1974 by Frank Howell. Used by permission of Bantam Doubleday Dell Books for Young Readers.

Quotations in Chapters 3, 11, and 14 from *The Phantom Tollbooth* by Norton Juster. Copyright © 1961 by Norton Juster. Used by permission of Random House, Inc.

Quotations from M.S. Wylie, "Looking for the Fence Posts" from *Family Therapy Networker*, March/April 1989 and Frank Pittman, "It's Not My Fault," January/February 1992. Used by permission.

Cover design by Monica L. Seifert.

Library of Congress Cataloging-in-Publication Data

Coale, Helen W.
    The vulnerable therapist : practicing psychotherapy in an age of anxiety / Helen W. Coale.
      p. cm.
    Includes bibliographical references and index.
    ISBN 0-7890-0480-1 (alk. paper).
    1. Psychotherapists—Professional ethics. 2. Psychotherapy—Moral and ethical aspects. 3. Psychotherapists—Job stress. I. Title.
RC455.2.E8C6 1998
616.89′14—dc21   97-37272
                                                                        CIP

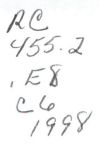
To my mother, Louella Mead Coale,
who inspired me to think creatively about ethics.

ABOUT THE AUTHOR

Helen Coale, LCSW, LMFT, is a licensed marriage and family therapist and social worker at the Atlanta Area Child Guidance Clinic in Atlanta, Georgia. An experienced supervisor and psychotherapist for children, adolescents, adults, and families, she has published on such topics as family therapy, divorce and remarriage, child welfare, brief therapy, use of humor and ritual in therapy, and the interface between psychotherapy and the law. In her spare time, she gardens, sings in a choir, constructs dollhouses, sews, and travels. Fluently bilingual, she has an international family—two daughters of Korean heritage and a husband, stepchildren, and stepgrandchildren who are Italian citizens. She also recently became a grandmother.

CONTENTS

Preface:
Informed Consent for the Reader

This is a passionate book. It is born out of my love of being a psychotherapist for twenty-eight years and my joy in supervising, teaching, and mentoring young therapists struggling to be creative, healing, and ethical in their relationships with clients. It is born out of my gratitude for how my experiences with clients and supervisees have enriched my life, stimulated my creative juices, and awed and humbled me in the presence of the human resilience and richness of spirit I have been privileged to witness.

It is also born out of my dismay and alarm at how the mental health professions are changing to accommodate the mentality of bottom-line market forces based on a narcissistic, exploitative self-interest that victimizes both clients and the professionals who serve them. It is born out of my anger that professionals are increasingly being held accountable for their own individual ethics in a context of professional sell-out to these unethical market forces.

In the very recent past, any gathering of therapists was a rejuvenating experience for me. I could count on nourishment and support, the exchange of creative ideas, and optimism and hope in the face of the difficult problems clients present to us. Now, any gathering of therapists is dominated by conversation about two primary concerns: shrinking resources and economic insecurity, and anxiety about litigation and ethics complaints. I leave such gatherings not restored and nourished, but anxious and depleted. What is happening?

About fifteen years ago, I supervised a clinical situation in which Stanley, an eight-year-old boy, had been referred to my training program for a diagnosis (Coale, 1989a). It was needed by the school system in considering whether or not to place Stanley in a psychoeducational setting for severely emotionally disturbed children. The attorney representing his mother also needed it as he litigated child custody arrangements with her abusive ex-husband.

Stanley had been in trouble at school for acting-out behavior and had gotten the family involved with Protective Services by breaking his younger sister's arm. His mother was at her wit's end, not only because of his behavior at home, but also because of her emotional drain from dealing with the school, the Protective Services agency, her lawyer, and her ex-husband. She was considering placing Stanley in a psychiatric hospital.

I understood Stanley's dilemma to be confusion in the face of his mother's unstated but powerful expectations that he function as a coparent to his two younger siblings and as the new man of the house to help with his mother's anxiety and depression. In expecting of himself what no eight-year-old could possibly do, the boy was failing abominably.

Because his mother wanted a diagnosis, I suggested to the supervisee that we diagnose him as an "emotionally disturbed pseudoadult." In presenting this to his mother, we told her that Stanley was capable of functioning like a normal eight-year-old, but was headed for additional trouble if he had to continue functioning as an adult. We asked her to tell us whether she wanted help in treating him as an eight-year-old or as an adult. If she chose the latter, she would have our help in researching psychiatric resources to assist him throughout the course of his lifetime. If she chose the former, she would probably not need this kind of assistance because Stanley was capable of being a normal eight-year-old. She, of course, chose the former and proceeded to prove to us that she could remove adult responsibilities from his life. There was a dramatic change in both Stanley and his mother after two weeks. The treatment then focused on helping her build a life for herself so that Stanley would no longer feel obligated to assume adult responsibilities.

At the end of the therapy relationship, we asked her to plan a celebration of her success. This was a training case, so there were several therapists participating behind a one-way mirror. She brought in a cake and a bottle of champagne for her last session and talked about her successes in therapy and her future goals (she was working on a psychology degree!). One by one, the therapist, the supervisor, and each of the therapists came into the room, toasted the mother with a glass of the champagne, and thanked her for something that she taught them during the therapy process. It was one of the most empowering sessions—for the client, for the therapists, and for me (the supervisor)—I have ever experienced.

I hope that I would come up with similar creative ideas if faced with the same kind of clinical situation today. However, I would probably be aware, somewhere in my consciousness, of concern about risks of misdiagnosis (emotionally disturbed pseudoadult is not in DSM-IV [American Psychiatric Association, 1994]), of authoritarianism (we did, after all, give the mother a kind of forced choice between two options), and of dual role allegations (we accepted the mother's gift of champagne and cake in her termination session). And if I let my awareness turn to anxiety about misdiagnosis or dual roles, I would probably not think or act as creatively. The client, the therapists in training, and I would all be lesser for it.

This is what is happening in the psychotherapy professions today. Our vision is colored by our anxiety about litigiousness and risk. This anxiety destroys trust and joy and hope and love and compassion and all of the values that led me to become a therapist in the first place. And it makes me *angry*. I do not like attorneys assuming such a powerful role in determining what I can and cannot do as a therapist. I do not like the fearful, anxious response to contextual problems that the mental health professions are taking.

So, in the spirit of informed consent, please be advised that this is not a neutral book. It is a book about the *heart* and the *soul* of ethical thinking—the *ethical being* of the therapist. It is a book with a passionate point of view.

It is not a book about the *rules* of risk management, the do's and don'ts of ethical practice, or the how-to's of ethical behavior. It *will* examine the impossibilities of some of our current ethics rules and critique the profession's adaptation to an inherently unethical business context. It *will* analyze how the professions have made clients and their therapists *more*, rather than *less*, vulnerable. It *will* suggest ways of using our vulnerability on behalf of our clients—of advertising rather than concealing the ethical dilemmas of the mental health professions.

My agenda is to stimulate critical thinking and to challenge the reader to become more proactive in questioning and changing, instead of adapting to and fearing what is happening in the arena of professional ethics today. The very survival of the psychotherapy professions *requires* change. We must either change or become obsolete.

Again, in the nature of informed consent, the price of reading this book may be costly. You may find yourself donating more time to pro bono work; withdrawing from a managed care contract or two; spending more nonreimbursable time reading or attending meetings with similar-minded professionals; volunteering to serve in some professional or politically active capacity; or renewing your artistic, spiritual, physical, and relationship interests. You also may find yourself challenging some of the ethics rules that are increasingly limiting the possibilities for you with your clients.

I hope that, after being so informed, you will still consent to read this book. I encourage you to read it as part of an ongoing dialogue— a conversation to create new ethical meanings in the practice of psychotherapy.

H. W. Coale

Acknowledgments

I wish to thank my husband, Carlo Finetti, for his unending support, nurturance, and faith in me as I wrote this book. To my daughters, Shinae and Myung, I am grateful for what they have taught me and continue to teach me—about ethics, morality, and different perspectives on life and the world. To my clients, supervisees, students, consultees, and colleagues, thank you for your continued presence and teaching in my life. To Kathy Couch, I am grateful for your help in editing this book.

Chapter 1

Introduction:
Ethical Contexts, Ethical Rules

. . . [W]e ask of a proposition not whether it is true or false, but in what kind of possible world it would be true.

—J. Bruner
Actual Minds, Possible Worlds

. . . [W]e do not relate to life "itself" but to our understanding of it.

—T. Andersen
"Reflections on Reflecting with Families"

This book is an exploration of therapist and client vulnerability in a professional context that is increasingly (and unethically) rule-based. While giving lip service to client protection, the mental health professions are equally concerned with risk management, i.e., with *protecting the therapist* from threats of litigation and ethics complaints by clients. This pits clients and therapists against one another and exacerbates the vulnerability of both.

What we need is a total revamping of our basic premises about ethics. We must move from rule-based ethics, which minimize rather than maximize healing possibilities in therapy relationships, to context-based ethics, which encourage ethical thinking, feeling, and behaving that are relevant to the uniqueness of each client and each client-therapist relationship. Context-based ethics facilitate ethical decision making as a *process,* not as a *regulation*, and rely on therapist use of self in relationships. Attention to the uniqueness of each client-therapist situation and the capacity of the therapist to facilitate an ethical process is the focus.

WHAT IS CONTEXT?

By context, I include not only the system of *people* involved in any therapeutic endeavor—the clients, their families, the professional helpers, their behaviors and interactions—but also the collective *meaning* in each system. This is consistent with constructivism's emphasis on the problem-determined or linguistically-determined system, the system of *meaning*, rather than people (Epstein and Loos, 1989; Goolishian and Anderson, 1988; Hoffman, 1985, 1990). Thus, context is how people talk, think, and believe about a problem.

To illustrate, take the simple example of a behavior such as drinking wine. Drinking wine has different meanings depending on the context. In a communion service it has a spiritual meaning. At a wedding celebration it has a ritual meaning. At a cocktail party it has a social and, perhaps, a business meaning. At an AA meeting it has a deviant meaning. In a therapy office it has an unethical meaning. In every context the meaning varies. And even within one context the meaning is different for each individual participant.

There are certain consensual meanings inherent in any therapy context. Therapy is a process in which one or more persons meet with a professionally trained therapist to solve a problem that they have been unable to solve, usually because they have become demoralized about the chances of doing so (Miller, Duncan, and Hubble, 1997). The therapist has expertise and power along with caring and compassion. The client gives up some power and trusts the therapist to work in her best interests, not exploiting her sexually or in any other way. Hopefully, by the end of therapy, the therapist will have helped her solve the problem.

Beyond this very general meaning, each therapy relationship—depending on therapist theoretical orientation, person of the therapist, practice setting, and individual client—varies in the meanings cocreated between therapist and client. The problem definition and resolution plan will be different in each situation. The same symptom can be defined in a myriad of ways. The same resolution behaviors between therapist and client can have many different meanings depending on the context of the therapist-client relationship.

The symptom of bedwetting, for example, can be viewed by the therapist as a physiological problem, a behavioral problem, a family organizational problem, a stuck problem/solution/problem cycle, a developmental crisis or delay, or a product of symbiosis in the parent-child dyad. From the child's perspective, bedwetting may be a nonproblem, a physical discomfort, an anxiety-provoking scene because it upsets his parents, a barrier to spending the night with other children, a way of getting back at perfectionistic parents, or a mysterious force that visits him in the night. From his parents' perspective, it may be something he will outgrow, a hostile rebellion, an ordeal, a sleep disturbance, a sign of parental deficiency, or a hereditary problem.

Putting together everyone's beliefs in a consensual meaning that conveys a plan for problem resolution, is the task of the therapist and clients together. Each situation will be different. The same behavior—bedwetting—can be resolved in a multitude of ways depending on how the clients and the therapist together define the problem's meaning.

If the resolution plan is taken out of the context of consensual meaning, it is useless. Hence, therapists who "apply" interventions "to" clients usually find that the solutions do not work because the therapist's meaning about the problem does not fit the client's meaning. A therapist who, for example, understands bedwetting as a symptom of cross-generational coalitions in the family, paired with parents who insist that the child will outgrow it, will encounter only resistance in trying to strengthen the marital bond and detriangulate the child. She has to first build some bridge between *her* meaning of the symptom and the *parents'* meaning that can then evolve into something with which the parents can agree. Many therapy failures occur because the therapist intervenes with *her* meaning before building such a bridge with the client. When the therapy fails, the *client* is then labeled resistant.

Perhaps, in the above example, the *child's* meaning will assist the therapist in building the bridge between her meaning of the symptom and the parents' meaning. Let's say that the child understands bedwetting as a kind of monster that overtakes him in the night. The therapist can combine her organizational theory and the parents' developmental beliefs with the child's monster theory. If a monster is disrupting the family by causing troubles upon which the parents must focus, keeping them from getting a good night's sleep in the marital bed (therapist's organizational theory), do the parents have hope that as the boy gets older (parents' developmental theory), he will have the strength to kick the monster from his bed (child's theory)? How old do the parents feel the child must be to do this? Do they think it is time to begin assisting him in this endeavor now?

If the parents agree with *this* meaning, then they, the therapist, and the child can begin developing a solution. Perhaps their strategy will be to establish ways of kicking the monster out of the child's bed (White, 1984). Perhaps they will make friends with the monster and "tame" it. The possibilities are endless; they all emanate from the consensual meaning that therapist and clients create together.

Suppose the therapist, in talking about the case, presents only the solution *behaviors* to her colleagues. She tells them that her latest solution for bedwetting is to ask the family to get up in the middle of the night and talk to the monster that causes the bedwetting. Depending upon theoretical orientation, the listeners might interpret this as a kind of ordeal therapy or as an exaggeration of the parental detour of marital problems through the child's symptomatic behavior and, hence, an attempt to restore appropriate hierarchy in the family. They might see it as a pattern disruption, or perhaps delusional thinking on the part of the therapist for accepting, rather than trying to correct, the child's primitive thinking. Unless the therapist explains the *meaning context* of the bedwetting cure, her approach cannot be understood by the listening therapists.

THE RELEVANCE OF CONTEXT
TO PROFESSIONAL ETHICS

Because the nature of the therapist-client relationship—and the meanings that evolve within it—are, by necessity, ambiguous, the context in which ethical decision making occurs is also ambiguous. What is ethical in one situation is not ethical in another. Ethical meanings vary. The imposition of the therapist's ethics on the client, without an attempt to build bridges to the client's ethics, does not work any more than the imposition of *any* therapist meaning on the client. Ethics are shaped in the context of the client-therapist relationship.

To continue with the bedwetting example, suppose that the monster-taming idea works and, at the end of the therapeutic relationship, the child and parents request closure through a ritual honoring the monster's retirement. The child, with the parents' full support, wants to have a ceremony by his bed to ban the monster from soiling his sheets. The therapist is invited to be a part of the ceremony and agrees to consider it. In the ethics of parents and child, inviting the therapist to their home for such a ritual is congruent with the therapist's involvement in taming the monster. For them, it is a healing way to terminate the therapy relationship.

In considering the family's request, the therapist takes into account the appropriateness of it from *their* point of view and decides that the ritual will be an important part of everyone's closure. She discusses with the family some of the possible complications regarding how the family will experience shifting from her office to their home and, in this conversation, realizes that the family is totally comfortable with this shift. She makes the home visit, participates in the monster's retirement ceremony, and celebrates the family's success.

Later, the therapist describes the termination session in a conversation with colleagues. Without understanding the entire treatment context created between therapist and clients, several colleagues challenge her on the appropriateness of her boundaries in shifting from office to home. They suggest the possibility that she was participating in a social, not a therapy, agenda with the family. They express concern that she could be accused of creating an unethical dual role with the child and his parents.

This is the kind of thinking that is prevalent in the mental health professions these days. Behavior taken out of context can be framed as unethical. The same therapist, working with a different kind of client, would not consider a home visit as part of the treatment. With the monster-taming family, however, a home visit was congruent with the treatment frame and was inherently ethical. To refuse to participate in the monster's retirement, based only on the profession's paranoia about the ethics police and without regard for the family's genuine and appropriate wish for this kind of closure, would be unethical.

Ethics are contingent on context. There is no way, given a few exceptions such as sexual or business exploitation of clients, that ethics rules can be legislated. What is ethical in one situation may not be ethical in another. As discussed in the following section, rule-based ethics circumscribe ethical thinking.

PROBLEMS WITH RULE-BASED ETHICS

> There is a saying, *tu puedes saber muchas cosas*, you can know about things, but it is not the same as *sentido*, possessing sense. (Estés, 1992, p. 188)

The problems with rule-based ethics include the following: their lack of attention to the variability of human need; their use as a substitution for ethical thinking; their privileging of professional over client voices; their ethnocentric representations of reality; their hidden agendas; and their legal, risk management emphasis.

The Variability of Human Need

As illustrated in the monster-taming case, rule-based ethics do not fit every situation. A home visit that is appropriate in one client-therapist relationship may be intrusive in another. Self-disclosure, touch, boundaries, and all of the other buzzwords in our current codes vary in their ethicality in each individual client-therapist relationship. Uniform truths simply cannot be applied to human relationships because they do not take into account the immense variability of human need, emotion, cognition, and mean-ing. Rule-based ethics rest on the assumption that clients are basi-cally alike and therefore require uniform therapeutic responses. They also ignore legitimate variations in therapist theoretical orientations and personal characteristics that inform treatment decisions.

The Privileging of Professional Truths

The uniform application of rules to different therapist-client rela-tionships is unethical because it favors the professions' needs and definitions of reality over the client's. It assumes that the various professional institutional bodies know the "truth." Not only does this disempower clients, but it is also problematic because professional "truths" have been responsible for grave harm done to many people. In the name of truth, psychiatry created tardive dyskinesia. In the name of truth, psychology proclaimed racial differences in intelligence. In the name of truth, marriage and family therapy blamed poor marriages for all schizophrenic offspring. In the name of truth, all of the mental health professions have contributed to pathologizing and disempowering the individuals and families they are purported to serve. As discussed in Chapters 5 and 6, nowhere is this pathologizing and disempowering more evident than in the traditional gender bias of many of the professions' beliefs.

The mental health professions have traditionally had a one-sided view of power, authority, and expertise (Marmor, 1983). A therapist-as-expert mentality disempowers the clients we serve.

> The "rights" may be the client's, but the therapist holds the power to define the client's reality and to set the terms of the therapeutic relationship. . . . Nowhere is the concept of shared power encouraged, or even discussed. (Ballou, 1990, p. 240)

In the real world of psychotherapy, clients *do* have power. They are not simply passive recipients of services given *to* them. Power imbalances beg to be rectified. Clients can "refuse" to get well, prematurely terminate treatment, or file an ethics complaint against the therapist as a way of doing so.

I was in the hospital for some diagnostic tests a couple of years ago, sharing a room with a woman who was scheduled for major back surgery the following morning. I listened as her surgeon brusquely reviewed the litany of things that could go wrong in her operation and then closed his monologue with "I'll see you in the morning," thereby staving off any conversation with her. While he was functioning according to the basic rules of informed consent, his whole manner screamed of protecting himself from malpractice claims; there appeared to be no genuine concern for the patient. When he left the room, I noticed that the woman was crying and asked if she felt like talking. With tremendous relief, she sobbed out her fears about the surgery and her pain in being treated like an object by the surgeon.

This example is from a medical, not a psychotherapeutic, setting. But all of the psychotherapy ethics codes are headed in this dehumanizing, rule-based direction. Even where there have been attempts to change ethical principles in ways that would enhance the healing potential of the therapist-client relationship, they have been absorbed into the rule-based approach. Feminist therapists, for example, challenged the hierarchical ordering of knowledge in psychotherapy and called for a more mutual process in which women's "knowing" is as privileged as therapist "knowing." One of the natural outcomes of this recommendation was an emphasis on talking *with* female clients, indeed with *any* clients, about all of the choices and possibilities available to them in the psychotherapy context.

The mutuality of this kind of informed consent model was quickly transformed into a hierarchical *method* in which therapists would talk *to* their clients about the possibilities and risks in therapy (e.g., Houston-Vega and Nuehring with Daguio, 1997; Lidz et al., 1984). The feminist emphasis on mutuality was reduced to a *method* of traditional hierarchical psychotherapy that is now incorporated into the legal and ethical standards in all of the professions (Brown, 1994). Therapists are supposed to give *to* their clients such information and get *from* their clients consent, preferably in writing. The official agenda is client protection; the unofficial agenda is risk management for the therapist. Mutuality is gone from the formula. The therapist is still the expert and the client loses her voice except to consent to the therapist's expertise.

Ethnocentric Representations of Normalcy

All of our ethics codes are ethnocentric representations of the mental health professions' views of normalcy (Bersoff, 1975). Without consumer input (of which there is very little), how can we know that *our* view of ethical behavior fits the *public's* view? The distance model of boundaries, for example, as discussed in Chapter 7, may not fit what most women and many men expect of an ethical therapist. The emphasis on legalistic versions of informed consent may feel unethical to many clients whose pain is magnified by the therapist's insistence on a self-protective, legally informed discourse at the beginning of the therapy relationship. The arrogance and self-serving nature of our ethnocentric ethics representations undoubtedly offend many clients and exacerbate the risk of complaints against therapists. Our delusion of knowing it all, which privileges professional knowledge over all other kinds, conveys the message that no one else has anything worth offering.

In addition, therapy and its promised results have been oversold (Dawes, 1994; Jacobson, 1995). Therapeutic allegiance to particular models, regardless of their documented effectiveness, predominates. Even with proven, established models, the effects of psychotherapy appear to be quite modest when examined under the microscope of clinical significance (Jacobson, 1995). In its promise to alleviate human misery, psychotherapy has climbed out on a dangerous limb. Many ethics rules that accompany such models—and, in part, derive from them—are also of questionable merit in their promises to protect vulnerable clients from potentially harmful therapists.

A Substitute for Thinking

The mind-set of rules frames everything in terms of compliance or noncompliance, acceptance or rebellion. One acquiesces or deviates, accepts or rejects. There is little room for the gray, the in-between. Knowing the rules—and abiding by them or discarding them—becomes the sine qua non of decision making and behavior. One no longer has to think for oneself. The *rules* are the truths that dictate ethical functioning.

Rules thus interfere with the *process* of ethical thinking. If the rule says "Don't touch," the therapist never touches—even though some clients might benefit greatly from an end-of-session hug. If the rule says "Inform the client of all treatment options and risks," the therapist informs the client—even though some clients may be in such crisis that informed consent is better postponed to a later time. If the rule says "Avoid all dual roles," the therapist peremptorily turns away a client in desperate need because the client lives in his neighborhood. The therapist is out of touch with the effects of his behavior on each individual client because the rules are his guidepost. If something goes wrong, the rules are to blame, not him. The rules thus interfere with his ethics. They dictate decisions and behaviors to him *regardless of client need.* They also dictate them in ways that tell him *what* to do but not *how* to do it because the latter is impossible across variable contexts.

Negative Implications

The formulaic approach of rule-based ethics implies that therapists are inherently untrustworthy and require artificial, external controls on their behavior for the protection of the public. Therapists, therefore, are in a position of having to prove their worth—to compensate for the suspiciousness and distrust fostered by rule-based ethics via attempts to prove to their clients that they really *do* care and really *are* ethical. But, as Gergen comments:

> Trying to prove one's love in the face of another's doubt is no longer loving in itself; rather it is a tendering of proof. In the same way, *trying* to be sincere robs sincerity of itself. If one must try, one is not doing it. And thus, as one seeks to compensate against doubt, the sincerity of one's initial commitment is obscured. (1991, p. 220)

The whole ambiance of psychotherapy practice today is one of doubt, in which practitioners must *prove* their worth—to clients, family members of clients, managed care panels, and the public in general. In our attempts to prove our worth, we jeopardize our credibility and enhance our vulnerability. Rule-based ethics amplify this problem by suggesting that *rules,* rather than therapist goodness and integrity, are all that protects an innocent public from the potential harmfulness of psychotherapists. In this environment, a shift has occurred in which the average therapist is viewed not as a "good enough" therapist who makes occasional mistakes in the ambiguous, often messy arena of therapeutic relationships, but as potentially "bad," capable of doing great harm, and therefore suspect and in need of detailed monitoring.

Theoretical Biases

There are approximately 400 schools of psychotherapy. What is considered ethical in one school may be different from what is considered ethical in another. A neurolinguistic programmer has a different idea about touch than a psychoanalytically trained therapist. A family therapist has different standards about confidentiality than an individual therapist. A feminist-informed therapist has different ideas about informed consent than a behaviorist. For each school of thought, ethical functioning is contingent, to a certain degree, on the integrity of theory and practice. Behind every ethics rule is some theoretical frame of reference. As long as we have so many theoretical orientations, it is impossible to legislate rules that accommodate all. *Every* rule has some theoretical bias. To hold all practitioners from all theoretical orientations accountable to the same rule is inappropriate.

In addition, many of the rules are based on psychotherapy models that give the therapist and client multiple sessions in which to work, and are no longer realistic in a managed care environment that continues to shrink psychotherapy services. In a brief crisis intervention or behavior change therapy, for example, the therapist may not have the time to follow all of the professions' guidelines regarding informed consent or termination. Nor may it be necessary or appropriate for him to do so. If he attempts to, it may be at the expense of the client whose brief time with the therapist dwindles as the ethics rule requirements consume it. In addition, doing so is contraindicated with some therapy models (such as strategic therapy) in which the effectiveness of the intervention may depend on *not* explaining everything to the client.

Hidden Agendas

Ethics rules are framed in terms of client protection, but they contain other thinly disguised agendas as well. One such agenda is the protection of the therapist. As increasing numbers of therapists are sued and/or reported to licensing boards and professional association ethics committees, such august bodies respond by legislating more rules to "protect" therapists in the face of their enhanced vulnerability. Rules are thus set to protect therapists from their clients, creating an adversary relationship that is not conducive to ethical functioning. If the therapist is concentrating his energy on protecting himself from the client (by implication, potentially "bad"), how can he truly relate to her in any way that resembles mutuality, collegiality, respect, and healing?

The extent to which risk management has become a primary focus is illustrated in a recent publication of the National Association of Social Workers in which the authors state that "[c]linical social work, practiced competently and ethically, is *in its essence* [italics added] a form of risk management (Houston-Vega and Nuehring with Daguio, 1997, p. 61). If the essence of competent social work is risk management, the presumption is that *all* social work is risky and potentially dangerous. While this description of social work is probably accurate in some respects (there *are* some dangerous clients), its uniform application to *all* clients creates a malignant practice context for therapists. A more appropriate—and less negative—statement would be that clinical social work is, in its essence, the ethical *process* of working with clients. Psychotherapy should be about ethics, *not* risk management.

Another hidden agenda of rule-based ethics is the protection of the mental health professions themselves. As they have fallen from grace in the public's eye, they have created rules as a vehicle for restitution, an avenue to restore their former status of power and authority. Rules enable them to sanction deviant *individuals* without having to examine the broader institutional and societal problems that have contributed to the current backlash against them. Rules can thus be understood as a form of self-preservation for the professions.

Tightening ethics rules and searching for violators gives the professions a temporary sense of competence and control in responding to society's complaints about them. Therapists who deviate—or appear to deviate—from the rules can be found and punished. Their "guilt" demonstrates that the codes are still needed in order to stop "offenders."

This is a total setup for the individual practitioner. She is held accountable by licensing boards, ethics committees, and courts to standards that are increasingly unrealistic, anachronistic, and authoritarian—and whose implicit agenda is to protect the turf of the profession under fire. This not only serves to justify the professions' ongoing existence; it also invites disgruntled clients to call on the professions' ethics police to sanction a therapist for any number of infractions from the ever-increasing list of dos and don'ts.

The reported violations, once investigated and either dismissed or acted upon, give the professional associations and licensing boards a sense that they are taking care of the public image problem by weeding out and disciplining offenders. There is no awareness that their very existence in the current form is an invitation to pass on the complaints against psychotherapy to the individual practitioner and to hold him totally responsible. In bypassing the crisis of meaning, the psychotherapy professions have temporarily dealt with the onslaught against themselves and, for awhile, delayed the need for total revision. This, however, is at the expense of individual therapists and their clients.

Legal and Risk Management Emphasis

Because of the litigiousness against therapists and resultant concerns about risk management, the psychotherapy professions are increasingly deferring to attorneys for the establishment of their ethics rules.

This is problematic because attorneys operate in a world of blacks and whites, rights and wrongs, truths and falsehoods. The legal profession does not relate well to the vast ambiguities and complexities of human relationships. In the courtroom, one is either guilty or innocent; in the psychotherapy arena, such polarities are usually inappropriate, useless, and nontherapeutic. Applying them to psychotherapy practice—in the form of ethics rules to protect therapists against suits and complaints and the professions from public criticism—is inappropriate and unethical. Chapter 8 discusses in more detail the problems of such legal supervision.

THE IMPOSSIBILITY OF FUNCTIONING ETHICALLY IN AN UNETHICAL PROFESSION

The mental health professions have compromised their ethics by adjusting to social and cultural contextual forces that are based on a bottom line of profit rather than human welfare. The mental health professions' buy-in to managed care is a glaring example. Managed care, in its privileging of corporate over client need, is inherently unethical.

Attempting to legislate ethics rules for the individual practitioner while the professions themselves are adapting to unethical practices, requires a kind of splitting not conducive to ethical thinking or action. For example, all ethics codes have provisions requiring therapists to treat client need as primary and not yield to unethical demands from third-party payers, agency policies, or lawyers that would compromise the primacy of client need. Yet managed care gatekeepers and payers often view client need quite differently from the therapist. And the mental health professions have "line[d] up at the trough . . . to make sure we have a space, . . . giv[ing] away our integrity to buy some semblance of economic security" (Passoth, 1995, p. 5).

The therapist is vulnerable to being held accountable for unethical functioning by adjusting to the managed care requirements so sought after by the professional associations. *All* of the responsibility and *all* of the risk for dealing with the ethical dilemmas resulting from the professional associations' courting of managed care rest on the therapist-client relationship—and burden it. Instead of confronting the ethical splits they participated in making, the professions have dealt with them by legislating ever-tighter ethics regulations for individual practitioners.

The therapist-client relationship is thus extremely vulnerable. The possibilities for healing in therapy are circumscribed when ethics rules and legalities, as well as managed care dictates, become primary lenses through which both therapists and clients view the therapy relationship. Clients can become the targets for therapists' frustrations when they "refuse" to heal in the six sessions allotted by their managed care gatekeeper. Therapists can become the targets of angry clients as consumers feel increasingly justified in filing complaints based on the latest buzzwords of rule-based ethics, e.g., *dual roles* and *boundaries.*

Therapists are thus being required to function ethically in professions that have become progressively unethical. I say this with some fear and trembling. Most of us who have invested our professional—and to a great extent our personal—lives in being therapists do not like to hear our professions challenged. I ask for the reader's patience in exploring what is happening in the professions and in the socially mediated realities and presuppositions that all of us bring to the table. Examine with me some other possibilities for our work that will restore a sense of meaning and purpose to it. My goal is to open up new dialogues, not to present any new truths. In so doing, I am challenging our current professional ethics as an unethical system of self-preservation. For the professions to function ethically, the entire system of mental health beliefs must be revamped.

This is a rather daunting challenge. What started out as a book about ethics has turned into much more—challenging the core beliefs of the mental health professions themselves. Ethics cannot be decontextualized from the professions that promulgate them. And the professions cannot be decontextualized from the sociocultural context in which they exist. The ethical functioning of every therapist cannot be separated from what is happening in the professional and sociocultural context. This is what we carry around in our heads when we are with our clients and what affects every aspect of our functioning as psychotherapists.

This book elaborates on these problems and proposes some possible solutions to address the crisis of meaning in the mental health professions. It also discusses self-care for the individual practitioner, assesses risk factors associated with "difficult" and "dangerous" clients (made more so by the current social and professional context), and makes suggestions at both individual practitioner *and* institutional levels for dealing with the ethical dilemmas that make therapists and their clients vulnerable.

SUMMARY

Ethical functioning cannot be separated from the context in which it occurs. The mental health professions' attempts to legislate ethics rules and standards of care jeopardize the safety and well-being of the individual therapist and client, burdening their relationship with the strains and risks of the professions' adaptation to managed care and other inherently unethical aspects of our overall social context. In such adaptations, the professions have created a split between institutional and individual ethics, holding the practitioner accountable for individual ethical behavior in a context of unethical institutional functioning. This renders both therapist and client extremely vulnerable. It also exacerbates rather than alleviates the crisis of meaning facing the mental health professions in today's world.

Chapter 2

The Crisis of Meaning in Psychotherapy and the Vulnerable Therapist

I have found more to life
In the travel of an ant
Than in the progress of the world
Which has fallen far behind
The place it started from.

—N. Wood, *Many Winters*

The mental health professions are faced with a crisis of meaning of tremendous magnitude. They are situated in a despairing sociocultural context that privileges individualism, narcissism, and marketplace concerns and operates from a mentality of survivorship and victimhood. Society has become disgruntled with a profession whose truths about individual pathology are increasingly irrelevant in a context of social malaise. In this atmosphere, the very existence of the mental health professions is threatened. This creates intense anxiety—at both the institutional and the individual levels of practice. The increasing proliferation of rules, as discussed in Chapter 1, is one response to such anxiety. Rules provide a transient illusion of safety in unsafe times, but ultimately increase, rather than ameliorate, anxiety. Other responses to the anxiety include a retreat to positions of neutrality about social advocacy, and an attempt to prove the veracity of the professional truths now under fire.

The following discussion explores the crisis in meaning and illustrates the responses of the mental health professions with an example from the current debate about the nature and meaning of memory.

LOSS OF MEANING

Once an individual's search for meaning is successful, it not only renders him happy but also gives him the capability to cope with suffering. And what happens if one's groping for a meaning has been in vain? This may well result in a fatal condition. (Frankl, [1959], 1984, p. 163)

Our sociocultural environment is characterized by despair, hopelessness, and a sense of crisis over the meaning of life. The rich are getting richer, and the poor and middle class poorer. We watch homeless women and children grovel for food, children kill each other, schools struggle to teach and students to learn in an atmosphere of violence, and men and women clamor for jobs in the face of company downsizing and outsourcing. We hear of multimillion-dollar bonuses for corporate executives who have just laid off thousands of employees to increase profit margins for their companies.

In a consumerist frenzy, we buy goods that have been produced with cheap labor in third world countries. We listen daily to reports of children dying from malnutrition and inadequate or nonexistent medical care. Hearing politicians suggest orphanages for children, we watch as they cut to the bone the already meager welfare supplements that increasingly are the lifeline for our nation's children. We talk of denying schooling to the children of immigrants and sterilizing the retarded, while we improve fertility technology for the middle and upper classes through artificial insemination and test-tube babies. We moan about the forty million Americans without medical insurance but have yet to create a unified health care plan available to all. We grow accustomed to placing profit ahead of people.

The last point in history when we felt energized and hopeful was during the 1960s. There was the promise then of a better life for all people, not just for some. Michael Harrington (1962) helped us "discover" poverty and we rallied to eliminate it in the War Against Poverty. Betty Friedan wrote *The Feminine Mystique* (1963) and kitchen table conversations grew into a mass movement, changing the consciousness of women—and men—in this country forever. The Civil Rights Movement forced the nation to look at the terrible impact of racism on the lives of African Americans. The Vietnam War stimulated fierce protests and challenges to our country's conscience and morality.

During the 1960s, there was *meaning* to our lives—a sense of people working together for the sake of all and a hopefulness that we *could* make a better world. The pursuit of a common good was fraught with conflict and passionate debate, but it was *alive*. For the first time, previously unheard voices spoke. And for a short time, we listened.

What has happened to us in the intervening decades? Where has our passion gone? Why do we sit by and watch ourselves lose ground in every arena in which the 1960s planted the seeds for change? How did we become deaf to the voices of hunger and despair?

Feminist voices might respond to this question with a discourse on the backlash against women (Faludi, 1991). Historians of the family might point to the diminishing economic value of children in an increasingly urban society. Psychohistorians might elucidate on our society's frenetic worship of youth as a defense against our anxiety about growing old and dying (Greenleaf, 1978). Economists might talk about the world's diminishing resources, the globalization of the economy, and the plundering of third world countries. Religious leaders undoubtedly would discuss the perils of secular views that privilege individual over communal and spiritual needs. Linguists and philosophers might analyze the ways in which we have transformed our use of language to silence voices of compassion and caring for others (Foucault, 1972). The New Right might talk about our abandonment of family values and the dangers of government intrusion. Therapists might say that our world is producing more sick people and sick families, more addicted people and addicted families, who are so dysfunctional they cannot mobilize their resources to help themselves, much less others.

An overarching theme in all of these explanations is one of individualism and self-interest—a preoccupation with self at the expense of community.

THE GODS OF INDIVIDUALISM, NARCISSISM, AND THE MARKETPLACE

The ideology of personal growth, superficially optimistic, radiates a profound despair and resignation. It is the faith of those without a future. (Lasch, 1979, p. 51)

The more a man . . . is mastered by individuality, the deeper does the *I* sink into unreality. (Buber, 1958, p. 65)

Lasch first coined the term *culture of narcissism* to describe a society obsessed with

> . . . competitive individualism, which in its decadence has carried the logic of individualism to the extreme of a war of all against all, the pursuit of happiness to the dead end of a narcissistic preoccupation with the self. (1979, p. xv)

Our narcissistic culture focuses on living for oneself in the here and now, with little concern for posterity and the historical continuity of generations; an abandonment of religious and spiritual values in favor of secular ones (such as therapy); and an emphasis on personal pathology, personal indulgence, and privatism. Our obsession with individualism has privileged separation, autonomy, and self-interest over connection, mutuality, and communal interest. Writes Bellah and colleagues (1985, p. 55), " . . . [T]he self has become ever more detached from the social and cultural contexts that embody the traditions . . . of equality, justice, freedom, morality, and common good." A "culture of separation" and self-interest encourages fragmentation, detachment, and a lack of coherence. The only threads that seem to weave us together in such a context are the dream of personal achievement and success, the expression of vivid personal feeling about our situations, and a consumer market that offers us pleasure (Bellah et al., 1985).

We are perhaps the most consumer-oriented society in the world. We value personal success and the acquisition of pleasure. We drive ourselves to work more so that we may spend more, which requires more work and generates yet more spending, trying to defend against our anxiety about the ever-increasing schism between rich and poor and the absence of social supports to catch us if we fall. We fill the void we feel in our disconnection from communal welfare with isolated pursuits of pleasure such as home entertainment centers and Internet surfing.

And we are doing this in an increasingly shaky work world of diminished resources. While industries and corporations have always been profit-driven, many used to provide decent wages for American workers and attend to safety, health, and ecological factors. As their production facilities are relocated in third world countries to capitalize on cheap labor, the resulting globalization of our economy has only exacerbated our problems. The bottom line that drives us is not collective human good, but profit (Lerner, 1995, 1996).

Psychotherapy, with its traditional focus on *individual* welfare, *individual* happiness, and *individual* rights and privileges, has not helped change the direction of our society's inevitable crisis in meaning fueled by the worship of the individual.

> Therapy has been the Holy Communion of individualism, granting each person his or her own private origin myth—childhood—and the right to face time with a secular savior, trained and paid for perfect, selfless love, to redeem the parents' fall. (Gottlieb, 1997, p. 45)

"People want to get out of their individuality and they don't know how," comments Hillman (1997, p. 55). Psychotherapy, a profession whose paradigms have traditionally been conceptualized solely in terms of individual mental health, has not helped people find meaning broader than that of individuality. Even in family therapy, the family as a circumscribed, isolated unit has been the model until very recently. Families simply replaced individuals as the unit of service. And, as is discussed further in Chapters 5 and 6, the language of mental health is still one of individual and personal pathology and treatment.

THE THEMES OF VICTIMHOOD AND SURVIVALISM

> . . . [P]eople committed only to survival are [more] likely to head for the hills. If survival is the overriding issue, people will take more interest in their personal safety than in the survival of humanity as a whole. (Lasch, 1984, p. 78)

> There are no qualifying exams for victims, not even any standards—victimhood is a self-designation. You get to be a victim just by announcing it to *People* magazine, a therapist or a stranger on a bus. (Pittman, 1992, pp. 60-61)

As Americans become more anxious about decreasing resources and try to salve anxiety with the narcissistic pursuit of pleasure, we increasingly search for someone to blame for our emptiness and lack of fulfillment. We blame African Americans, the poor, women, homosexuals, political liberals, and immigrants. We have become a culture of victims and survivors as well as a culture of narcissists.

The individual no longer has to answer for misconduct because he is a victim—of his employer, of the bartender who sold him drinks, of his family, of a mental disease. Even the normal suffering of living has become equated with abuse and victimization (Hillman and Ventura, 1993). Victims have come to enjoy an exoneration from responsibility in their lives and a kind of moral and political correctness.

Victim and survivor mentalities are intertwined. Survivors are those who have endured some kind of hardship, who were once—or continue to be—victims of something they must endure. The language of survivorhood has been watered down so that victims now not only survive severe trauma and abuse; they also survive dysfunctional families, bad marriages, bad therapy, and hard days. Even the pursuit of success in work and closeness in relationships is seen as a daily struggle for survival (Lasch, 1984).

Survival, always an issue for the poor, is currently a buzzword for the middle class as well, contributing to a preoccupation with the present and a pessimism about the future that exacerbate the "me first," hedonistic mentality so prevalent in our culture today. Survivors, in their preoccupation with self-in-the-present, do not make good contributors to the common welfare or stewards of the world's resources.

Survivor and victim mentalities are thus not future-oriented. Neither are the psychotherapy professions that have traditionally focused on the past—on the events and traumas from childhood that affect present life. Strategic, solution-focused, and other brief therapies were developed originally to offer an alternative, more present-focused model for psychotherapy. As managed care dictates ever faster approaches, however, brief therapy has evolved very quickly from a therapeutic alternative to an economic necessity required by payers. The primary emphasis is on fixing the problem in the present as quickly as possible. The past is of little interest and there is no concern for the future, except in preventing a relapse that might drain the managed care coffers.

Neither the traditional nor the brief approach offers much future-directed energy. One focuses on helping people survive the past, the other on surviving the present. And yet it is the future about which so many people despair. The emphasis on survival, past or present, does not address the need for hope in the future.

The psychotherapy professions have begun using survivor and victim language, not just in reference to their clients but also in reference to themselves. Articles such as "Endangered Species: Is Private Practice Becoming an Oxymoron?" (Wylie, 1994) and "Surviving the Revolution" (Butler, 1994) are surfacing more and more frequently. Advertisements for workshops and marketing materials reflect the same trend, for example, "The Resilient Self: Rising from Adversity" and "From Surviving to Thriving: Business Planning for Today's Market."

While the psychotherapy professions are potentially faced with extinction unless they make significant changes and, therefore, *do* have very real survival concerns, the increased anxiety about survival does not enhance the public's confidence in our capacity to address and take a leadership role in our society's current crisis in meaning. A survivor mentality interferes with planning for and hope about the future both for ourselves and for our clients.

Frankl ([1959], 1984) wrote of the concentration camp prisoners who, losing all meaning in life and all hope for the future, became preoccuppied solely with survival concerns. They were doomed to die more quickly than the prisoners who could sustain some kind of ongoing meaning and hope. Like the doomed prisoners, the mental health professions will not endure without transforming concerns for survival into a more meaningful hopefulness about the future.

FROM INDIVIDUAL TO SOCIAL PATHOLOGY

In an age of cynicism and despair, psychotherapy spread its expertise to almost every institution of American society: education, corrections, parenting, business, government, even religion (Bellah et al., 1985; Dawes, 1994; Lasch, 1979; Peele, 1989). Our concepts and beliefs infiltrated everything and entered the mainstream. We became secular priests (Lasch, 1979) ministering, not just to a small minority of individuals and families, but to the misery of a troubled society. We increased in numbers and became essential in creating many of the truths now being challenged by a disgruntled public.

Our promises to alleviate human suffering were overrated (Jacobson, 1995). Renewed interest in holistic approaches to healing, mushrooming self-help movements, and articles about healing yourself and "firing your shrink" (Weiner-Davis, 1995) are signals that the public is reclaiming what has traditionally been professional turf. The fact that the mental health professions are full of "decaying truths" (Minuchin, 1982) has become ever more apparent.

In addition, as the women's movement brought the problems of violence and sexual abuse toward women and children into the public arena and challenged patriarchy as the root cause of such abuse, therapists could no longer work with psychological problems without also addressing social problems. This further expanded the boundaries of psychotherapy turf and made many therapists a target of blame for transforming what was heretofore considered individual pathology into social pathology.

As long as we did not equate psychological with social pain, we were able to monitor our own standards, licensing requirements, and ethics codes. Once we "went social," positioning individual problems in their societal context, we lost control and found ourselves increasingly the target of criticism and attack. This has been exacerbated by the loss of public trust and the tarnished image of all of the professions, as discussed in Chapter 8.

The false memory debate, as discussed next, is an example of this phenomenon and of some of the problematic responses to it in the mental health professions today.

THE MENTAL HEALTH PROFESSIONS' RESPONSE TO THE CRISIS OF MEANING

The False Memory Debate: An Example

As more therapists began hearing the stories of women's childhood sexual abuse, they deconstructed the individual pathology themes of the stories and reconstructed them with the social theme of patriarchal context. *Context,* not *person,* thus became the problem, and it was context that had to change. The addition of post-traumatic stress disorder to the DSM-III-R (American Psychiatric Association, 1987), a diagnosis originally created for the benefit of Vietnam War veterans, validated the notion of external rather than internal causes of psychic stress. This new diagnosis opened the door for the social themes of childhood sexual abuse to be included in mainstream psychiatry. Psychiatry co-opted a *contextual* and *social* problem in a diagnostic manual of *individual* disorders but, in so doing, it lent credence to the notion of iatrogenic trauma as a cause of pathology.

So far, so good. What happened next is just one example of the backlash that can occur and, in fact, has occurred in the past when psychotherapy addresses social problems. The False Memory Syndrome Foundation, started by the wife of an accused child abuser, began challenging child abuse survivors and their therapists, accusing them of falsely creating memories of childhood sexual abuse. Therapists began getting sued for implanting false memories in their clients. A tremendous flurry of articles and books on the nature of memory, especially traumatic memory, hit the press (Butler, 1995; Calof, 1993; Courtois, 1988; *Family Therapy News*, 1997; Ganaway, 1989; Herman, 1992; Loftus and Ketcham, 1994; Loftus and Yapko, 1995; Ofshe and Watters, 1994; Spiegel, 1994; Terr, 1994; Waites, 1993; Yapko, 1994).

The mental health professions responded to the debate about the nature of memory with new standards of care, cautioning psychotherapists that their job was not to differentiate between historical and narrative accuracy of memory, but rather to treat the client according to whatever story she brought to the treatment room. It didn't matter whether the client's story was true or false in order for the therapist to work effectively. There were also cautions against confusing a therapeutic role with an advocacy role, a message which translates as "Keep the therapy in the office, not in the world." The safety of a neutral position was encouraged.

Challenges to the veracity of women's memories thus became incorporated into professional standards of care, further reinforcing a division between private and public, individual and social. The professions neatly bypassed the opportunity to challenge the social context in which child sexual abuse occurs. Even psychology, the profession most under attack in the false memory debate because of its historical expertise in the field of memory, continues a bitter war within its own professional ranks that has divided its membership into two distinct camps (Barasch, 1996). This fight detours its energy from concerns about social context to concerns about individual memory.

Pandora's box, once opened, is difficult to close. The professional associations might retreat to safety behind the "it doesn't matter if it's true or not" bunker, but the individual practitioner who is dealing daily in his office with the repercussions of child sexual abuse has a more difficult job. How can he listen to survivors, most of whom are telling stories that they *never* repressed, without being able to *believe* them? It makes sense to maintain a both/and approach to women with repressed memories, but how does this approach make *any* sense with the vast majority of women who *do remember and have never forgotten* their abuse experiences? How can the psychotherapist honor both the standards of care being promulgated in the professions (which caution against believing the truth of survivor stories) *and,* simultaneously, the need of his client to be believed and, under some circumstances, to be advocated for outside the therapy office?

Freud abandoned his original beliefs that the stories he was hearing from women about childhood abuse experiences were, in fact, true. His reversal occurred in a social and professional context that could not support such knowledge. Much of his psychoanalytic theory thereafter was built on a foundation that ignored contextual realities and attributed abuse memories to fantasy. The current struggle is like an eerie déjà vu.

Our mental health professions have responded to the social pressures of groups like the False Memory Syndrome Foundation by retreating to a noncommittal stance. While this is not the same as total denial, it creates a huge question mark once more about the veracity of women's voices, *not* just the veracity of the voices of the few women who, for various reasons (all occurring within a patriarchal context) might fabricate memory, but of *all* women's voices. The professions have gotten detoured and frightened by the false memory debate instead of taking a clear position that, as long as we live in a patriarchal society, women and children (both boys and girls) will be abused and therapists will be the containers for many of their abuse stories. In their fear, the professions have avoided opportunities to participate in social transformation. By focusing on the occasional false memory, they avoid taking a proactive stand on the prevalence of child sexual abuse in our society.

Even the social work profession, historically the most socially oriented of the mental health professions, has retreated into neutrality. *Social Work Practice Update*, a production of the National Association of Social Workers' Office of Policy and Practice, for example, states the following:

> Clinical social workers should explore with the client who reports recovering a memory of childhood abuse the meaning and implication of the memory for the client, rather than focusing solely on the content or veracity of the report. The client who reports recovering a memory of sexual abuse must be informed that it may be an accurate memory of an actual event, an altered or distorted memory of an actual event, or the recounting of an event that did not happen. (1996, p. 2)

This might be an appropriate stance to take with *some* clients but not with the vast majority who *do* remember what happened to them and would feel totally unsupported and discounted. While the policy statement is about *recovered* memory, because of the conflictual, litigious nature of sexual abuse in our society, there is a tendency for therapists to generalize the precautionary stance to *all* abuse memories. The long and the short of it has become that dealing with *any* sexual abuse puts the therapist in a higher-risk category of practice.

NASW could have taken a clear position on the social nature of all abuse stories, both "real" and "fabricated," if it had framed its policy position within the broader social context in which there *is* a very high rate of childhood sexual abuse. It could have stated clearly its support of clinical social workers who empower clients by pathologizing context and depathologizing individuals (Coale, 1994), with guidelines on how to bring the social nature of every client's discourse into the therapy room. This would have supported practitioners in dealing with the social (rather than just the private) nature of clients' stories. Instead, NASW chose, as did the American Psychological Association, to focus on the recovered memory debate rather than on the socially constructed meaning of the debate and the contextual conditions in which it is occurring.

In addition, in a section titled "Risk Management," the NASW policy position discourages advocacy for clients, encouraging "great caution," directing the social worker to remain "neutral and objective," and advising clinical and legal consultation prior to any meeting with both client and family member(s) accused of abuse. The policy recommends that such a meeting only occur if it fits client self-determination and therapist judgment about its therapeutic indications and consistency with the treatment plan. If the meeting *does* meet these criteria, then it should only be undertaken with great caution and an awareness on the social worker's part that it would "be difficult to argue that this session is not part of the treatment plan" (1996, p. 3). This cautionary statement most likely stems from the recent proliferation of lawsuits against therapists by disgruntled family members and confusion about *who* the client is when family members are also seen.

One major crucible for client healing—the family—is depicted as potentially dangerous and therapists are thus discouraged from inviting them to participate in the client's therapy. While inviting family members to participate is not appropriate in all situations, it is in many. The tone of dangerousness such invitations have now assumed interferes with family member inclusion, and contributes to the schism between clients alleging abuse and their families. On a larger scale, it fuels, rather than diminishes, the rage of groups such as the False Memory Syndrome Foundation.

Instead of challenging the false memory debate and addressing the social context in which it is occurring, the profession yields to it and advises its members on how to stay neutral and avoid litigation. Again, with some kinds of situations, the policy makes sense. With the vast majority, it does not.

In not taking a stand on the more typical situation, the profession is actually subjecting its practitioners to risk by tying their hands as they struggle in the trenches to deal with the psychological consequences of social realities. It is creating fear-based standards of care that are officially in the best interests of clients, but unofficially help practitioners manage risk. These standards do not apply to many clients.

Standards of care are the backbone upon which hangs the flesh of lawsuits, licensing board actions, and professional association ethics committee complaints. Social workers have to abide by them or risk professional sanction, loss of license, or the consequences of lawsuits. This creates a crisis for the individual practitioner, who must look at the client through the haze of such standards, constantly making decisions between the safe (i.e., the official) position and what the client and she together determine is in that particular client's best interests. The latter often is in conflict with the former; choosing it takes courage and, increasingly, the willingness to risk one's very right to practice.

Attempts to Protect Turf

The false memory debate illustrates how the mental health professions have responded to the crisis of meaning in society. In addition to their retreat to neutrality, the professions (especially psychology) have responded by attempting to preserve their "scientific" beliefs. If we can just learn more about how the *individual* brain receives, stores, and retrieves memories, then we will solve the false memory debate. Then we will know which *individual* memories are true and which are false. A search for what is and is not true about recovered memories of individuals is a decontextualized dialogue which does not take into account the social construction of *all* memory. It serves to protect the professional expertise and turf of psychology as well as to provide new research data about memory.

The other disciplines have also responded to the crisis in meaning by staking their claims to knowledge and expertise. Psychiatry's escalated attempts to medicalize, pharmacologize, and individualize all human unhappiness and social deviance reflect its efforts to hold onto turf, to protect and expand its body of "knowledge," and to survive in a context of public disenchantment with and economic squeezes on the medical profession as a whole. Even though psychiatry has added *social* psychiatry as a specialty, its preeminent focus is on the decontextualized individual. Its success in controlling the diagnostic labeling of *individual* pathology, as discussed in Chapter 5, is one of its major coups d'état.

Social work's first and most important identity was rooted in societal change. *Psycho* was added to *social* during the New Deal years in the sweeping development of child guidance clinics following the Great Depression. Social work's split into *casework* and

community organization specialties reflects its fundamental dichotomizing of individual and social. It considers social reform still to
be its turf, as is illustrated by its ambivalence about the validity of
private practice and its reluctance to accept the changes in the
profession as more and more social workers become private practitioners. Two respected academicians and leaders in the field go so
far as to describe the social work movement into private practice as
a movement of "unfaithful angels" (Specht and Courtney, 1994).
Others discuss not only the movement into private practice, but the
preoccupation with mental health services at all, as regressive
(Rothman, 1984) and self-serving (Brieland, 1990). These lamenta-
tions about social work's abandonment of the social in favor of the
psychological reflect concerns about turf as well as about clients.
After all, if "social" is dropped out of social work, what is left?

Social work's resistance to transforming its turf from public to
private will be no more effective than the efforts of the other mental
health professions to add social issues to their predominantly individualized beliefs about human beings and their problems. None of
our sacred cows hold much milk anymore. The medical model,
which dichotomizes mind and body, is being eroded by challenges
to its efficacy and accuracy. Feminists have challenged every mental health belief that pathologizes women; this includes almost all of
our beliefs. Self-help movements have attempted to wrest turf from
professionals, even as they are increasingly co-opted by professional takeovers of their concepts. Managed care has reduced us to
the level of machines which must produce or become extinct. Turf-
guarding will only facilitate our survival over the short haul. In the
long haul, it will contribute to our demise.

THE NEED FOR TRANSFORMATION
IN THE MENTAL HEALTH PROFESSIONS

The false memory debate is an example of how the mental health
professions have responded to society's crisis in meaning by reinforcing their claims to knowledge and by adopting policies and
standards for *individual* clients and therapists rather than taking
clear stands on the societal problems that exacerbate the sexual
abuse of women and children in this culture. In so doing, the crisis

in meaning is bypassed by the professional institutions and laid in the laps of individual therapists and their clients.

Each profession is attempting to deal with society's crisis of meaning in general and in the professions in particular. But they are scrambling like hamsters repetitively going round and round in the same cage instead of transforming, or possibly leaving, the cage. In their struggle, they stake out escalating claims to knowledge at a time when the exact opposite is needed. In their struggle, they establish rule-based ethics which disempower and render vulnerable both therapists and their clients.

If the mental health professions are to survive into the future, they must stop standing on the ashes of individual practitioners who get caught in the crunch of the current crisis. This does not mean an elimination of all ethics codes; nor is it a denial that there *are* some individual practitioners who commit grievous violations against their clients and should be sanctioned and/or weeded out of the field. What it *does* mean is that the mental health professions must examine their investment in maintaining outdated beliefs, their efforts to police their memberships according to such outdated beliefs, and their avoidance of overhauling their repertoires of "truth" so that they can play a leadership role in our entire society's crisis of meaning. The more they focus on survival, the more they move toward extinction.

Protecting their turf and policing their memberships based on beliefs whose hidden agenda is to protect the professions is a poor substitute for substantive change and for the necessary search for new meaning with which to energize and transform the field—and the society we were created to serve—from survivalism into a new ethos of caring and healing.

> When there is a breakdown in a culture . . . it can usually be traced to one of several things. The first is a deep disagreement about what constitutes the ordinary and canonical in life and what the exceptional or divergent. . . . A second threat inheres in the rhetorical overspecialization of narrative, when stories become so ideologically or self-servingly motivated that distrust replaces interpretation, and "what happened" is discounted as fabrication. . . . The . . . phenomenon expresses itself in

> modern bureaucracy, where all except the official story of what is happening is silenced or stonewalled. And finally, there is the breakdown that results from sheer impoverishment of narrative resources. . . . It is not that there is a total loss in putting story form to experience, but that the "worst scenario" story comes so to dominate daily life that variation seems no longer possible. (Bruner, 1990, pp. 96-97)

The professions have all of these symptoms of cultural breakdown. First, we are in tremendous turmoil and disagreement about what constitutes the ordinary and what the exceptional. The false memory debate is just one illustration of this. Second, our stories have become extremely ideological and self-serving as we compete for managed care dollars and carve out new markets, all the while functioning under the official story lines promulgated by the ultimate authorities of the profession: the licensing boards, professional association ethics committees, and courts. Third, as I have already discussed, the ever-increasing policing of mental health professionals by such bodies has shifted the very nature of psychotherapy from best-case to worst-case scenarios. Clients are viewed as prospective victims and therapists as prospective perpetrators.

The impoverishment of our narrative resources is occurring in the context of our society's crisis in meaning. As long as the primary focus at the professional level is on survival rather than on transformation and change, the individual practitioner and her client are vulnerable. The client can be hurt by therapists who, in their attempts to manage risk, try to practice by all of the ethics rules. The therapist can be hurt by *not* going by the book when he and the client determine that this is not in the client's best interests. If not going by the book comes before a licensing board or an ethics committee at some later time, the therapist can receive sanctions for an ethics violation, even if the decision made sense in the therapist-client context at the time it was made.

SUMMARY

The psychotherapy professions are situated in a social context characterized by a loss of meaning; an emphasis on individualism, narcissism, and the forces of profit and the marketplace; themes of victimhood and survivalism; and a lack of public trust in our professional knowledge and expertise.

The professions' response to the crisis of meaning has been to attempt to prove their beliefs, claim their turf, legislate increasingly impossible standards and rules, and thereby pass on to the individual practitioner-client relationship all of the risk of practicing in an unsupportive, antagonistic social context. In so doing, the mental health professions exhibit many signs of cultural breakdown as described by Bruner (1990): deep disagreement about what is ordinary and what is exceptional, overspecialization of narratives with an adherence to official stories and a repudiation of all others, and an impoverishment of narrative resources.

Chapter 3 discusses the social construction of all realities and the futility of the psychotherapy professions' attempts to preserve traditional "truths."

Chapter 3

Social Constructionism and Its Implications for the Mental Health Professions

> . . . "[R]ealities" are the results of prolonged and intricate processes of construction and negotiation deeply embedded in the culture.
>
> —J. Bruner, *Acts of Meaning*

> . . . [If] we claim that the therapist cannot have access to the objective knowledge of any pathological mechanism, how can we still define the therapist as a healer and still call the practice a cure?
>
> —L. Fruggeri, "Therapeutic Process as the Social Construction of Change"

One of the reasons for the crisis in meaning in the mental health professions is the postmodern challenge to *all* knowledge in *all* of the professions. Even in the so-called hard sciences, knowledge is increasingly understood as a product of social construction rather than as something which is objectively true or false. Knowledge is more or less true or false depending on the context in which it is created. What is true in one context may not be true in another. Expert truths, therefore, are context-dependent and do not stand alone. This has profound implications for all of the mental health professions.

THE EVOLUTION OF SOCIAL CONSTRUCTIONISM

Prior to the 1960s, the predominant beliefs in our society reflected an objectivist stance that the truth was knowable and existed objectively out there in the world. It could be measured, assessed, and analyzed; was real in its own right; contained stable principles that persisted over time; and should instruct human action. The objectivist stance favored scientific truths over humanist truths. It supported a dualism between the hard knowledge of science and the soft knowledge of folk wisdom and literature, the objectivity of the outer world and the subjectivity of the inner world, with little or no awareness of their interconnectedness (Bruner, 1986, 1990).

Objectivist truths helped contain the unexplainable and frightening. Science promised stable, solid truths on which to hang uncertainties in a post-World War II society that was racing to the moon, stockpiling weapons to allay Cold War anxiety, frenetically creating new appliances to keep women at home and to fuel the greediness of a growing consumer market, dealing with government leaders being shot and killed, and listening to the rumbles of minority voices threatening the status quo. Science promised salvation from impending chaos, indeed from extinction itself. Science was also the valued truth of a patriarchal society vested in maintaining power and control.

The 1960s witnessed massive challenges to scientific truths through the voices of women, African Americans, and other minorities, who began to question the relevance of such truths to *them*. In the late 1950s and early 1960s, a Cognitive Revolution began to acknowledge and explore how "mind" is a part of the sciences (at least the human sciences). It looked at science not simply as knowledge to be "discovered," but also as a product of cognitive thought. Anthropologists were among the first to explore *how* we know what we know. As they studied primitive cultures, they discovered that the "objects" of their analysis were often curious and found the beliefs and behaviors of the anthropologists strange. The very lenses through which they were viewing primitive cultures superimposed their own meanings on whatever they saw and affected their conclusions. They began to shift to an approach that no longer focused on roles, social classes, and other constructs of Western culture. Instead, they searched for the underlying meanings and commonsense beliefs about human behavior that gave rise to whatever structures had been created in the culture under study.

Historians originally looked for facts that could be remembered in a unified, continuous way—facts that, when grouped into temporal frames or series, stood on their own as documents of the past and explained relations of causality, circular determination, and expression. As anthropology shifted to a more meaning-based exploration of how we know what we know, so did history. History no longer was *memory*. Discontinuity, rather than continuity, became a major organizing premise. Thus, the historian looked for specific events— dislodged from a unified temporal sequence—to describe and analyze, with a clear recognition that his observing voice was part of the history being analyzed (Foucault, 1972). History, in other words, shifted from the event out there to the work of the historian who could select *any* event and give it meaning without being required to put it into a longitudinal temporal sequence.

By the mid-1970s, all of the social sciences had moved away from a traditional positivist, objectivist stance to a more interpretive, or narrative, stance. Even the hard sciences began to address how the hypotheses they sought to verify derived from folk wisdom and, thus, were socially created.

PSYCHOTHERAPISTS: LATECOMERS TO SOCIAL CONSTRUCTIONISM

> Never was the idea that reality is socially constructed more evident, but at the same time, never has it been so unwelcome. At the same time, never has it been so necessary. (Hoffman, 1992, p. 10)

> There is more in a human life than our theories of it allow. (Hillman, 1996, p. 3)

The mental health professions have been latecomers to social constructionism. Traditional beliefs and practices are slow to change. Following is a discussion of the evolution of social constructionism in psychotherapy and its implications for the professions.

Preservers of the Status Quo

Psychotherapists have been privileged as expert knowers of (flimsy) bodies of "scientific" knowledge upon which each profession has built itself (Dawes, 1994). Shifting to a notion of nonobjective, socially constructed realities challenges all of our beliefs. Out of these original beliefs, the professions and the society that sustains them have developed mammoth institutions that preserve the status quo. We affect and are affected by the insurance industry, the court systems, educational institutions, hospitals, industrial settings, and pop psychology, all of which sustain traditional psychotherapy beliefs. We are an instrument to preserve society as it is. At the core, we are an instrument of social control.

> . . . [A] willingness to cooperate with the proper authorities offers the best evidence of "adjustment" and the best hope of personal success, while a refusal to cooperate signifies the presence of "emotional problems" requiring more therapeutic attention. (Lasch, 1984, p. 49)

Shifting from being an instrument of the status quo, of social control, is an incredible challenge. Nevertheless, the shift is occurring. Like a slow lava flow, it is transforming the entire landscape of psychotherapy.

Psychotherapy's Shift to Social Constructionism

The Cognitive Revolution

Bruner credits Lev Vygotsky (1962), a Russian psychologist, as the first to place importance on the role of culture in creating human meaning. His early work, *Thought and Language*, was first written and suppressed in Russia in 1934 and translated into English in 1962. Vygotsky emphasized the shared meanings to which children are acculturated through language and the products of language (e.g., literature, science, technology, etc.) so that their actions become mediated in response to the world by cultural consciousness or reflection. Adults serve as a kind of "vicarious consciousness" for children as they gradually learn to modulate action themselves with socially created reflection. A collection of Vygotsky's papers titled *Mind and Society*, first published in the United States in 1978, described this transmission as occurring in a "zone of proximal development"—the distance between what the child is currently capable of and what he is potentially capable of under adult guidance.

In 1955, a year prior to the official beginning of the Cognitive Revolution, George Kelly published *The Psychology of Personal Constructs*. His work and others that soon followed shifted emphasis from what we know to the personal constructs that form and shape our knowing. But the Cognitive Revolution got detoured into "mind as machine" metaphors (Bruner, 1986, 1990). The concept of the mind as a transactional entity, already established in the social sciences, did not really penetrate the psychotherapy field until the 1970s and 1980s.

Family Therapy and Social Constructionism

Even the blossoming field of family therapy had, from the 1950s onward, simply displaced the individual unit as the primary focus. The unit to be diagnosed and treated was the family and its interactions, a closed system isolated from and devoid of context. Structural machine models that described families as resistant to change predominated. Families were believed to calibrate themselves in response to therapist interventions out of their need to preserve homeostasis and avoid change. Symptoms were seen as playing an integral part in preserving the family's status quo.

Thus, a field that had particular promise for appreciating and exploring socially mediated realities missed its first opportunity to do so; but it did not miss its second. Family therapy's first shift was to a position in which the therapist was no longer seen as an objective observer of the system being treated, but rather a coparticipant in the system, creating *with* the client(s) new meanings to facilitate problem *dis-solution*. The reification of membership and interactional patterns in families yielded to the concept of *system* as the shared meaning in the minds of the people who defined and were attempting to solve a problem. The therapist's job was to introduce new possibilities for meaning, to perturb the system in such a way that the problems could be dis-solved (Anderson, Goolishian, and Windermand, 1986; Boscolo et al., 1987; Goolishian and Anderson, 1988; Hoffman, 1985, 1990; Keeney, 1983; Keeney and Ross, 1985). This shift was labeled *constructivism* because the members of the therapist-client system were *constructing* together the realities of problem definition and resolution.

So far so good. However, the context still only included the meanings of those people defining and trying to solve the problem; the social and cultural biases of both therapists and families were ignored. Therapists still had privileged truths from the socially constructed well of professional knowledge—truths which guided them and with which they influenced families.

The gender bias of many of these truths was glaring. Goldner's seminal articles (1985, 1988), which questioned traditional models of family therapy for ignoring gender altogether in their theories and for assuming that male and female experiences in families were the same, paved the way for many other feminist challenges to the view of the family as a private unit isolated from its social context (Goodrich, 1991; Hare-Mustin, 1989; Knudson-Martin and Mahoney, 1996; McGoldrick, Anderson, and Walsh, 1989; Walsh and Scheinkman, 1989; Walters et al., 1988). The social creation of all realities, including professional realities, began to be obvious.

With the focus on the social construction of all beliefs, therapist neutrality—a primary principle of constructivism—was criticized. In treating the therapist-family system as an isolated unit that created its own realities, constructivism ignored the social inequities and hardships that impinged upon families in the real world—unequal power distributions between men and women, child abuse, poverty, and so forth (Fish, 1993; Minuchin, 1991). In constructivism, the world was still seen as external and each family as responsible for constructing its own realities. The role of the therapist, as part of the problem-solving system, was to help the family deconstruct and reconstruct these realities in ways that made problems more resolvable, lives more hopeful. Therapists were to remain neutral in the process.

Nowhere was the criticism of therapist neutrality stronger than over the concept of power. Constructivists saw power as just one among many possible realities in any therapeutic setting and tried to divest themselves of its tyranny by basically ignoring its existence. If power could be constructed, then it could be deconstructed. And yet, as therapists saw the effects on families of spousal and child abuse, rape, poverty, and other catastrophes of patriarchal culture, the brutal social facts of power abuses in the social context were not so easily deconstructed.

The debate over therapist neutrality contributed to a growing awareness that the realities clients (and therapists) bring into the therapy arena are socially constructed and that neutrality is impossible. Any position, even a so-called neutral one, is biased by its social context. The mind is not separate from the transactional nature of human interaction, but, in fact, exists only in relation to others, as a social construction, or what Hillman calls an "interiorization of the community" (Hillman and Ventura, 1993, p. 40). Both clients and therapists bring social constructions of reality into the therapy room. Social construction is not just "out there" impinging upon families; it is in the minds of family members. Social construction *is* mind. Tick describes it eloquently in his treatise on working with Vietnam veterans:

> . . . [T]herapy is inevitably a psycho-historical enterprise . . . [As we experience] secondary trauma from exposure to [client] memories, we, too, are wounded and we, too, must heal. . . . [W]e are participating in the diseases and the healing not only of our clients but of ourselves and our culture. (1995, p. 35)

And states Hillman:

> Any individual's grief and panic is, at this moment in history, in part a grief and panic at the dying of our culture. And if psychotherapy doesn't deal with that, it's in a state of denial of one of the root causes of our pain. (Hillman and Ventura, 1993, p. 225)

Narrative Themes

With a growing awareness of the *psychological* story as a *social* story, family therapy turned to a narrative theme, paying attention to the (socially constructed) narratives that clients bring into the therapy room. If stories could be constructed, they also could be deconstructed and reconstructed in ways that would expand possibilities for client healing (Sluzki, 1992; White, 1995; White and Epston, 1990) and acknowledge the *social* creations residing in any individual story. Individual pathology could be understood more in the context of the social pathology in which it was generated (Coale, 1994).

Family therapy was only able to take this leap by opening itself to the other human sciences that had already evolved to social constructionist theories in psychology, philosophy, and linguistics (Berger and Luckman, 1966; Foucault, 1972; G. Lakoff, 1987; G. Lakoff and Johnson, 1980; R. Lakoff, 1975, 1990; Middleton and Edwards, 1990; Shotter, 1990, 1993). Feminist thinkers also moved the field along, despite great resistance to their contributions. But family therapy is still a marginalized modality (Shields et al., 1994) and its impact on the entire field of psychotherapy tenuous.

IMPLICATIONS OF SOCIAL CONSTRUCTIONISM FOR PSYCHOTHERAPY

[F]rom here that looks like a bucket of water . . . but from an ant's point of view it's a vast ocean, from an elephant's just a cool drink, and to a fish, of course, it's home. So, you see, the way you see things depends a great deal on where you look at them from. (Juster, 1961, p. 108)

If what is psychological is also social and what is social is also psychological, the beliefs upon which each mental health discipline is founded are all up for grabs. How can psychotherapists, who by definition are healers of the mind, do so when the mind is a product of social construction? When the mind is no longer private and individual but rather totally interdependent with culturally mediated realities? When the social realities we see in our offices, through the experiences of our clients, are not a part of traditional psychotherapy turf which focuses on individual rather than social pathology? When, every day, families bring their own variations of social problems into our offices?

Social constructionism requires that we see everything through the lens of culturally negotiated meanings. Depression and anxiety are not just within the individual or family; they are within the society that defines their terms and contributes to their creation. The same condition, experienced in another culture, might have a different meaning. The same psychotherapeutic response, experienced in another culture, might also have a different meaning.

I worked recently with a family in which the mother was Iranian and the father Australian. They had lived in several countries before settling in the United States. They presented with concerns about their seven-year-old son, who was doing poorly in school and was having behavior problems at home. Each parent had constructive ideas about how to manage the son's problems, but the ideas did not fit the school's definitions of competent parenting. After months of trying to cope in their own culturally specific ways and being criticized by the school for it, they had simply given up. The result was an escalation of the son's problematic behavior. A discussion with them about the culturally created beliefs of *everyone* in the situation (which honored their beliefs as well as the school's) empowered them once again to problem solve with the school. As long as their beliefs had been relegated to a deviant status and the beliefs of the school to a superior status, the family had been immobilized. Fortified with the therapist's support for their beliefs, they could function, even though that meant adapting to some of the school's beliefs.

Unfortunately, the disempowerment of clients through the imposition of dominant discourses about health and pathology is one of the problems of the mental health professions today. Scientific beliefs, when misused, can have a constricting effect (Newmark and Beels, 1994). In the case just cited, the parents' disempowerment was easy to see because of the explicit differences between American culture and the cultures of the parents. With many clients, it is less obvious but still ever-present.

Perhaps the biggest implication of social constructionism for psychotherapy is the honoring of *all* stories equally and the emphasis on multiple truths. No story is more true than any other. Although some stories may be more useful than others in solving certain problems, it is their utility rather than their veracity which is emphasized. All stories, including all psychotherapy stories—scientific or otherwise, are cultural variations of truth. This dramatically changes the expertise of the psychotherapist from purveyor of expert knowledge to facilitator of conversations with clients which (hopefully) assist in expanding the possibilities for healing.

SUMMARY

Social constructionism explores not what we know but how we know. And how we know is mediated through culture. Even the so-called hard sciences derive their initial hypotheses from folk psychology and are thus socially created. Social constructionism represents a shift from traditional positivist, objective stances toward knowledge to more interpretive, narrative approaches in which the stories individuals tell are viewed not as objective truths but rather as subjective variations of the larger stories of culture.

The implications of social constructionism for the mental health professions are profound. We must stop viewing our clients' stories as indications of individual and family pathology but rather as contextual, social creations. We must also understand that *all* of our beliefs about psychotherapy are culturally created and, hence, no more or less true than other stories. In doing so, our role shifts from expert knower to co-creator of stories that facilitate hope and healing.

Chapter 6 examines some of our traditional beliefs and how they must be deconstructed and either discarded entirely or reconstructed in a social constructionist frame. Chapter 7 does the same thing with respect to our ethics codes. Since language is the tool through which we communicate and through which social meanings are created and transmitted, the next two chapters discuss language and its uses in psychotherapy.

Chapter 4

Language:
Some Theoretical Considerations

> . . . [T]he presumed neutrality of science, like that of language itself, gives way to the recognition that the categories of knowledge are human constructions.
>
> —C. Gilligan,
> *In a Different Voice:*
> *Psychological Theory and Women's Development*

Because language is the primary tool of social construction, understanding its power in the creation of all of our truths is essential. The following discussion addresses some of the key theoretical aspects of language development and usage, laying the groundwork for an understanding of its power in creating the psychotherapy truths inherent in our diagnostic labels and other psychotherapeutic constructs that inform the mental health professions.

LANGUAGE: THE MEANING MAKER

Language is more than a tool of communication. It is both a reflector and creator of the social constructs each of us carries around in our heads and through which we understand and give meaning to the world. I have always been fascinated with it, from the first time I struggled with learning another language and became frustrated with the impossibilities of word-for-word translation into English. I had to learn not only the words but how the words were put together into sentences and how the sentences were used in everyday discourse in a context of meaning that did not always make sense to me.

One simple example was the sentence *j'ai peur* which, translated literally from French into English, means "I have fear." That's odd, I thought to myself. How can one *have* fear? Fear is not something you *possess*; it's something that possesses *you*.

Later, as an adult struggling to learn Italian, I was struck with the same phenomenon. There it was again, *ho paura* ("I have fear"). I started introducing the French and Italian formulations into my (English) work with clients. If one can *have* fear rather than *be* afraid, new possibilities appear. If I *have* fear, then I can pass it around, throw it away, temporarily place it somewhere else, tell it to leave me alone, and so forth (Coale, 1994).

Elsewhere, I have described a clinical example in which I used the two different expressions for "I love you" in Italian to help transform the stuckness of a couple working with me in therapy (Coale, 1994). The husband, feeling desperate about his wife's threats to leave him, continued to pursue her for reassurances of her love. The more he pursued, the less loving she felt and the less able to reassure him. Both wanted to make their marriage better but their impasse had become increasingly toxic. I explained the difference between *ti amo* ("I love you" in the romantic sense) and *ti voglio bene* ("I love you" in the sense that I care, am concerned about your welfare, and, literally, wish you well). Could the wife say the latter and the husband accept it while we worked on the relationship to see if it was possible to restore the former? The impasse was resolved and a safe space was created in which to work.

I was once involved in a fierce child custody case that wound up in court. As I was trying to describe the complexities of the child's attachment to both parents and his need for ongoing relationships with both, the mother's attorney, whose agenda it was to win custody, aggressively asked me, "Do you think that this father really *loves* his child? After all he's done?" This was followed by an oratorical, negative listing of the father's behaviors. My response was to question the attorney's assumptions about the word *love*. Did he mean the kind of love that a noncustodial parent exhibits when he sees his child twice a month? The kind of love that a full-time parent exhibits when he sees his child every day? The kind of love that would make a father give up his struggle to see his child? The kind of love that would fuel a father's struggle to see his child? What kind of love did he mean?

In so doing, I made my point about the complexity of love and its definitions. The lawyer withdrew his question. In refusing to respond to it without some explication of the attorney's *meaning* of the word *love*, I did not accommodate his attempts to concretize and trivialize the word.

Language is socially constructed and, for therapists, is the most important tool in our work. The following sections describe some relevant conceptual and theoretical aspects of language.

CLASSICAL THEORIES OF LANGUAGE

The objectivist assumption that words name stable realities in the world informs classical theories of language. For the mind, which functions as a mirror of the real world, symbols (language) are a representation of this reality. Human reason is accurate when symbols correspond to entities and categories in the world without any influence from the mind of the knower. Language, in other words, is seen as describing the truthful order of the world out there.

> Existence and fact are independent of belief, knowledge, perception, modes of understanding, and every other aspect of human cognitive capacities. No true fact can depend upon people's believing it, on their knowledge of it, on their conceptualization of it, or on any other aspect of cognition. Existence cannot depend in any way on human cognition. (G. Lakoff, 1987, p. 164)

Language, in the classical view, is factual in that it corresponds to a natural order in the world. This is fine when it comes to words like *chair* but difficult for words like *love*. And, even with such concrete words as *chair*, there can be confusion. Is it an armchair, rocking chair, desk chair, recliner? Is a beanbag chair a chair?

Classical theories of language privilege objective over subjective language because the latter *appears* to conform to factual realities in the world. Subjective language—the language of feelings, imagination, fantasy, emotion, perception, hypothesis, memory, body, society, and culture—is perceived as less true than the language of facts. But, as I shall describe in greater detail in Chapter 5, the objective language of facts is socially constructed in the same way as the more subjective language of human nature. We construct our worlds linguistically, all of them.

THE SOCIAL CONSTRUCTION OF LANGUAGE

Language is socially constructed. It is a product of the interaction between environmental stimuli and what our nervous systems are expecting (Bruner, 1986) as mediated by culture. An Arab in the desert has different expectations for a chair than does a business executive in New York. An Eskimo has different expectations for snow than does a Floridian. Language, the symbols for social construction, both reflects and creates these expectations.

Context is shaped by what Bruner (1986) calls our "folk psychology"—the collective wisdom of the culture, which contains normative descriptions about how human beings tick and what self and world are all about. Through language, we create narrative about ourselves and our worlds, narrative that gives meaning to our lives. Biology constrains us by limiting what we can and cannot do physically. Much as we might like to fly, we are limited to airplanes, gliders, and other mechanical means. Culture constrains us by linguistically shaping our beliefs about what is true, functional, right, workable, and moral.

CATEGORIES, PROTOTYPES, AND IDEALIZED COGNITIVE MODELS

Language contains categories that organize our experiences in the world. Categorization begins at the level of distinctive action, at the level which is learned earliest, and at the level in which things are first named. *Dog*, for example, is a category that precedes *German Shepherd*. Prototypes are the most representative members of a category and become what George Lakoff (1987) describes as "idealized cognitive models." Thus, for Westerners, *chair* is something that has four legs, a seat, and a back. Variations would be *modified* versions of the idealized cognitive model, e.g., rocking chair, armchair, beanbag chair.

Now, to the interesting, and less objective, part. What is a *family*? Is it a group of biologically related human beings, consisting of first-married parents and their offspring, who live together? Is it a single mother raising children after a divorce? Is it a remarried couple with combinations of children from previous marriages? Is it a married couple with adopted or foster children? Is it a lesbian couple who had a child through artificial insemination? Is it an unmarried couple who live together with their child?

In this culture, the idealized cognitive model of family is a first-married, biological, legally sanctioned family with children. This model contains subthemes about what a *good* family is—themes of "blood is thicker than water," good parents do not put their children through a divorce, they are heterosexual, and so forth. As with *chair*, there is a clear idealized cognitive model. Families who do not fit this model are described with modifiers, e.g., stepfamily, foster family, adoptive family, divorced family, single parent family. These modifiers signifiy a variation from the idealized cognitive model and carry powerful social meaning.

There are some kinds of families that are not included in the category *family*, even with a modifier. Lesbian couples with children, for example, may not be named *family*. Naming something legitimizes it, even if the modifier is considered second best or pejorative. Not naming something conveys deviance. It was not very many years ago when the majority of stepfamilies did not use any "step" words to describe themselves because of the deviant status the word conveyed (Lewis, 1981).

There are some modifiers which, in a language of polarities, have silent power. The words *natural, real, intact, complete* used to describe the prototypical family denigrate without even specifying the *unnatural, unreal, nonintact, incomplete* descriptions of nonprototypical families. And the stated modifiers for such nonprotypical families are often pejorative, e.g., *broken, single, second time around, reconstituted* (Abramovitz, 1991; Coale, 1994; Lewis, 1981, 1985). My younger daughter, in hearing the word *broken* to describe the family of one of her friends, expressed to me at the tender age of seven, "I hope I'll never have a broken mother." Her understanding of the modifier *broken* was a mother who was both financially and physically destroyed (Lewis, 1983).

In the use of modifiers, negative implications for women are rampant. Robin Lakoff (1975), for example, describes how we assume that *doctor* or *sculptor* or *CEO* are of masculine gender. If the doctor or sculptor or CEO is a woman, we preface the word with *woman—woman* doctor, *woman* sculptor, *woman* CEO.

LANGUAGE DEVELOPMENT IN CHILDREN

There is evidence that meaning-making begins before children actually speak words (Bruner, 1986, 1990). Once they have mastered some basic skills in the manipulation of objects, they seem to develop an understanding of how to hand objects back and forth, pass them around in a circle, exchange them for other objects, and so forth. By age one, they can point to things in their environment that they want from their caregiver. Bruner sees children's "mutuality of action" in passing objects back and forth and the "reference" to desired things in the world around them as transactional precursors to the actual development of language. In other words, children have some semblance of socially constructed, transactional meaning before they have words. They act first and, in acting and experiencing the responses of caregivers, begin to incorporate cultural meanings. This makes them more receptive to learning the specific words because they have already begun to grasp the *contextual meanings* of words. After language acquisition, they then learn that it is important not only to *act* right but also to tell the right story about the action (Bruner, 1990).

Observing my own children and those I have had as clients over the years has been instructive and fits Bruner's assessments of children's preverbal sense of meaning. As they struggle to master new vocabulary, children often understand the context before they grasp the correct word or phrase for describing it. Thus, one of my daughters (at age six), described a television show in which a woman was knocked unconscious in a fight, by saying, "That woman was knocked obnoxious." She had accurately described the odiousness of the violent interaction without yet having the technically correct vocabulary (Lewis, 1983).

On another occasion, in describing the dilemma of a classmate whose mother had abandoned her and whose father and stepmother had taken her in, she said, "She went to live with her father and his new wife will be her gardener." What a lovely description of the child's hopes to be nourished in her new family (Lewis, 1983). I had a seven-year-old client, whose father was opposed to his ex-wife's remarriage, stage a marriage ceremony with puppets in which the minister said "Do you take this woman to be your *awfully* wedded wife?" She did not have the language exactly correct, but she certainly understood the context of her mother's intended remarriage!

THE POWER TO DEFINE GOOD AND BAD, SANE AND MAD

> Somewhere, and I can't find where, I read about an Eskimo hunter who asked the local missionary priest, "If I did not know about god and sin, would I go to hell?" "No," said the priest, "not if you did not know." "Then why," asked the Eskimo earnestly, "did you tell me?" (Dillard, 1974, pp. 121-122)

Language: An Internalized Social Control Agent

Language has enormous power to shape and control meaning. Foucault (1972) describes how social control functions can shift from *person* as monitor to *discourse* as monitor. Social discourse, in defining what is right and wrong, good and bad, feminine and masculine, moral and immoral, ensures compliance with normative behaviors and explains deviations from and exceptions to normative behaviors. Since we all carry social discourse in our heads, we all also carry our own internalized social control agents.

In defining the meanings of words and the contexts in which they are used, language excludes some words from use except in particular contexts (by, for example, determining what is polite and what is coarse), defines who can and cannot use certain words (e.g., so-called male-speak and female-speak, professional-speak and lay-speak), and divides the world between truth and untruth, reason and folly. "From the depths of the Middle Ages, a man was mad if his speech could not be said to form part of the common discourse of man. His words were considered nul[l] and void. . . . " (Foucault, 1972, p. 217).

The Power of the Unsaid

There is often a fascination with what is not said and a tendency to credit the "mad" with strange powers. Women who have spoken "subversive dialogues" (Brown, 1994) have been incarcerated, burned at the stake, institutionalized, clitorectomized, denied their civil rights, medicated, diagnosed, and pathologized when they have said what should not have been said, according to the dominant patriarchal discourse of society. They have also been objects of fascination and fear. Their "madness" can be viewed as both an attempt to speak the unspeakable and a response to the madness of the dominant discourse that excludes them. Punishment often follows the speaking of the unspeakable as Chesler ([1972], 1989) so eloquently describes when she talks of women as being "colonized" and then devalued and punished for the way they protest their colonization.

I worked with a woman recently who came from a powerful patriarchal Southern family in which the men throughout the family history had all held public office or been eminent attorneys, judges, and doctors. The women had all either died young or been considered eccentric. My client was struggling to find her own voice in the context of this family history and in the context of a human services agency that had squelched her voice when she threatened the organization's (unethical) status quo. She plummeted emotionally, crushed by the historical discrediting of her voice by her father, brothers, and a long genealogy of misogynous men, and the present threats to her right to practice her profession.

I began a dialogue with her about the voices of women and how they have been silenced over the centuries. She became energized and passionate instead of lethargic and pitiful as we talked about finding her voice in the familial, cultural, and professional context that had squelched it. At the end of the session, she described how she had always felt most powerful when she could gather a group of girls (and later, women) in her home for girl talk about ideas, the world, hopes, dreams, and life. In the safety of her home, she could be powerful. Outside of her home, it was more difficult. We created together a treatment goal of finding her own voice *outside* as well as *inside* her home.

The Squelching of Nondominant Discourses

It is not just women whose voices are silenced. Children, ethnic, racial, class and caste minorities, and the disabled—*any* nondominant group member is less likely to be heard than the dominant one. The early work of family therapy demonstrated how, within the family system, symptomatic members were often those who uttered the unspeakable in the family and then suffered for it. And because the social construction of reality privileged men and discounted women, women have been more likely to be symptomatic and to seek help.

Men, however, can also be the bearers of the unspeakable and be labeled as crazy for it. I worked with a middle-aged rabbi and his wife, for example, who came to me after a very painful expulsion from the religious congregation in which he had served for several years. Although there were many complex and complicated factors in operation within the congregation, I began to understand the rabbi's life mission as the carrier of the unspeakable and his wife's life mission as the denier of the unspeakable. By age fourteen, he had lost both his parents. She had been the peacemaker in a violent alcoholic family. In their marriage, they had become increasingly polarized into carrier and denier positions in the face of the intense systemic stressors in the congregation. The more polarized the couple became, the more he spoke the unspeakable to the congregation and the more she tried to silence him. This dynamic contributed to his ultimate dismissal from the congregation.

His defense against the immense pain of losing both parents as a child was to talk about any and everything; her defense against the pain of the alcoholic violence in her family was to smooth it over, keep the peace, and *not* talk about anything. Therapy consisted of creating a safe place to talk about the unspeakable in both of their families of origin and in their marriage.

The Mental Health Professions'
Difficulty with the Unspeakable

It is extremely interesting to me, a therapist, that our professions are having trouble speaking the unspeakable. We have many official party lines: the line of diagnosis and pathology, of individualism and self, the lines of child and adult development, of victimization, of business, of professionalism, of survivalism, of ethics. All of these dominant discourses are currently up for grabs. The professional institutions, instead of reflectively considering the nondominant discourses that challenge the dominant ones, are hunkering down to defend their traditional beliefs.

SUMMARY

The classical approach viewed language as a symbolic tool to express the objective realities of the external world and the non-objective realities of human nature. Postmodern social constructionism views language as a socially constructed tool that both creates and reflects the realities of all of our worlds, both scientific and subjective. Through interaction with our environment in a transactional context that conveys meaning via language, we grasp social meanings even before we can actually speak the culture's words.

Language involves not only the use of words but the use of words in meaning-laden contexts. Much of our language conveys prototypical thinking in which, as we categorize meaning, we select representative models that are seen as normative. Modifiers, used to describe variations in prototypes, often convey second best or pejorative status. Language, thus, has the power to define the goodness and badness, health and pathology of our social realities.

The next chapter explores the power of language as it is used in diagnostic labels.

Chapter 5

Diagnosis: The Power to Name

One of the most obvious illustrations of the power of language in the mental health professions is in the use of diagnostic labels. The following discussion addresses the gender bias of such labels and explores the professions' resistance to change that perpetuates their continued usage.

THE SOCIAL CONTROL FUNCTIONS OF DIAGNOSIS

Diagnosis reflects the worldview and phenomenology of the dominant class; like history, it is written by "the winners." Diagnosis, the power to call behavior pathological as opposed to normative, or to define it as illness rather than criminality, carries extraordinary weight in dominant culture. (Brown, 1994, p. 127)

Via diagnosis, mental health professionals have the power to define normal and abnormal, crazy and sane. Via diagnosis, they are the gatekeepers for disability benefits, insurance reimbursements, incarcerations, hospitalizations, and educational placements. They are also the gatekeepers and hence, the social controllers, for an entire society's concepts of normalcy and deviance.

One of the the most obvious examples of this social control function is the gender bias in diagnosis. Women have been called histrionic, labeled as unfeminine when they pursue "masculine" careers, called codependent, hysteric, and borderline. Many of these labels pathologize the very qualities considered to be normative female qualities in this culture. For example, the *self-defeating personality disorder* diagnosis, which was placed in an appendix of DSM-III-R (American Psychiatric Association, 1987) for further study after there was protest to its inclusion in the main text, pathologizes the feminine quality of putting the needs of others first. Like its ancestor, *masochistic personality disorder*, it individualizes social pathology and ignores the conditions that create women's defeat in this culture (Gove, 1972; Hare-Mustin, 1991; Miller, 1991). Writes Tavris:

> When men have problems, it's because of their upbringing, personality, or environment; when women have problems, it's because of something in their very psyche. When men have problems, society tends to look outward for explanations; when women have problems, society looks inward. (1992, p. 175)

Broverman and colleagues' classic research from 1970, almost three decades ago, demonstrated that clinicians' concepts of a healthy mature man do not differ significantly from their concepts of a healthy mature adult. Their concepts of a healthy mature woman, however, differ significantly from their concepts of a healthy mature adult. The authors speculate that the different standards stem from clinician acceptance of and adjustment to the environmental notion of mental health that automatically leads to a double standard of mental health for men and women.

Others have come to similar conclusions (Avis, 1991; Bayes, 1981; Chesler, [1972] 1989; Holder and Anderson, 1989; Howell, 1981). Brodsky and Holroyd (1981) found the following biases in a survey of *women* psychologists done in 1974: fostering of traditional sex roles via equations of mental health with wife and mother roles; insensitivity to women clients' career, work, and role diversity; assumption that women are primarily responsible for childcare; deference to husbands in the treatment of women clients; biases in expectations of women; using demeaning labels to describe women; and sexist use of psychoanalytic concepts such as the myth of the supremacy of vaginal orgasm and labeling women as masochistic who have been victimized by violence.

In the family therapy arena, women's sensitivity, empathy, and ability to communicate have often been pejoratively labeled as enmeshed, undifferentiated, fused, and intrusive while the more male terms of autonomy, differentiation, hierarchy, and boundary are defined as fundamentally healthy (Walters et al., 1988). The labels may not come from the DSM, but they are powerful pathologizers of women just the same.

Tavris hypothesizes that if the normative were female rather than male, our mental disorders and the diagnostic system used to classify them would also change. For example, we might be more concerned about the prevalence of narcissism and

> [T]he National Institutes of Health would fund field studies of Sadistic Personality Disorder and Delusional Dominating Personality Disorder . . . [and we would have] independency groups . . . to help the men, and some women, who are too independent and too unresponsive to the needs of others. (1992, p. 205)

To follow Tavris' line of thought, we might, from a family systems point of view, look more closely at the "male" problems of emotional disconnection, pseudo-autonomy, power confusion, and the absence of consensual and collective problem-solving skills as contributors to individual and family distress.

Why, if we *know* that we privilege male standards of mental health over female standards, do we continue to pathologize women with gender-biased diagnoses? Because diagnosis is, at its heart, political. Diagnosis occurs by consensus and vote. It has little, if anything, to do with science, in spite of its masquerade to the contrary. Diagnosis serves to maintain the status quo by pathologizing deviations from normative models. Thus, diagnostic labels define women as disordered and hold them accountable for their own pathology (Anderson and Holder, 1989).

More women than men are diagnosed as depressed. They are taught to "see their resentment and despair about their place in the social structure as an individual problem, an emotional disorder," as their own fault (Stephenson and Walker, 1979, p. 122). Women also receive more antidepressant medications than men (Cooperstock, 1981). Women, especially married ones, have higher rates of depression, even when taking into account that they are socialized to seek help more readily and earlier and that they evaluate stress differently (Weissman and Klerman, 1981). *Women are simply under more stress* and the explanations are more of social than biological or genetic origins.

PROFESSIONAL RESISTANCE TO FEMINIST REVISIONS OF DIAGNOSIS

At the most visible level, images of science and of masculinity are mutually edifying: Both are signified through language as tough, rigorous, unemotional, rational, independent, competitive. This gender symbolism is now entrenched in contemporary psychology. (Morawski, 1990, p. 166)

Professional resistance to feminist revisions of diagnoses occurs in a context that struggles to preserve mainstream ideas and to contain deviant and frightening behavior in categories that explain the non-normative.

Preservation of the Mainstream

The psychotherapy professions have been slow to hear the voices of feminism, which have made little headway into mainstream mental health practices. Such voices are often relegated to the sidelines under *women's studies, women's issues,* and the *special needs of women.* Framed as an appendage to traditional theories, their relevance to the field as a whole is thus discounted.

Even in family therapy—the field which arose as a challenge to the whole notion that psychopathology is individual and which recognized early the interactional nature of symptomatology—the voices of women have been often ignored. All of the family therapy models have within them hidden gender dimensions (Walsh and Scheinkman, 1989). Writes Taggart as recently as 1989:

By continuing to produce "family therapy" as if the feminist critique did not exist, family therapy theorists intensify the patriarchal project of presenting as comprehensive and normative that which is partial and atypical. (p. 101)

Family therapy, although still marginalized, has become a major treatment modality in this country and abroad. Yet, despite the clearly established notion of the relational context of pathology, our diagnostic system is still completely individual in its focus. Attempts to incorporate a "Global Assessment of Relational Functioning" into the DSM-IV (American Psychiatric Association, 1994) continue to be an uphill struggle (Group for the Advancement of Psychiatry Committee on the Family, 1996; Kaslow, 1993; Strong, 1993).

I question the wisdom of even trying to add a relational model to a system that is totally individualistic. The DSM-IV requires a clinician to eliminate the possibility of physiological and medical problems first and problems caused by substance abuse or medication second before assessing individual mental and emotional factors, personality traits, and, finally, relevant social and relational issues. Thus, it *forces* clinicians to think first from an individualized medical model perspective. Psychosocial stressors on Axis IV are considered last (Wylie, 1995). What is the point of trying to add a "Global Assessment of Relational Functioning" that will just be subsumed under such an outdated model? In the meantime, the continued use of DSM-IV poses ethical problems for therapists due to its myopic focus on individual pathology (Dell, 1983; Denton, 1989).

In addition to the relational model proposed by family therapists, social constructionists have proposed contextual models in which the therapist's role is to facilitate dialogue with clients—dialogue acknowledging the socially constructed realities constraining "landscapes of action" and "landscapes of consciousness" (Bruner, 1986)—dialogue focused on opening up new possibilities for action and meaning rather than on labeling. Feminists have also proposed more contextual and mutual models. All of these models are interactional and nonpathologizing. None of them have made much headway against the DSM-IV.

Traditional Diagnoses as Containers for Nonnormative Categories of Reality

If we *know* that our diagnostic system individualizes relational and social problems, that it pathologizes and marginalizes along the lines of gender, class, caste, ethnicity, age, and culture, why are we still using the DSM? Gergen speculates that

> . . . the vocabulary of the mental health professions does serve to render the alien familiar, and thus less fearsome. Rather than being seen as "the work of the devil" or as "frighteningly strange," for example, nonnormative activities are given standardized labels, signifying that they are indeed natural, fully anticipated and long familiar to the sciences. (1994, p. 148)

By naming nondominant discourse phenomena as pathological, such phenomena become more manageable. Naming also controls the eruption of nondominant discourse,

> . . . [relieving] its richness of its most dangerous elements; [organizing] its disorder so as to skate around its most uncontrollable aspects . . . , [and symbolizing a] profound logophobia . . . of this mass of spoken things, of everything that could possibly be violent, discontinuous, querulous, disordered even and perilous in it, of the incessant, disorderly buzzing of discourse. (Foucault, 1972, pp. 228-229)

As they are normalized in this manner, they are segregated into defined categories of reality that must be dealt with in specialized ways by professionals. The "disease," the person who has it, and that person's family are labeled, often as one and the same. The person with alcoholism is an alcoholic and his family is an alcoholic family. The person with schizophrenia is a schizophrenic and his family is a schizophrenic family.

> Learning the language of medicine contributes to the reconstruction both of the person who is the object of medical attention and of sickness as well. . . . Both the sufferer and the sickness are transformed from common realities into very special realities. . . . (Newman and Gergen, 1995, p. 3)

In addition to rendering the strange less frightening and organizing official categories of response, there is also the agenda of professional self-preservation. For if the mental health professions can control the language of normalcy and pathology, they can survive.

INSTITUTIONAL SELF-PRESERVATION: A HIDDEN AGENDA OF DSM

Disciplinary Turf

> . . . [T]here are more therapists (lay and credentialed) using many more scientific or pseudo-scientific medicalized or quasi-medicalized pictorially-based descriptions of many more clients than at any previous time in history. (Good and Good, 1989, pp. 307-308)

The history of the mental health professions is a history of economic and institutional self-preservation as well as a history of healing. The origin of medicine and of psychiatry as a specialty branch of medicine is illustrative.

Healing of all kinds was originally the domain of women. During the late eighteenth and early nineteenth centuries, men entered the practice of medicine, professionalizing it, banning women from its ranks, and destroying the traditional networking, skill sharing, and accumulated knowledge of women over the generations. Men were drawn to the profession of medicine for economic and status reasons. Medicine held the promise of a lucrative career, afforded membership in an increasingly exclusive club, and conferred on the practitioner the status of gentleman (Ehrenreich and English, 1978).

As men took over healing, much of the pathology created in the context of a patriarchal social order became medicalized and individualized and femininity itself became viewed as a medical disorder. The new physician experts ". . . were the first to pass judgment on the social consequences of female anatomy and to prescribe the 'natural' life plan for women" (Ehrenreich and English, 1978, p. 4). Because the "natural life plan" for women only reinforced the femininity-as-pathological mentality, a continuous stream of women patients was practically guaranteed.

Mental illness—originally an issue of concern to (predominantly female) social reformers—became the turf of medicine as the specialty of psychiatry evolved in the late eighteenth century.

From Freud and Janet and Charcout and Ferenci onward, the definition of sanity and insanity became the turf of the male medical profession, whose pathologized beliefs about women prevailed.

Women's emotional and psychological deficiencies were thought to reside in their ovaries and uteri, and horrendous interventions such as clitorectomies were performed to "cure" women of depression and hysteria. Psychiatrists thus established their expert turf on the basis of the body as an avenue to the mind (Masson, 1984, 1986).

It was not long before the psychiatry profession faced competition. Although already considered a profession before World War I, psychology became more firmly established through administering routine IQ tests to military personnel during the war. The acceptance of the IQ test as a valid instrument to measure intelligence ultimately propelled psychologists into every social institution in this country as the experts on measuring all conceivable cognitive and emotional aspects of human functioning. As with medicine, psychology also was historically a male profession.

Social workers, whose turf was originally social, found themselves moving more and more into the psychological arena as they worked in child guidance clinics founded during the New Deal era. The term *psychiatric social worker* crept into usage to indicate not just the shift in the field to a casework approach, but also the growing allegiance to and fascination with psychoanalytic theory. With the establishment of child welfare services, family service agencies, mental hygiene clinics, and other casework settings, social work expanded its turf to include the *psycho*social. In 1955, the National Association of Social Workers was formed, thus establishing social work as a *professional* career and as the only predominantly female mental health profession.

Psychiatry, until the 1960s and 1970s, was still in the lead position among the mental health professions. But, in the face of the tumultuous social upheavals of the Women's Movement, the Civil Rights Movement, and the Vietnam War, the individualized diagnosis and classification of mental disorders arose as a grave conceptual problem for the profession. What had heretofore been viewed as individual pathology was showing its social roots, potentially compromising the entire theoretical orientation upon which psychiatry was founded.

Psychiatry's response to this dilemma was to enlarge its diagnostic system and to reinforce its *medical, disease-oriented* expertise. Until this time, the DSM-I (American Psychiatric Association, 1952) and the DSM-II (American Psychiatric Association, 1966) had a modest number of categories in the fairly loosely constructed descriptions of mental and emotional disorders. By 1980, however, when DSM-III was published, the number of categories expanded considerably and revisions occurred at more and more frequent intervals. DSM-III-R, for example, was published in 1987 (American Psychiatric Association) and DSM-IV in 1994 (American Psychiatric Association).

The rapid expansion of diagnoses enabled psychiatry to continue to pigeonhole issues of social concern into problems of *individual* diagnostic reliability (Kirk and Kutchins, 1992). In focusing on the creation of DSM-III and on its use as a scientific taxonomy, psychiatry was able to exploit what had been a little-known technical manual into *the* major resource on diagnostic nomenclature, supported by a rhetoric of research and scientific technology. Not only did psychiatry bypass the entire question of the social and contextual nature of mental and emotional problems by tightening up and selling its own diagnostic model; it also ensured its own survival. "DSM-III saved psychiatry from professional oblivion, wresting it away from psychoanalysis, re-medicalizing it and establishing its preeminence throughout the mental health field" (Wylie, 1995, p. 24).

With the advent of managed care, the DSM-III-R and the DSM-IV became so entrenched in the mental health systems that working with *any* client who is using third-party payer benefits mandates that the clinician give a DSM diagnosis and justify treatment on the basis of medical necessity. It has become *the* standard of classification and psychiatric nomenclature and *the* basis for third party treatment authorization (Maser, Kaelber, and Weise, 1991; Wylie, 1995).

Big Business and Its Controlling Influence

The growing power of the DSM in the naming of mental illness and its use in managed care to control treatment resources also has facilitated the escalation of biological psychiatry and the increased partnering of managed care, psychiatry, and the pharmaceutical industry (Breggin, 1991; Dumont, 1990; Lexchin, 1988). This is big business, not science (Kutchins and Kirk, 1988). And it is business with a powerful social control function. It masks the societal conditions that spawn many mental health problems in the first place.

> When it diagnoses, drugs, and incarcerates the homeless poor, psychiatry covers up the political issue—society's unwillingness to provide jobs, housing, or an adequate safety net. People victimized by socioeconomic conditions are turned over to psychiatry for further abuse. All of us then rest more easily—except for the victims. (Breggin, 1991, p. 66)

Managed care's use of the DSM has been particularly dangerous because its benchmark for determining the reimbursable status of illness is a medical necessity. Medical necessity tends to inhere in those diagnoses that take the least time to treat and respond to standardized treatment models, such as depression, anxiety, and learning disorders, but not post-traumatic stress or dissociative disorders (Wylie, 1995). Increasingly, medication is the standardized treatment model and the rights of clients to refuse medication are being jeopardized.

The DSM, with its individualizing, medicalizing, and pathologizing of all human problems—and especially those associated with socially created inequities—is the antithesis of contextual and social constructionist thought. The ethicality of its continued use must be questioned. It is, as Gergen (1991, p. 13) so aptly describes, a "vocabulary of human deficit."

THE ACCOMMODATION OF OTHER DISCIPLINES TO THE DSM

As the DSM-III, DSM-III-R, and DSM-IV cornered the managed care business of mental health, the professions of psychology, social work, marriage and family therapy, and professional counseling lobbied for the privilege of being included instead of challenging its usage. Psychology was the first to be included on provider panels, followed by social work and, with more struggle, counseling and marriage and family therapy. Each inclusion was met with resistance from those already in—with much scientific and standard-of-care rhetoric to substantiate their opposition.

Instead of questioning the ethics of using an individualized and decontextualized diagnostic system and perhaps attempting to work *with* the early managed care groups to change the diagnostic model of DSM, the professions clamored to jump on the managed care bandwagon. Much of the rationale for such a position was framed in terms of *client* need, but the underlying issue was one of professional self-interest and economic survival.

The outcome of going with the managed care flow has been that we are evermore wedded to the use of the DSM and evermore subject to ethical conflicts created by the juxtaposition of the business requirements of managed care with the ethical guidelines still promulgated by the professions. To cite but one example, as the number of therapy sessions allocated by managed care gatekeepers continues to shrink, the therapist is faced with the dilemma of fighting with the managed care company to justify additional services for the client, or terminating and referring the client to another resource. Feminist ethics suggest a third alternative, to continue with the client pro bono or at reduced rates.

The first alternative potentially jeopardizes the clinician's participation on the provider panel since managed care companies are known to drop those who provide "too many" sessions to a client. The second alternative is very difficult since even the public mental health clinics, which used to be the referral source of last resort, are now going to managed care models of service in order to compete for funds. The third alternative jeopardizes the economic survival of the clinician and, with some managed care arrangements, would be considered a breach of contract. All of the ethics codes have standards about not abandoning clients, yet compliance is becoming increasingly difficult in a managed care environment of shrinking resources.

This is just one example of how the mental health professions, in lobbying to participate in what is inherently an unethical system, both lost an opportunity to take a more ethical stand and subjected individual practitioners to dealing with the ethical fallout at the individual level.

Ironically, inclusion in the managed care provider panels has, temporarily at least, enhanced the prominence of nonmedical providers in the mental health arena. Social workers and other masters-level providers receive lower reimbursement rates and hence are more likely to be used as primary providers of psychotherapy services. The medical model, however, still predominates and there are some predictions that psychotherapy sessions will ultimately shrink to brief medication management appointments provided by psychiatrists (Lerner, 1995). The policy of many managed care companies to *require* medication trials with certain diagnoses is an ominous harbinger of such an approach. In the meantime, the ethical conflicts posed by the incongruity between the standards of managed care and the ethical codes of the professions will continue to jeopardize the individual practitioner and the clients he serves. The DSM and its continued use pose ethical conflicts that are becoming more and more glaring.

SUMMARY

The DSM-IV has been established as *the* diagnostic manual for *all* of the psychotherapy professions. Its acceptance by insurance companies and managed care corporations as the required nomenclature for justifying third-party payments for mental health services makes it essential. The fact that it medicalizes, pathologizes, and individualizes all problems at a time when the exact opposite is needed demonstrates the power of what Laura Brown (1994) calls "the winners"—the people and institutions who define what is normal or abnormal, diseased or criminal, sane or insane. Currently, that power resides with the American Psychiatric Association and the corporate minds of insurers and managed care companies. Diagnosis, at its very core, is a social control mechanism.

The gender bias of DSM-IV is perhaps the most obvious example of the problems inherent in its continued use. But it is also skewed in its generic privileging of white (male) medicalized beliefs over other ethnic and cultural beliefs about mental health and illness and in its decontextualized, intrapsychic view of pathology as residing *within* the symptomatic individual. This is particularly problematic at a time when the relational, contextual aspects of mental health problems have become increasingly obvious and when other diagnostic systems, such as "The Global Assessment of Relational Functioning" (Group for the Advancement of Psychiatry Committee on the Family, 1996) *are* available.

When psychology, social work, and marriage and family therapy bought into managed care, lobbying with great energy to be included alongside psychiatry on provider panels, they also bought into the use of DSM-IV. They are now stuck with the results. Mental health professionals of all disciplines must utilize a diagnostic system that is not only no longer relevant to a postmodern stance of honoring multiple truths but is, at its very core, unethical.

The next chapter discusses additional examples of mental health truths that have been socially constructed and whose utility is questionable.

Chapter 6

Social Constructionism's Challenge to Traditional Mental Health Beliefs: Some Additional Examples

Questions that are overly directed by a methodology risk squelching the therapist's opportunity to be led by the clients into their own world.

> ——H. Anderson and H. Goolishian,
> "The Client Is the Expert:
> A Not-Knowing Approach to Therapy"

People can become obsessed with their own theories and miss the point of everything. In Tibet we say: "Theories are like patches on a coat, one day they just wear off."

> —S. Rimpoche,
> *The Tibetan Book of Living and Dying*

Just as we must challenge diagnoses that deconstruct from scientific truths to labels that control social deviance, privilege professional power, and pathologize large groups of people, so must we challenge many of our other socially constructed mental health beliefs. These include our ideas about the self, child development and developmental stages, feelings, intelligence, and family, to name but a few.

In deconstructing these beliefs, I am not suggesting that they are not useful in some client-therapist contexts and should therefore be discarded. What I am advocating is that therapists must be aware of their social creation and not present the traditional ideas so prevalent in the field as truths to clients. This is particularly important because so many of our truths are "only tentative, tradition-bound human inventions [that, in the mental health field] have not had a very good track record for longevity" (Efran, Lukens, and Lukens, 1990, p. 40). It is also important because beliefs, like diagnoses, can be pathologizing, disempowering, and potentially harmful, closing down rather than opening up possibilities. Keeping possibilities open is ethical, yet many of our beliefs, standards, and codes require the opposite.

IDEAS ABOUT THE SELF

> . . . [S]ocial complicity and identity walk hand in hand; without others there is no self. (Gergen, 1991, p. 178)

> Only by replacing [the] transactional model of mind with an isolating individualistic one have Anglo-American philosophers been able to make Other Minds seem so opaque and impenetrable. (Bruner, 1990, pp. 33-34)

Early concepts of the self were rooted in scientific objectivity. The self was something that was observable and reified. Debates about the nature of the true self led to the idea that it was conceptual rather than essential, and was dependent on culture and dialogue. These debates dwindled away as psychology developed standardized research paradigms to define self, which then became what the standardized tests measured.

In the 1970s and 1980s, self began to be understood as a product of social context and interaction—self as a storyteller who incorporates self-descriptions as defined both by the individual and the culture. From this point of view, self is revealed in the relationship and transactions between teller and listener. The narratives of self define the meanings of self. Collectively, these narratives create and are created by our folk psychology, our culture.

The Implications of a Narrative Definition of Self

The narrative definition of self challenges traditional beliefs about an autonomous self capable of independent, noncontextually based thought and action. In narrative, there is no clear distinction between the self and the object, the self and the other. We are all different selves in relation to different people and in different contexts. We are all interdependent. The self is constantly changing, a fluid narrative in time and context rather than a fixed and differentiated reality (Bruner, 1990; Hoffman, 1992; Rosenbaum and Dyckman, 1995; Spence, 1984). Writes Gergen (1991, p. 164), ". . . [W]e find *auto*biography is anything but *auto*nomous; it is more properly *socio*biography."

The implications of narrative for psychotherapy are staggering. If stories are fluid and changeable according to relation and context, then selves can change as narratives and the actions that emanate from them change. Stories of disempowerment, pathology, incompetence, disease, hopelessness, and despair can be reauthored to define self in more powerful, competent, healthy, and hopeful ways (Epston and White, 1992; White, 1995; White and Epston, 1990).

> One might say that the search for new meanings, which often comprises searching for a new language, is a search for us to be *the* selves with which we feel most comfortable. . . . "[T]herapeutic" talk might be regarded as a form of search. . . . (T. Andersen, 1992, p. 64)

The traditional beliefs about self as stable, objectified, individual, real, and separate from other selves interfere with the process of exploring new possibilities in therapy. Therapists who are invested in imposing their own narrative about self cannot hear their client's version of self and cannot help him create alternative versions that are healing and empowering. They only see the client's self through the lens of privileged therapy beliefs about self. Thus, descriptive terms such as self-abusing, self-defeating, self-blaming, self-righteous, and self-esteem all carry with them the narrative of self in isolation, self boundaried from context, self as individual. Any of these self terms can only be understood in the transactional and social contexts in which they occur. The following case example illustrates how therapists' assumptions about the client's self were disempowering and damaging to him.

Case Example

Bill was utterly demoralized by the labels several well-meaning therapists had put on him and that he had also internalized from reading numerous pop psychology books. He was narcissistic, immature, fragile, and depressed. It was only when he left psychotherapy, began to pursue his artistic interests, and welcomed feedback from friends that he changed his self-identity. He sought me out for couples counseling because his wife, Melanie, had lived anxiously for years, constantly waiting for his new facade to melt, and for him to "decompensate."

It took almost six months of regular couples therapy sessions for Bill to accept that I *believed* that he had indeed changed him*self* and for Melanie to relax her hypervigilance about his self's supposed fragility. Once this corner was turned, Bill and Melanie joined together in their rage at how previous psychotherapy experiences had reinforced his negative self-image instead of helping him change it and had, in fact, created more problems for him than he had when he entered therapy. Their understanding of how the therapists' beliefs about self as internal, objective, and disconnected from the transactions of the couple and of the therapy, enabled them to generate and sustain new self-concepts.

Ethical Problems in Our Current Beliefs About the Self

The case above is just one illustration of how therapy beliefs about the relatively fixed nature of character structure *within* the individual self can create severe problems for clients. Nothing about such pathologizing of a client's self would be considered unethical in our current codes, but it should be.

Our current codes and standards interfere with possibilities for expanding people's self-definitions. One of the standards in the treatment of domestic violence, for example, cautions therapists against doing any couples work when the man has been violent until he has gone through a treatment program with other men. This standard assumes that the man's whole *identity* is violent and will continue to be so without group intervention. While this may be true for some men, there are many others for whom violent behavior is ego-dystonic. These are men who feel horror and shame in their loss of control and desperately want to eliminate violence from them-*selves*. There is no reason why couples work with such men should be contraindicated except that it violates the current party line about violence (Lipchik, 1991). It is based on an outdated notion that violence resides in the self of the man. Although the approach appropriately emphasizes the cultural context of male violence against women, it still isolates the man from his partner, his most significant other, even when couples therapy would not place the wife in jeopardy and could help the man define himself in terms of qualities other than violence.

There has been a certain advantage for mental health professionals in seeing clear distinctions between self and other. It has enabled us to deny the powerful impact we can have on someone else's selfhood, to distance from the pain of the other, and to minimize our responsibility for change. If the self is, after all, relatively immutable and objective, we are limited in how we can help shape and change it. If self refuses to change, we can blame it for its resistance to our efforts. If self is mutual, relational, and contextual, the limits become blurred. Our own selves become more connected to the self of the other, more implicated in whatever resistance we encounter and help cocreate in the client-therapist relationship. We become aware of our power to affect the client's self and of our vulnerability to the client's impact on our own selves.

In recognizing the mutuality of selves in psychotherapy, the therapist is doing *with* rather than doing *to* his client. His only role is as a facilitator of dialogue and action that open up new possibilities for selfhood for his clients, new narratives that situate self more positively and hopefully. This is a joint process for which the client must be (almost) as fully responsible as the therapist. Yet our standards of care and ethics codes continue to perpetuate the self-other dichotomy, to hold the therapist responsible for *everything* that transpires in therapy, to exonerate the client from any responsibility, and to avoid the ethical dilemmas posed by such a position.

An article titled "Rights of Clients, Responsibilities of Therapists" (Hare-Mustin et al., 1979) portrays the dichotomizing of self and other in the therapeutic arena. The expertise and responsibility of the therapist are privileged while the expertise and responsibility of the client are discounted. The rights of the client are privileged and the rights of the therapist discounted. This renders both therapist and client vulnerable when something goes awry—the therapist because of the unrealistic expectation that he can control the client-therapist relationship and be *totally* responsible (without many rights) for what happens in it, and the client because of the diminishment of his responsibility (and credit) for the treatment process.

IDEAS ABOUT CHILD DEVELOPMENT AND DEVELOPMENTAL STAGES

Ever since people took notice of children, they have been formulating theories of how to rear them. (Greenleaf, 1978, p. 142)

Our lives may be determined less by our childhood than by the way we have learned to image our childhoods. (Hillman, 1996, p. 4)

Traditionally, psychotherapy has focused more on the past than the future. The idea has been that, for clients to have better tomorrows, therapists must first help them create better yesterdays. (Miller, Duncan, and Hubble, 1997, p. 141)

The Social Construction of Developmental Stage Theories

References to child development and developmental stages permeate mental health literature. Assumptions about the tasks which children did or did not complete developmentally; the role reversals, traumas, or neglect they experienced; the developmental milestones they achieved early or late; and how their progression through each stage is dependent upon completion of the preceding stages are embedded in our theories. Who each person is is viewed as the inevitable result of the events through which he has journeyed developmentally.

Theories of child development evolved in the social context of the turn of the century. Industrialization removed production from the home, eliminating chores for both women and children. Child labor laws and other reforms for the benefit of children were enacted to protect against the horrors of industrial capitalism and promote the yearning for home as a safe haven from the outside world. Until child labor laws banned children from the factories to the "safety" of the home, children worked alongside adults and were included in adult social and community activities. It was only as they were gradually segregated from the workforce and into compulsory education that they were seen as special and different from adults. Childhood became a stage.

The "century of the child" was a talisman for changing conditions of the family and for the development of not only a new interest in childhood, but also what Ehrenreich and English (1978) call a "cult of motherhood." For if children were so important, then the mothers who raised them were crucial. Developmental theories about the child thus reinforced the expanding power of women. Motherhood, like housework, became a profession. Women, however, because of their restriction to the private sphere of home, could not be trusted to raise boys who would go into the world. Enter the experts to assist them—experts who, by the 1940s and 1950s, encouraged them to stay home and devote their full energies to motherhood, and who held them totally accountable for the mental health of their children (Ehrenreich and English, 1978).

Adolescence is a stage we invented during the early 1900s, in the context of the development of secondary education, the mass production of automobiles, the arrival of motion pictures, and the reign of the flapper. During the Great Depression, when survival was a national concern, adolescence went underground. It resurfaced in the 1940s and mushroomed through the 1950s and 1960s as the pill, a new openness about sex, and the fight for women's rights and the rights of African Americans exploded onto the social scene.

Since the 1950s, developmental stage theories have expanded to include almost every age and condition. Gail Sheehy's *Passages* (1976), for example, introduced us to the notion of stages in adult development at a time when the excitement and enthusiasm of the 1960s had begun to sour and people were turning their vision to inward concerns. Individual malaise and discomfort, seen through the lens of stage theory, seemed to reassure people that what they were feeling was part of a normal developmental stage rather than a reaction to social problems.

In today's electronic age, in which children and adolescents have access to information previously restricted to adults, the stages of childhood and adolescence are deconstructing (Meyrowitz, 1985; Pipher, 1996; Postman, 1982). Conversely, as adults function like children, we hear terms such as *parentified children* and *parental abdication* to describe the blurring of age boundaries.

Stage theories have also been developed in reference to families. Books and articles addressing the stages of divorce (Ahrons and Rodgers, 1987; Beal, 1980; Kaslow, 1984) and the stages of remarriage (Ahrons and Rodgers, 1987; Lewis, 1985; McGoldrick and Carter, 1980; Visher and Visher, 1979, 1982; Whiteside, 1982) reflected the increasing prevalence of such phenomena in the 1970s and 1980s. As with *Passages*, the stages described in such publications provided anchoring in the unknown seas of family dissolution and serial marriage, and normalized divorce as a solution to problems rooted in patriarchy.

Stage theory also has been applied to illness, death, and dying (Kübler-Ross, 1969), trauma recovery (Waites, 1993), and to almost every other conceivable life experience. Normal life pains and problems are explained as stages through which one must journey.

Problems with Developmental Stage Theories

For all of the anxiety-relieving reassurance of normalcy that stage theories provide, they also have their downsides.

Assumptions About Truth

Stage theories are problematic when they are presented as truth. People tend to expect that they should comply with them, questioning their normalcy if they are not "in stage."

I had a young woman client who had recently been diagnosed with a recurrence of cancer. She had survived her first bout with the illness well, learning much about her own inner strengths and the strengths of her support system. With the second diagnosis, she was upset but not devastated, sad but not depressed. Her presenting concern in the initial therapy session was that perhaps she *should* be more devastated and depressed. Her referring oncologist was worried that she was suppressing the normal feelings that would ordinarily be present in the second stage of the cancer.

In my conversation with the young woman, I expanded on all of the possible normal ways to learn to live with cancer, deconstructing the oncologist's beliefs. Via an exploration of all of the things that past experience had taught her about *her* strengths, together we empowered her to believe in her own stages. Relieved to be divested of beliefs that did not fit her situation, the young woman regained confidence in her own style of coping.

Another young woman presented in therapy with the concern that her child was not grieving his parents' recent divorce. All of the books she had read about divorce and children taught her to expect the child to be angry with her, to express wishes for the parents to get back together, and to regress behaviorally. Her child was doing none of these things. In an interview with him in his mother's presence, he said that his father had been extremely abusive to both of them and he was relieved to no longer live in the presence of such violence. He felt happy to be living his life without such overwhelming stress. His mother was relieved to hear that her son's processing of the divorce was working well for him and that he did not *have* to experience all of the things about which she had read.

Detour of Social Concerns

Stage theories detour social concerns into an individual model of health and pathology. One is no longer depressed because of the mundane and insecure nature of a depressing job but because of a midlife crisis. One's anxiety is not because of worries about retirement in a country which provides few social supports, but because of the empty nest syndrome.

Risk of Disempowerment and Pathologization

Stage theories can create disempowering and pathologizing realities for many people. In the stage theory of menopause, for example, women are taught to expect hot flashes, irritability, depression, loss of sleep, inertia, hysteria, and night sweats. Their ovaries are described as atrophied and failing to produce. As in past theories of women's mental health, biology is seen to rule psyche; women's reproductive systems are defined as abnormal and deficient because they are different from the (normal) reproductive systems of men (Fausto-Sterling, 1985; McGoldrick, 1989; Tavris, 1992). Menopause was even called an estrogen-deficiency *disease* by the World Health Organization in 1981 (Tavris, 1992), one factor which paved the way for the massive use of estrogen replacement therapy currently in vogue in this country. The fact that many women experience only mild discomfort or no symptoms at all during menopause becomes obscured in the overarching beliefs associated with the stage theory of menopause.

That culture plays a significant part in the symptoms of menopause is evidenced by the historical fact that, in the nineteenth century, the more a woman violated social laws, such as promoting women's suffrage or using birth control measures, the more likely she was to experience the symptoms of menopause (Smith-Rosenberg, 1973). Madeleine Goodman (1977) and her colleagues researched the rate of incidence of menopausal symptoms in a sample of Caucasian and Japanese women in Hawaii in 1977. They found that 75 percent reported no remarkable menopausal symptoms, with the rates lower for Japanese than for Caucasian women. Other studies have found even higher percentages of nonsymptomatic women (Boston Women's Health Collective, 1984). Yet, the negative view of menopause as a disease is the prototypical model in this culture and therefore affects *all* women.

> The negative view of menstruation and menopause is part of a larger perspective that regards female anatomy as designed entirely for reproduction. When it starts to "fail" and "run down," therefore, it can only be seen as a "problem," a "crisis"; the relevant body parts become "superfluous" or in need of a little medical bolstering. (Tavris, 1992, p. 161)

The view that women go through a *diseased* stage in menopause is a way to silence their voices. As the *diseased other,* they can be more easily dismissed. How many times in couples therapy sessions have I heard *both* husband and wife discount what she has to say because she is menopausal (or "PMSing")? It is often revealed in subtle comments but is a powerful presence in the room. My immediate response as a therapist is to question their beliefs. "How did you come to believe that menopause would affect you this way? Do you think that hot flashes reduce the power of your brain cells? What makes you think that you are more irritable and depressed than usual?"

Gender Bias

Assuming that male development is the norm, stage theories have generally privileged the development of boys and men over that of girls and women. Differentiation, autonomy, and identity are emphasized over connection and intimacy. Even Erikson (1950), who stated that developmentally, girls achieve intimacy before identity, still used the male sequencing of identity followed by intimacy as the model for his chart of life cycle stages.

The early socialization of girls into their more passive and adaptive roles is illustrated by feminist researchers and clinicians. Maccoby (1988), for example, found that as early as age three, girls begin deferring to boys in their play. Gilligan (1982) describes how girls begin to stop speaking up at about age eleven or twelve, as they become socialized into the voiceless role of women in this culture. Goldner (1985, 1988) examines the role of gender as well as generation in the developmental lives of families and discusses how the family is experienced in two very different ways for men and for women.

Obsession with Survival

Stage theories reflect our societal obsession with survival, with getting through things with as little pain and suffering as possible (Lasch, 1979). They imply that if you just "do it right," suffering can be minimized. This promise is another way of placing on the individual the responsibility for society's crisis in meaning.

The Application of Stage Theories to the Mental Health Professions

Stage theories are also relevant to the way the mental health professions conceptualize themselves. Our entire system of training, supervision, credentialing, and licensure is built on the notion that therapists must progress through certain stages of learning and supervised practice before they are equipped to provide therapy, and that the more experience they have, the better therapists they will be.

The fact that much research debunks the stage theory of professional development is ignored. Robyn Dawes (1994, p. 106), for example, in a review of over 300 research studies, found that "[t]he empirical data indicate that mental health professionals' accuracy of judgment does not increase with increasing clinical experience, just as their success as psychotherapists does not." Furthermore, much training and supervision are based on mental health mythology and on theories and techniques that have no demonstrable success.

Stage theories in the mental health professions are officially promulgated to protect the public from untrained and inexperienced practitioners. But they also enhance professionalism by controlling access to the professions, establishing pecking orders among the professions, and preserving the mystique and privilege of professional language and knowledge. Since professionalism is responsible for the creation and maintenance of the middle class in this country, stage theories, in limiting access to the professions, restrict access to the middle class and its economic benefits. In so doing, they also isolate the professions and their bodies of knowledge from the influence and benefit of nonprofessional theories, "seem[ing] to assure that no outsider has anything to offer [and preserving] the delusion of knowing it all" (Ehrenreich, 1989, p. 140).

IDEAS ABOUT FEELINGS

The intense emotions we all feel—anxiety, anger, and despair—all have been labeled pathological and "treated" by therapists. (Pipher, 1996, p. 117)

Feelings: Psychotherapy's Turf

If there is anything that the mental health professions stake a claim to it is human emotion. People seek services because they are depressed, anxious, fearful, unhappy, conflicted, or angry. Normal feelings are framed as problematic. Psychotherapy is supposed to make people feel better. Psychotherapy is predicated on the belief that feelings reside *within* the human being. Even the interactional theories of family therapy treat feelings as individual. You may "carry" your mother's depression as a way of helping her out, but the feelings are within *you*. A child may be behaving in an angry and rebellious fashion to distract his parents from their marital problems, but, in the process, *he* is the angry and rebellious one. Feelings are conceptualized as *entities* with a fundamental existence of their own.

The Social Construction of Feelings: Anxiety and Depression

When feelings are understood as *constructs* rather than entities, their meaning shifts from something *within* the individual to something that is socially constructed in relation and in context. To illustrate, Sarbin (1964, 1968) traces the social construction of the word *anxiety*. The word itself derives from the Middle English word *anguish* which came from the Old French word *anguisse,* meaning a choking sensation in the throat. *Anguish* in Middle English was a kind of spiritual suffering. Sarbin hypothesizes that the meaning of *anguisse,* a condition with clear causation, was used metaphorically to describe the anguish of spiritual suffering, a condition without clear causation. In everyday usage, the metaphorical, "as if" quality was forgotten.

Anxiety is not just a response to an environmental stimulus; rather it is a result of the threat created when a person cannot accommodate what Sarbin calls "cognitive strain . . . a state of not having answers (or having incompatible answers) to vitally important questions" (Sarbin, 1964 and 1968, as cited in Hallam, 1994, p. 151). An anxious response to an environmental stimulus, is, in other words, culturally and socially mediated.

Weiner and Marcus (1994) elaborate on the kinds of socially constructed contexts that might produce another feeling, that of depression. In their view, depression does not reside *within* the person but rather is generated by transactional contexts of hopelessness, helplessness, worthlessness, and/or powerlessness. This suggests a diagnosis of depression-producing *contexts* rather than of depressed *people.*

The Social Construction of the Lack of Feeling

The social construction of the *lack* of a feeling is also instructive. *Frigidity,* the absence of sexual feelings in women, for example, was a term coined during Freudian times to refer to women who were unable to enjoy the pleasures of marital intercourse. *Vaginal* intercourse was believed to be optimal, *clitoral* orgasm to be immature. Freud's solution to the problem of frigidity was to encourage women to submit to their husbands, to define femininity on the basis of women's capacity to enjoy sexual pleasure in such submission, to teach women to think of themselves as less sexually mature than men, and to call them diseased if they were unable to have sexual feelings (Boyle, 1994). Both the definition of frigidity as an absence of sexual feeling *and* the remedies proposed were socially constructed. Rachael Hare-Mustin addresses similar problems regarding modern women's sexuality in an article titled "Sex, Lies, and Headaches: The Problem Is Power" (1991).

Ethical Problems in Dominant Discourses About Feelings

As mental health professionals, we make assumptions about the normalcy and appropriateness of feelings *as defined by social context.* In accepting the standard assumptions about feelings, we may miss the client's own unique story. Dominant discourses prevail; nondominant discourses are the variations, as with the young boy's relief to have his father out of the home. This suggests that the ethical stance of the therapist should be to listen to the *client's* story about feelings rather than to expect the client to conform to the professional narratives about feelings that we are trained to believe.

IDEAS ABOUT INTELLIGENCE

> . . . [R]esearch on *anything* will yield findings that mirror its procedures for observing and measuring. Science always invents a conforming reality in just that way. (Bruner, 1986, p. 104)

The Social Construction of Intelligence

Tests that measure intelligence are socially constructed. Their early usages were often to "discover" biological and racial differences that were used to justify status and economic inequities. The poor, according to these early tests, were at the bottom of the social pecking order because they were less intelligent. Intelligence was seen as something deep within the individual, as hardwired and unalterable (M. L. Andersen, 1994).

Even though we *know* that intelligence tests are socially and culturally biased, we continue to use them *and* to believe in their veracity. In addition, we take little into account about the nature of the testing situation in determining outcome, such as the power differential between tester and subject, the meaning of the test outcome to the subject and her family, the social control functions of test results in determining educational placements, institutionalizations, and job and corporate tracking.

Alternative Models of Intelligence

M. L. Anderson suggests that we move from current conceptualizations of intelligence as something that really exists within the brain to a more generative model committed to the idea of indeterminate potentiality:

> The most important kinds of intelligence are truly social and collective, and not properties of individuals. . . . If the ability to survive is the measure of intelligence, then we will soon discover whether we are all very smart, or very, very stupid. (1994, pp. 135-136)

Andersen's challenge to the mental health professions is clear. We must transform our beliefs about intelligence to more collective, socially constructed, and mutual ideas that facilitate communal well-being and continuity over generations. The ethics of continuing the current format of intelligence testing, which closes down rather than opens up possibilities for our clients, is questionable at best. How many parents learn to expect less from their child after being told that his IQ is average? How many parents push their child to super achievement after being told that she is bright? How many applicants for graduate school are rejected because they are not good test takers? How many men and women, because of various test results, are steered into nonacademic high school tracks that offer little opportunity for career satisfaction?

The Individual Therapist's Ethical Dilemma

Meanwhile, in the trenches, the individual therapist is forced to comply with what is considered standard knowledge about intelligence. The risk of deviating from the standard can be high, particularly if ethics complaints or lawsuits are filed. Children must be referred for testing in schools, child welfare settings, psychiatric settings, and juvenile courts. Adults receive testing in child custody disputes, probationary situations, job placement facilities, psychiatric hospitals, military organizations, and prisons.

While not all such tests are *intelligence* measures, they are all socially constructed measures of human characteristics and functioning. Whatever is being measured is simply what the tests measure, no more and no less.

IDEAS ABOUT FAMILY

Family is a collection of people who pool resources and help each other over the long haul. Families love one another even when that requires sacrifice. Family means that if you disagree, you still stay together. (Pipher, 1996, p. 24)

The Social Construction of Family

In Chapter 4, I discussed idealized cognitive models and used the word *family* as an example. The idealized cognitive model for family is a first-married, biological, legal unit consisting of two heterosexual adults of the opposite sex and their child(ren). All other family types are described with modifiers to indicate their deviation from it or are simply not described at all. In this model, families are observable, "real" units of people.

From a social constructionist point of view, the term family is more a description of how we organize and represent social relations than a unit of people (Holstein and Gubrium, 1994). All of our beliefs about what constitutes the ideal organization and representation of social relations are social and political. Current debates about what kinds of structures should be permitted to describe themselves as family are political issues. Rhetoric that privileges some family structures as more "natural" than others is simply rhetoric. As more diversity in family organization surfaces, more debate occurs.

Linguistic and Legal Limitations in Psychotherapy Beliefs About Family

Most of the psychotherapy professions' beliefs about families are products of and contributors to socially constructed beliefs. They reflect society's biases regarding what is healthy and what is not. Even it we accept with open arms the addition of new kinds of family organizations, we are stuck with linguistic difficulties in relating to them. Chapter 4's discussion of the meanings of words like *natural* or *real* to describe families is but one example of this difficulty. So is the total absence of words available to refer to many kinds of families.

We are also constrained by legal definitions of family and parental rights to the extent that such definitions often circumscribe whom we can and cannot see in a therapy session, even if clinical wisdom dictates otherwise. A colleague recently had a case, for example, in which the mother, Mrs. Jones, and her children, Ann and Travis, needed supportive therapy following an extremely litigious divorce. Mr. Jones and his attorney did everything within their power to vilify Mrs. Jones and to wrench custody from her. The agenda just under the surface was the husband's wish for revenge against his wife for leaving him.

Although Mrs. Jones retained physical custody, the judge gave the couple joint legal custody in order to mollify Mr. Jones. The therapist was subpoenaed to testify in court, not as the child custody evaluator, but as Ann's and Travis' therapist. In his testimony, he reported that both children were doing fine with Mrs. Jones. Post-divorce, when Mrs. Jones requested a continuation of therapy for the children, Mr. Jones threatened to sue the therapist if he provided this service. Under the joint custody agreement, Mr. Jones had the right to approve all medical services for the children. His right superseded what was in the best interests of the children.

The "blood is thicker than water" mentality continues to be privileged in most legal definitions of family, as evidenced in the frequent struggles stepparents have in maintaining postdivorce relationships with their stepchildren. Adoptive parents have similar problems with the security of adoptive placements when biological parents contest. Legal presuppositions about family also interfere in the rights of gays and lesbians to perform primary functions in the dying process of their partners if extended family members object, and with the rights of foster parents to contest removal of foster children from their homes.

Honesty About Our Biases: An Ethical Imperative

Therapists are a part of the culture that is struggling with how to relate to the diversity of family organizations currently present in our society. As members of a culture (and of a profession) that privilege some kinds of families over others, the least we can do ethically is to be honest about our own biases and to make them a part of our conversations.

In the case just cited, the therapist told Mrs. Jones that as long as Mr. Jones objected to his children's treatment, continuing to see Ann and Travis would place them in the middle of ongoing conflict that was not in their best interests. He could have stopped there but he also was honest with her in acknowledging that although he did not agree with the legal privilege her ex-husband had in determining what professionals his children could see, he was forced to comply with Mr. Jones's legal rights. He also told her that he was anxious about going out on a limb by seeing Ann and Travis because he did not trust either the professional or the legal context to support him. He felt that it was very important for her to know *all* of his thoughts and feelings in making the decision not to see her children, not just the "official" story.

Psychotherapy's Pathologization and Disempowerment of Family

In addition to beliefs about what kinds of family structures are optimal, there are beliefs that the family (regardless of its structure) is the crucible of all psychopathology in individuals. Dysfunctional families, enmeshed families, codependent families, toxic families cause all the problems of individuals. "Families can be dangerous to your health" is the clear message. We have what Pipher (1996) calls a "socialized antipathy" to families, which is primarily of psychotherapy's construction. We have pathologized love, connection, sacrifice, and hard work for the benefit of others as disease entities requiring the attention of specialists rather than as real life issues that must be faced by everyone. Armed with such beliefs, therapists have encouraged clients to stop being helpful to their families (that's overfunctioning), to confront their parents about their inadequate parenting, even to cut off their families totally.

Psychotherapists not only support the view that families are potential disease entities, they also then promote themselves as the antidote. Therapists help clients "differentiate" and heal from the sicknesses their families "caused." Yet no therapist brings chicken soup when you are sick or foots your college bill. No therapist keeps your sick baby or picks you up when your car is in the shop. The family as bad is perhaps the most destructive of all of our psychotherapy beliefs. As it has entered mainstream culture, it has had tremendous impact on all of us and has disempowered our most important unit of care and love.

SUMMARY

All of our professional beliefs have been socially constructed, even the so-called scientific ones about intelligence and its measurement. To present the beliefs as true may be helpful to some clients; it may be unhelpful and disempowering to others. When beliefs are presented as true, they can close down rather than open up possibilities. Many of our beliefs about self, developmental stages, feelings, intelligence, and family are powerful examples of this constriction of potential.

The professions, in requiring their members to practice according to standardized beliefs, limit options in the therapist-client relationship and subject the practitioner to risk if she deviates. The individual therapist must be honest with her clients about the biases in professional and societal beliefs, giving an "unabashed presentation of who [she is] and where [she stands]" (Efran and Clarfield, 1992, p. 205) and not pretending that her beliefs come from some privileged objective reality.

The next chapter examines some of the key buzzwords in the ethical codes and standards of care in the mental health professions and describes how, when decontextualized and framed as truths, they disempower clients and their therapists and render both more vulnerable.

Chapter 7

The Language of Professional Ethics: Some Buzzwords

Formal moral codes have limited utility; they are neat general-
izations in a world of messy particularities.

—M. S. Wylie, "Looking for the Fence Posts"

Just as with diagnostic labels and mental health constructs of self,
intelligence, developmental stages, and so forth, the language of
professional ethics has dominant discourses that empower certain
standards of ethical functioning, while disempowering and making
suspect others. This chapter discusses three examples of these dominant discourses: touch, boundaries, and dual roles.

TOUCH IN PSYCHOTHERAPY

Touch in psychotherapy is highly controversial. If it is not cov-
ered specifically in every ethics code, it is certainly a hot topic in
standard of care guidelines and is used by courts, licensing boards,
and ethics committees in evaluating professional behavior.

Touch became controversial as the sexual transgressions of therapists (primarily male psychiatrists) with their clients (primarily
women) came to light in the 1970s. The use of touch became suspect due to a number of factors: the human potential and encounter
group movements of the 1960s in which sexual boundaries with
clients were loose, a growing feminist movement, increased consumer education, and an emphasis on "good touch/bad touch"
education in child sexual abuse prevention programs.

The Equation of Touch with Sexual Abuse

As cases of sexual exploitation in therapy came to public attention, profiles of perpetrators were formed. One of the behaviors identified as leading therapists down the slippery slope into sexual violations was touch (Pope, 1988, 1994). Touch thus became equated with potential sexual abuse in the therapy room. This made all touch suspect even though there are many therapeutic situations in which it is a potential resource for healing. In fact, in many kinds of therapies, touch is a primary aspect of the therapy contract.

The equation of touch with sexual abuse is problematic. There is a big difference between the therapist who drugs clients and has repeated sex with them in his office and one who gives his client a hug at the end of a session. Increasingly, the distinctions between these two very different kinds of behaviors have become blurred.

Even though no ethics code expressly forbids nonsexual, nonexploitative touch, it has become a red herring in assessing ethical violations. The anxiety practitioners thus feel in using touch as a therapeutic resource is illustrated in a recent article published by the American Psychological Association. The authors state that a handshake is the limit of physical contact a therapist should ever make with a client and give suggestions regarding how to discourage hugs from clients who insist on them. After stepping back and catching the client's wrists in a blocking maneuver, the therapist is to say: "Therapy is a talking relationship; please sit down so we can discuss your not doing this any more" (Gutheil and Gabbard, 1995, p. 222). This is an example of how toxic the issue of touch has become in psychotherapy and of how suspect *all* touch has become. Touch is strongly discouraged, regardless of the motivations of the therapist, the needs of the client, and its meaning in the psychotherapeutic context.

Problems with the Slippery Slope Theory

Generalizations from Perpetrators to All Therapists

One problem with the slippery slope theory and the assumption that all touch in psychotherapy is bad is that it generalizes from proven perpetrators to the entire therapy profession. It assumes that because *some* therapists use touch inappropriately, *all* therapists will.

This generalization is especially problematic when numbers are taken into consideration. While previous studies showed a sexual violation rate ranging from 2.5 percent to 3.1 percent for female and 7.1 percent to 12.1 percent for male therapists, Borys and Pope (1989), found a rate of .2 percent for women and .9 percent for men in a study of psychiatrists, psychologists, and social workers. And in the April 1995 *NASW News* (the official publication of the National Association of Social Work), it was reported that the organization's Committee on Inquiry (the ethics committee) substantiated the complaints of only 72 out of a total of 226 adjudicated cases from 1982 to 1992. Out of these 72, 29.2 percent were for sexual violations. While the percentage sounds high, the actual number (21) is low considering a membership of over 150,000. Twenty-one cases out of a potential of 150,000+ represents an approximate percentage of .00014.

In a 1994 national study (Brock and Coufal, 1994), marriage and family therapists also reported a low rate of 1.7 percent of respondents who said they had engaged in erotic contact with a client.

The anxious focus on touch should therefore be restricted to a very small percentage of therapists who either intentionally or unintentionally *do* fall down the slippery slope from nonerotic to erotic contact with their clients. Those who do so intentionally should be prosecuted in the criminal courts, as more and more states are mandating (Strasburger, Jorgenson, and Randles, 1991). Those who unintentionally (out of countertransference issues, life crises, substance abuse, and other reasons) engage in erotic touch should be assessed for rehabilitation and remediation potential and, where the prognosis is dim, should be denied the right to practice.

The Risks of Touch Going Underground

The vast majority of us should be made aware as part of our training and ongoing supervision and consultation that we are *all* potentially vulnerable, in the right combination of circumstances, to act out our own issues (either sexually or otherwise) in our relationships with clients. This means being totally free to own and discuss sexual and other feelings for and fantasies about clients with colleagues, supervisors, and teachers.

It is the majority of us about which I am concerned. Because touch has become such a red herring, based primarily on a perpetrator profile that represents a very small percentage of mental health professionals, practitioners are reluctant to talk about how they use (or try to refrain from using) touch in their practices. And if *touch* is difficult to talk about, then how much more difficult is it to discuss *sexual feelings and fantasies?* Yet the risk of *not* talking about these things with consultants, supervisors, and colleagues is that the therapist has no reality check other than himself and his clients to ensure that he is using and/or not using touch in an appropriate manner. Denial, concealment, and making taboo the issues of touch, sexual feelings, and fantasies increase the risks to both therapist and client.

> . . . [T]he horror at harm done to the patient, shame that some in the profession victimize those who come for help, and other powerful reactions to therapist-client sexual intimacies (i.e., *behavior*) can make therapists turn away from their own sexual *feelings* as "too dangerous," as reflecting an abusive or pathological nature, or as a temptation to be blotted out of existence and awareness. Thus, the small, atypical group of therapists who have violated the prohibition against therapist-client sexual intimacies have not only exploited their clients but also helped to create an atmosphere in which acknowledging, accepting, and learning about sexual feelings seem dangerous and daunting for the vast majority of therapists who, whatever their sexual feelings toward patients, would never seriously consider violating the prohibition and placing their patients at risk for great and lasting harm. (Pope, Sonne, and Holroyd, 1993, pp. 4-5)

The Many Meanings of Touch

Another problem with the generalization from perpetrator profiles to the entire therapy profession is the lack of distinction among various kinds of touch in therapy and the appropriateness or inappropriateness of each for different clients and therapists.

Examples of appropriate kinds of therapeutic touch include anchoring in neurolinguistic programming, physical containment in work with children, psychomotor work, rolfing, massage, sculpting, ritualized hugs to mark session completions, and, in some situations, nonerotic holding and containment.

Touch is inappropriate for clients who do not want to be touched and would regard it as an intrusion. It can also be inappropriate for clients who would misinterpret nonerotic touch as erotic and for clients who want it as a defense against facing issues necessary to their own healing. Some very narcissistic clients, for example, demand touch and other special concessions from the therapist as a defense against grieving for early childhood deprivations and abandonments (Stark, 1995).

Touch is also inappropriate when it passes the therapist's zone of comfort. Even if the client has appropriate reasons for requesting a particular kind of therapeutic touch, if the therapist is not comfortable with it or trained in giving it, then it will not be healing. Rather than force a nongenuine response, it is far better for the therapist to tell her client that his need is valid but that she is unable or uncomfortable in responding to it in the way he has requested. Out of this kind of conversation, other ways of responding to the client's need can then be negotiated.

The particular configuration of the therapist-client relationship and its context are also relevant to decisions about the use of touch. The client may have a therapeutically appropriate need to be touched and the therapist may be comfortable in doing so. But a gender difference between them would change the meaning of the touch in some way that makes therapist, client, and/or client family member uncomfortable with the behavior.

The Effects of Touch Phobia

Problematic Contexts

Touch phobia has contributed to the creation of some contexts in which there is such anxiety that *any* touch is automatically considered suspect. Our current mania about sexual harassment in elementary schools, for example, takes normal childhood interactions vis-à-vis touch and attributes malevolent adult meanings to them in ways that make *any* touch dangerous. A therapist involved with a family in an elementary school "sexual harassment" situation, for example, would have to take into consideration the contextual meanings of touch both inside and outside of the therapy office before deciding on its appropriateness in the client-therapist relationship.

Privileging the White Male Dominant Discourse

Touch phobia favors a dominant (white male) point of view at the expense of all others. Certain groups' customs with regard to touch are privileged at the potential expense of others. Nonsexual hugging, for example, is more of a female than a male behavior in mainstream American culture. Nonsexual hugging and cheek kissing are routine greetings in Latin cultures among both men and women. Hugging and holding are normal expressions of connection with children; when children resist all touch, in fact, it is often diagnostically indicative of an abuse history. Many physically disabled and ill people require touch to feel connected to, rather than shunned by, humanity.

Reinforcing Mind-Body Dualities

Touch phobia reinforces mind-body dualities that artificially separate mental and physical health. Just as we are becoming ever-more aware of the integrative, holistic nature of human functioning and of both the emotional and physical etiology and interconnectedness of symptoms, our standards of care about touch have become increasingly incongruent with this awareness.

An Ethical Approach to Touch

Therapists must be free, without anxiety about litigation, to touch clients when it is an appropriate part of the therapy relationship. They must also be free to discuss touch without fear of being judged unethical. It is in openness, not secretiveness, that ethical thinking and behavior occur.

The current dominant discourse about touch, which guides licensing boards, courts, and professional association ethics committees, must be deconstructed from its current usage, which tends to lump it into the category of sexual (or potential sexual) violation and malpractice risk. *Sexual violation* should be the ethics buzz-word, not *touch*.

In the meantime, therapists who touch clients are at more risk than therapists who do not. And both our clients and ourselves are constrained by this awareness.

BOUNDARIES

> Is it that time has blurred the form, or have two men fused in some mysterious way, for they appear, one bending over the other, almost as one seamless curve, breathing together, the boundary between them erased? Does nurse join patient or patient blend with nurse? One cannot tell. The entire atmosphere has softened. All around them boundaries appear to be dissolving. (Griffin, 1992, p. 209)

The Confusion of Boundary Problems with Sexual Violations

Boundary is another buzzword in our currents ethics codes and standards of care. As with touch, boundary has become confused with sexual misconduct, with an implication that any boundary violation contains sexual overtones. Sexual misconduct and exploitation are not just about boundaries or touch. They are about violence against women and children. Sexual misconduct and exploitation, therefore, should be labeled as such and not euphemistically called boundary problems, a label that camouflages the real problem of violence and makes suspect the ordinary boundary issues that occur in negotiating *any* relationship, therapeutic or otherwise. Boundary issues are part and parcel of every therapeutic relationship and cannot be legislated away.

The Privileging of Rigid and Distant Boundaries

The pathologizing of all boundary problems and their equation with sexual misconduct have, as with the issue of touch, led to some rather rigid and paranoid emphases on the maintenance of clear boundaries in therapy. Gutheil and Gabbard (1995), for example, frame transactions between client and therapist as boundary *crossings* and caution the therapist against any self-disclosure, any acceptance of a gift, however small, any use of a client's first name, any clothing which could be in the least bit provocative or intrusive, and so forth. Their recommendations are for therapist risk management (another current buzz phrase) and convey the clear message that all boundary crossings except verbal ones are potentially perilous.

Setting boundaries that eliminate everything except verbal communication is impossible. Putting physical touch aside for the moment, there are an infinite number of ways in which both we and our clients communicate nonverbally—body posture and language; behaviors of all kinds; pregnant pauses in conversation; the decor, seating, arrangements, and location of offices; the ambiance of waiting rooms; our clerical arrangements; and so forth. These are *all* nonverbal communicators to our clients and can *all* be experienced as a kind of boundary crossing in the therapeutic relationship.

Favoring verbal communication over all other kinds of communication privileges some kinds of clients over others. What about clients who, for example, feel intruded upon by too much emphasis on verbal communication? Have speech and language problems? Speak English as a second language? Are from an ethnic group or socioeconomic class that values actions more than words? What about children, who communicate through play more than talk? For these clients, insisting solely on verbal communication could be considered unethical in its favoring of risk management strategies over client need (Coale, 1992).

The illusion that therapy is solely about verbal communication and that boundaries should never be crossed is an absurd example of how reactive and fearful some therapists have become in their attempts to put up walls to protect themselves from their clients. The language of boundaries brings up

> . . . relationships with hard borders between enclosed individuals [in which d]istance is enshrined; connection is seen as inherently tainted and untrustworthy [and t]he danger zone is thought to reside in any manner of person-to-person touching—physical, emotional, or spiritual—that might take place in the therapy relationship. (Greenspan, 1995, p. 53)

This is a distance model of relationships, not a connection model. Relationships are about both distance *and* connection, separateness and merger, disengagement and passion. The balance fluctuates within every relationship and varies among relationships. Some clients need more connection, others more space. Some therapists can sustain more intensity than others. Variations in the client-therapist relationship occur according to both client need and therapist capacity. Both distance *and* connection are necessary.

Connection and Mutuality as Crucial in Boundary Setting

Most therapists would probably agree, in principle anyway, that the balance between distance and connection is generally slanted more toward the connection end of the continuum with long-term therapy and more toward the distance end of the continuum with short-term therapy. But even in short-term therapy, the capacity of the therapist to *engage* with the client is highly relevant to treatment success. In *both* long- and short-term therapy, connection is crucial.

Therapy is about compassion, caring, empathy, empowerment, interconnectedness—the *being with* another's pain so that he feels heard, seen, understood, and accepted. Therapy is not about holding the client at a distance through the application of expert knowledge and risk management procedures. Therapy is, by definition, boundless in the sense that it connects the therapist and client in a mutual journey of healing, impacting both client and therapist in the process, and breaking old boundaries of distrust, isolation, suspicion, and despair (Greenspan, 1995).

Establishing therapeutic relationships based on mutual interconnectedness involves working within therapeutic paradoxes—establishing equality in a hierarchical relationship, mutuality in a nonmutual relationship, empowerment in a power-imbalanced relationship, and respect for *client* meaning and belief within a frame of therapy theories and beliefs (Kottler, Sexton, and Whiston, 1994). Setting boundaries in the context of such therapeutic paradoxes is a joint process between therapist and client. It is not just something that the therapist can do *to* the client but rather something that, in interaction, the client and therapist do together. The client must agree to respect the boundaries that he and the therapist set together. He must be open to what the therapist has to give (Fruggeri, 1992;

Kottler, Sexton, and Whiston, 1994). In a recent review of studies about the therapeutic relationship, client (as well as therapist) alliance behavior has, in fact, been seen as a powerful determiner of outcome success in psychotherapy (Marziali and Alexander, 1991).

Laura Brown addresses the interactional nature of boundary setting and the joint responsibility of both therapist *and* client in the process:

> [The] myth of the invariant, concrete frame for therapy generates [a] sort of fiction, akin to the dominant ethical notion of clearly right and wrong, well-dichotomized modes of action. It is the myth that a boundary violation can always be identified readily because it will be overt and observable in the therapist's behaviors. This image of the boundary violation as clearly contained in the therapist's behaviors ignores the manner in which a client's unique personal symbologies or the specifics of the social and political context, may lend meaning to a particular behavior. (1994, pp. 212-213)

All of the professional association ethics codes hold the therapist totally responsible for the maintenance of boundaries in the therapy relationship and seem oblivious to the power of the client in complying or not complying with the agreed-upon boundaries. In today's current merger of boundary violation with sexual misconduct and the inevitability of crossing boundaries in *any* therapy relationship, a boundary violation thus is a useful charge against *any* therapist by an upset client.

Boundary Setting as Contextual

Just a therapists tend to be cautious about appropriate, nonerotic therapeutic touch, they have become cautious about any therapeutic interventions that might look like boundary violations if taken out of context. Home visits, in situ interventions, and other kinds of outreach are being put on the shelf as "not therapy" and are relegated to protective services workers, nurse practitioners, mental health technicians, and social workers defined by their contexts as *not* therapists. The acceptable frame of what is considered appropriate therapeutic intervention is thus diminished, at the expense of many clients who cannot work effectively in the middle class, boundaried milieu of most therapy offices.

This trend is a good example of viewing a behavior and assessing it without taking context and meaning into account. A home visit can be a genuine outreach to a client in need; it can also be an attempt to form an out-of-office friendship with a client. The former meaning is ethical; the latter is not. The same behavior, a home visit, can have multiple meanings.

The key issue is not the boundary per se but what happens within the therapeutic relationship. The structure of the relationship and its boundaries do not determine its health or pathology; the way in which boundaries facilitate or impede the therapeutic process *on behalf of the client* is key. Is the client being objectified or exploited in any way? Is the therapist aware of the *client's* experience of the boundaries? Is the therapist open to discussing the boundaries and being honest about why she prefers certain kinds of boundaries over others with the client? Is she able to adjust herself in relation to different kinds of boundary needs with different kinds of clients? Is she getting enough of her own needs met outside of the office to prevent their intrusion into the therapy relationship?

These are the relevant issues, not the structure of boundaries. With some clients, boundaries need to be very permeable, with others very impermeable. The variations depend on client need, therapist discipline, theoretical orientation, and personal comfort, and must be individualized to fit each situation.

Boundary Violations as Secretive Role Reversals

Boundary violations are about the misuse of therapist power (Lerman and Rigby, 1994). I like Marilyn Peterson's (1992) approach to defining boundary violations as a reversal of roles between client and therapist characterized by the *therapist's* rather than the *client's* needs in first place, a secretive collusion between therapist and client not to talk about the reversal, an inability on the part of the client to leave the treatment relationship and a loss whether he leaves or stays, and an indulgence of privilege and power on the part of the therapist. The boundary violation is not a function of any specific and identifiable behavior but rather of the secretive reversal of roles between client and therapist.

> Since each violation is shaped by the context of the relationship, violations restrict classification, which makes them even more difficult to pinpoint. (Peterson, 1992, p. 76)

The therapist who violates a client's boundaries is generally portrayed as one who leans on the client in some way to take care of himself—talking about his problems and needs instead of the client's, asking for personal favors, becoming friends with the client, and so forth. All of these violations are intrusive. But boundary violations can also occur when, in the name of client need, the therapist is overly distant in order to protect himself.

I had a client one time who volunteered her professional services to help terminal patients in their dying process. She was truly one of the most compassionate human beings I have ever known. She had a gift for being present in a way that facilitated her patients' peaceful deaths. The pain that brought her to therapy was not what one would expect. She was not burned out from sitting day after day with dying people, but rather from her supervisor's criticism for giving too much, an indication of her "loose" boundaries.

In exploring the situation, I found nothing inappropriate about the compassionate connection my client had with her dying patients. I was able to help her understand that criticism about boundaries was a way her supervisor used to protect herself from the pain and anxiety of being around dying people on a daily basis. My client's capacity to connect made her supervisor anxious. In the name of boundaries, the supervisor criticized my client's ethics.

Therapist Need: An Implicit Agenda in Boundary Setting

An unacknowledged agenda of the boundary buzzword is often for the protection of therapists as well as clients. After all, it is difficult to sit with wounded people all day and take in their pain and suffering. The fifty-minute hour and all of the other trappings of our therapeutic rituals and practices *do protect us* as well as our clients. Yet, all of our professional rhetoric emphasizes boundaries as protective of clients and ignores their functions for us. Like so many aspects of psychotherapy, the needs of the practitioner are minimized and denied and *everything* is framed in terms of client need.

For therapist as well as client, protection is a valid function of a boundary. After all, if we do not use boundaries for our own as well as our clients' needs, our usefulness to clients can be jeopardized. Both client *and* therapist have needs for protection and safety if they are to work together effectively. There are some kinds of clients, life situations, and personal issues faced by the therapist that require very firm boundaries. Others require very little boundary setting. A client who is in constant crisis and demands frequent responses from the therapist needs different boundaries than a client who rarely, if ever, reaches out for help. The therapist also needs different boundaries in the presence of varying situations in her own life.

The danger in the one-sided emphasis on client protection is that it makes secretive, and therefore suspect, the agenda of therapist self-interest and protection—yet therapist self-interest and protection is a part of *every* therapist-client relationship and needs to be owned as such. To follow Peterson's formula for a boundary violation, rigid ethics codes that make our *own* needs for boundaries secretive, are in and of themselves a boundary violation. They ask clients to collude with us in the myth that all of the boundaries in the therapy relationship are for *their* needs rather than our own.

The Catch-22 for the individual practitioner is that owning therapist self-interest may be perceived as a boundary violation in the rigid, rule-based ethics codes of professional associations and licensing boards. We are not supposed to make professional decisions based on anything but client need. The Feminist Ethics code, which embodies a more collegial, honest approach, is not the standard by which our august professional and legal bodies operate. The therapist who owns her own as well as her client's needs in justifying a professional behavior is, therefore, ethical, but vulnerable.

DUAL ROLES

Another example of an ethical red herring is the controversy over dual roles. With the exception of sexual relationships with clients, no ethical code has prohibited dual roles; yet the term dual roles carries with it a connotation of sexual or other exploitative malfeasance just as do the words touch and boundary. Some experts go so far as to suggest that practitioners engaging in dual roles *of any kind* should lose their licenses and professional association memberships (Kagle and Giebelhausen, 1994). The irony is that there is no way to avoid dual roles in psychotherapy and that they, in fact, can be useful treatment resources when used appropriately (Biaggio and Greene, 1995; Bograd, 1992; Hedges, 1993a, b, c; Tomm, 1991; Tomm et al., 1993). As with touch and boundary decisions, there are dangers in sending dual roles underground by making them suspect in all situations.

Unavoidable but Suspect

There are a multitude of dual roles in many contexts: the minister, priest, or rabbi who both counsels *and* ministers to members of his congregation. The school social worker who counsels families *and* follows up on the social control function of truancy. The protective services social worker who provides counseling to families *and* has the power to recommend removal and placement of the family's children. The private practitioner who both provides therapy *and* defers to the managed care company's directives. The psychiatrist on an inpatient service who both treats *and* has the power to involuntarily incarcerate a patient. The list is endless. Employee assistance programs; small communities shaped by ethnic, racial, or gender preferences; small towns; and many other contexts expand the inevitability of dual roles.

In addition to the dual role probabilities in certain settings, there are the various dual roles inherent in *any* human relationship. When I am working with a couple, I am aware that as a female therapist I have potential dual roles just by virtue of my gender. I must be aware of my role as a *woman* as well as a therapist with each person in the couple and also recognize the nuances of sexual tensions and power differentials present in the room. When I am working with a therapist as a client, there are automatic dual roles inherent in the relationship. I must be aware of any tendency to move from the role of therapist to one of supervisor or colleague so as not to interfere with my client's freedom to be fully himself (Bridges, 1995; Fleischer and Wissler, 1985). When I am working with a child, I am aware that my role as a parent as well as a therapist is present in the therapeutic relationship and I must pay attention to any tendency to inadvertently usurp or undermine the real parent's competence.

All relationships, therapeutic or otherwise, involve multiple roles. My husband is sometimes my nurturing (or critical) parent and sometimes I am his. My children are sometimes my caretakers and, more frequently as they mature into adulthood, my peers. My clients are often my teachers and, rarely (but sometimes) my caretakers. They do, after all (at the very least) pay my bill and sometimes offer words of condolence for stressors in my life of which they are aware.

Dual Roles as a Treatment Resource

The problem is not *occasional* dual roles. They can be invigorating, healthy, and conducive to healing, as along as they are not secretive or skewed toward therapist interest at the expense of the client. There are ample opportunities in most therapy relationships, for example, for the client to contribute something of value to the therapist in a way that is empowering. I frequently ask parents who devise creative solutions for discipline problems, bedwetting, or temper tantrums if I can use their ideas with other parents facing similar difficulties. When a client's story of courage and hope in the face of overwhelming obstacles touches my heart, I occasionally tell her how her story helps me in some way to cope with pain in my life.

I once had a client who, at the end of therapy, insisted that I accept a token gift and a heartfelt thanks for my help. When I started to refuse, attributing all of the success of the therapy to her, she reached out, touched my hand, and said, "Please learn to accept thanks, to be the recipient rather than the giver. I need to do this for me as well as for you." I accepted the gift and the gratitude and thanked her for teaching me something important. For the moment, she needed to change roles with me for her own empowerment.

Flexibility in roles is not the problem, rigidity is. If I always have to be the expert, the giver, the controller of determining what is right for the client, then the client is always the nonexpert, the taker, and the helpless participant in the relationship. This is not ethical. By only presenting one aspect of my humanity and expecting the client to present all aspects of hers, I am disempowering her as I protect myself.

Outside of the therapy relationship, dual roles also are inevitable in our clients' lives (and our own) and can be invaluable treatment resources. For example, distinguishing when a child is functioning as his parent's parent from when he is functioning as a child can be an effective treatment intervention to help him and his family get unstuck from the disempowering expectation that he will simultaneously function in both roles (and succeed in neither). Prescribing alternating parent-child roles in couples therapy can help partners who are both functioning as passive children, controlling adults, or where one is always the parent and one always the child (Coale, 1989b). Using children as occasional helpers in marital therapy or asking them to "supervise" parental happiness in some way (Madanes, 1984) involves prescribing dual roles for therapeutic purposes.

The Dangers of Forbidding Dual Roles

Dual roles are a resource that can be used or misused. My concern is that, as the term becomes prohibited in our ethics language, we shall be more reluctant to use the richness of dual roles in our work *and* will unwittingly be involved in dual roles without the freedom to explore them thoroughly with our clients. As with touch, the freedom to acknowledge and discuss is the best prophylactic against exploitation. I often suggest that clients use their regular therapy session time and the money to pay for it to go out to dinner. This makes the monetary arrangement in our relationship (and its benefits to me) explicit. I sometimes thank them for helping to pay for my vacation or my dental bill. I occasionally tell them that I might be tempted to continue working with them because I like them, and therefore, want their permission to ask periodically if the therapy is still addressing their needs. In doing so, I am acknowledging to them my multiple roles of healer, salaried employee, and human being.

Lest I be misunderstood, I am certainly not advocating throwing all caution to the winds; nor am I suggesting that all dual roles are positive. There are many dual roles, in addition to sexual or exploitative business relationships, that are generally contraindicated. I do not think that becoming a client's friend post-therapy is appropriate. The power differential that is part of the therapy relationship can never be totally eliminated and permeates the friendship in potentially destructive ways. I also think that it is complicated to be the therapist of a member of one's religious community or neighborhood.

But relationships are messy and there are circumstances in which *not* participating in a dual role can be more destructive than doing so. I had a new client whom I recognized as a member of my church when I greeted him in the waiting room. He also recognized me. I immediately offered him a referral to another therapist. He was obviously distraught, and told me, with a shaking body and flushed face, that it had taken every ounce of courage he could muster to show up for the appointment with me. If I refused to see him, he didn't think he could make it to another therapist's office. I saw him.

I had another client who, several sessions into her work with me, recognized my daughter's picture on my desk and told me that she and my daughter had been in many of the same classes in high school. She was already very connected to me and working well in the therapy process, so it made no sense to refer her to another therapist. Instead, the acknowledged dual roles became an opportunity to enrich the work we were doing together on the trust and betrayal issues that had brought her to therapy in the first place.

In any small community, dual roles are inevitable. And even in large communities, the longer a therapist practices, the more likely she is to participate in dual roles. Chains of referrals create them, as when a former client refers her friend or her brother-in-law or her colleague; serving as a therapist to other therapists creates them; serendipitous coincidences create them.

Assessing for Appropriate Use of Dual Roles

Rather than trying to eradicate dual roles, we should be openly discussing their potential benefits and problems, and establishing guidelines for how and when to engage in them. M. C. Gottlieb (1993) proposes a model for their use based on three dimensions: the power differential between therapist and client, the duration of the therapy relationship, and the clarity of termination in the therapy. The choice to have a dual role with a client outside of the therapy frame is contraindicated when the client has been in a long-term relationship with a therapist, the nature of the therapy termination invites the client to return in the future for additional therapy, and the power differential between therapist and client is high. When even two out of the three dimensions are present, the choice is contraindicated. However, when at least two out of the three dimensions reflect low levels of connection, the choice to engage in dual roles may be more appropriate. An example of the latter might be a brief and clearly terminated evaluation in a job interview process.

Pope (1991), on the other hand, warns against *any* chosen dual role based on the possibility that the therapist could unexpectedly be called upon in the future to provide court testimony about the client's treatment, because a power differential is always present in the relationship, and because the consideration of dual roles changes the entire nature of the psychotherapy process. Where dual roles are inevitable, he identifies the warning signs that a dual role is becoming detrimental to the client. The first is selective inattention on the part of the therapist to the dual role by charting only the official relationship and splitting off any discussion about other roles between therapist and client from the therapy record. The second sign is justifying the dual roles as beneficial or necessary for the client without a full exploration of them.

As with touch and boundary setting, what is key is the full acknowledgment and exploration of dual roles in the therapy relationship. The current mind-set in the mental health professions does not encourage this openness. The equation of dual roles with exploitation and danger discourages discussion and supports the opposite of what is in the best interest of both client and therapist, rendering both more, rather than less, vulnerable.

THE RISKS OF RISK MANAGEMENT

The professional red herrings of touch, boundaries, and dual roles are all framed as potentially risky business and are thus discouraged and pushed to the realms of the unspeakable. This not only discourages beneficial possibilities for healing with many clients, but also makes more likely possibilities for abuse by some therapists.

In addition, and perhaps more significantly, discouraging anything risky illustrates the reactive, fear- and anxiety-based mentality of the mental health professions in today's world. Therapy *is*, by definition, risky business. If we cloak ourselves in risk management strategies to protect ourselves, what are we conveying to our clients as we encourage *them* to take huge risks in their lives? And how are we discouraging therapists from working with higher risk populations of clients, e.g., children, abuse survivors, clients with Axis II diagnoses? Our ethical thinking has become too rigid to support the therapist in dealing with the inevitable, messy complexities such clients present. As they become too risky, will we banish them from our offices in favor of the "worried well?" Is this ethical?

I overheard an attorney advise a colleague of mine that the only "safe" approach to a borderline client was to plan on keeping her in treatment forever. To terminate at any point would open the therapist to abandonment charges. My colleague challenged the attorney by describing her fears that treating such a client often involves difficult decisions about touch, boundaries, and dual roles. What about these risks? The attorney's response was that these ethical dilemmas would only become problematic if the client became angry at the therapist post-termination; hence the advice never to terminate. My colleague subsequently told me that she planned to screen all clients carefully from this point on to weed out any with an Axis II diagnosis. Unfortunately, my colleague's decision is not uncommon.

SUMMARY

The ethical buzzwords of touch, boundaries, and dual roles are examples of the problems in the mental health professions' decontextualized, rule-based thinking about ethics. The tendency to equate *all* of these buzzwords with sexual violations simplifies the complexities of human relationships and renders the therapist less effective and potentially less ethical in making appropriate therapeutic decisions.

Such simplicity and rigidity are creating a climate in which there is great confusion about what may truly be in the best interest of clients and what is brazen risk management for professionals. Despite more egalitarian, pluralistic, mutual, and empowering approaches to therapy introduced by feminist and social constructionist thinkers, our ethics codes and standards of care are increasingly legalistic, anachronistic, authoritarian, disempowering, and anything but mutual. In focusing on how to prevent wrong rather than how to facilitate right behavior in therapists, the codes and standards circumscribe possibilities for healing. They also convey powerful negative messages that depict both therapists *and* clients as risky and potentially bad. Such an environment renders both therapists and their clients helpless and vulnerable.

The following three chapters discuss the legal and psychological hazards of practicing psychotherapy in such a reactive, fear-based professional context.

Chapter 8

Legal Vulnerabililty: Context

In our current psycholitigious world . . . we only have left brains, and . . . only what is "appropriate" is thought to constitute therapy. Forget "excellence". . . . Our profession is now defined by those who want to make the word safe for mediocrity! (1996, p. 31)

—L. Bergantino,
"For the Defense: Psychotherapy and the Law"

Psychotherapists of all disciplines are legally vulnerable. This chapter discusses the increase in licensing board complaints and malpractice actions against therapists and explores the characteristics of the sociocultural and professional contexts that fuel the increase.

INCIDENCE OF COMPLAINTS AGAINST PSYCHOTHERAPISTS

Recently, litigation against psychotherapists has become something of a growth industry. (Wylie, 1989, p. 24)

Therapists of all disciplines increasingly find themselves the target of malpractice suits and complaints from licensing board and professional association ethics committees. Exact statistics are difficult to obtain. No malpractice carrier has all of any one profession's business and, because of antitrust laws and competition among carriers, they are reluctant to release statistics to the public (Marine, 1997). The national associations of regulatory boards for each discipline only receive adjudicated complaints in which the individual practitioner has received formal disciplinary action for a violation of the licensing law in his state. They do not keep records of the numbers of complaints filed and dismissed, or complaints heard without formal disciplinary action. The professional associations have data covering a longer period of time since they were in operation before most licensing boards were established, but they are still struggling to develop databases that adequately reflect the escalating incidence of complaints (Berliner, 1989; Stanley, 1997a,b; Sturkie, 1997).

Professional Association Ethics Complaints

Professional associations have different membership sizes and vary in their methods of complaint adjudication and record keeping. The data reported below, therefore, are not intended to depict anything other than trends and are not comparable among disciplines.

Social Work

Between 1979 and 1985, there were 292 cases filed with the National Association of Social Workers for which records were available. Forty-one percent were sustained allegations and *59 percent were dismissed*. Of the sustained allegations, 25 percent were for conduct as a social worker; 27 percent were for ethical responsibility to colleagues; 28 percent were for ethical responsibility to organizations, the social work profession, or society; and the remaining 20 percent were for ethical responsibility to clients, including sexual misconduct, breach of confidentiality, fee splitting, and soliciting another's clients (Berliner, 1989). The largest categories are also the vaguest.

By 1993 there were 1,000 adjudicated cases closed and on record at NASW's national office (National Association of Social Workers, 1995). Of these cases, 29.2 percent were from 1979 to 1985 and 70.8 percent, more than double the earlier amount, were from 1985 to 1993. A random sample of 300 of the 1,000 cases was studied. Of these, 226 involved an alleged violation of the Code of Ethics (National Association of Social Workers, 1996), 32 percent (72) of which were substantiated. Of these 32 percent, 29.2 percent were for engaging in sexual activities with clients, 16.9 percent for relationships that conflict with the interests of clients, 16.4 percent for exploiting professional relationships for personal gain, and 16.7 percent for precipitous withdrawal of services. The balance was for fraud, not resisting the influences and pressures that interfere with the exercise of professional discretion and impartial judgment, personal conduct that compromises the fulfillment of professional responsibilities, and inappropriate transfer, referral, or continuation of services (National Association of Social Workers, 1995).

Psychology

Complaints against psychologists received by the American Psychological Association's Ethics Committee show a steady increase from 288 in 1985 to a peak of 488 in 1993 (a 62.9 percent increase), with a drop to 407 and 420 in 1994 and 1995 respectively (American Psychological Association, 1996). In 1995, the largest number (37 percent) of cases opened were for loss of licensure (cases that had already been reviewed by a licensing body). Thirty percent were for sexual misconduct and 16 percent for a nonsexual dual relationship. Fourteen percent were for insurance/fee problems, and the rest for a variety of charges.

Marriage and Family Therapy

Complaints against marriage and family therapists peaked in 1991 at 172 and then showed a steady decrease to fifty-eight in 1996 (Stanley 1997b). Currently, approximately sixty complaints per year are received by the American Association for Marriage and Family Therapy (Haug, 1994). For 1994, 1995, and 1996, out of a total of eighty-four fully deliberated complaints, fifty received some kind of disciplinary action. Major categories were nonsexual dual roles (9), sexual dual roles (11), confidentiality violations (4), competence/integrity problems (6), disciplinary action by a licensing board or a professional association (10), and miscellaneous violations (10) such as sexual harrassment, impairment, improper fee arrangement, and so forth (Stanley, 1997b).

Trends

The data reported by the professional associations are relevant only in that they show an increase in complaints followed by a more recent leveling off. This trend seems to be accompanied by a growth in licensing board complaints. Elizabeth DuMez (1997), manager of the Office of Ethics and Adjudication for NASW, states that while the overall number of complaints to the association's Committee on Inquiry has remained about the same, in some states there has been a dramatic drop in professional association complaints as licensing board complaints have increased. Berliner (1989), in a study of Committee on Inquiry Complaints with NASW from 1979 to 1985, found that half of the jurisdictions with the most professional association complaints lacked regulatory boards, making the professional association the primary channel for complaint processes. The states with regulatory boards had fewer professional association complaints. His study supports the idea that professional association complaints decrease when licensing board complaint channels are available to consumers.

Lincoln Stanley (1997a,b), ethics case manager for the American Association for Marriage and Family Therapy, also states that professional association complaints against marriage and family therapists seem to be leveling off as licensure board complaints increase. In addition to the increase in licensing board complaints, he attributes the trend to improved professional ethical awareness, the move toward briefer and more standardized models of therapy, and the completion of adjudication procedures in the association's accumulated backlog of complaints.

Licensing Board Complaints

Statistics reported by the national regulatory board associations do show an increase in the numbers of adjudicated licensing board complaints resulting in disciplinary actions against mental health professionals.

Social Work

The American Association of State Social Work Boards (1997), for example, reported 610 disciplinary actions taken against 469 social workers since 1983, most of them occurring within the last five years (*NASW News*, April 1995). These are data reported by forty-seven states. After subtracting 202 miscellaneous actions, the categories of offenses most often cited include: unprofessional conduct (288), incompetence/malpractice/negligence (53), and a variety of other categories (alcohol and substance abuse, narcotics violations, felony, fraud, mental disorder, allowing unlicensed persons to practice, and disciplinary action taken in another state [67]). The largest categories—unprofessional conduct and incompetence/malpractice/negligence—are also the vaguest and the most difficult to define.

Psychology

The Association of State and Provincial Psychology Boards, which receives reports from sixty-one member psychology boards, reported 1,406 disciplinary actions *above a reprimand* between August 1983 and January 1997 (Association of State and Provincial Psychology Boards, 1997). Of these, 492 were for a sexual/dual role relationship with a patient. All but forty-five were received after January 1988. The second largest category was unprofessional/unethical/negligent practice, with 385 disciplinary actions. In 1988 this category was a total of twenty-nine. The number of disciplinary actions for inadequate or improper supervision doubled between August 1993 and May 1994 and breach of confidentiality showed a 51 percent increase in this same time period.

Other categories on the top ten list included fraudulent acts, conviction of crimes, impairment, fraud in application for license, improper/inadequate record keeping, and failure to comply with continuing education requirements. As with social work, the largest categories of disciplinary action are behaviors potentially open to a variety of interpretation: sexual/dual role relationships and unprofessional/unethical/negligent practice. As discussed in Chapter 7, the fact that sexual and dual role relationships are even linked together is problematic as it equates the sexual exploitation of a client with all other dual roles.

Marriage and Family Therapy

The Association of Marital and Family Therapy Regulatory Boards has no data yet compiled (Sturkie, 1997).

Malpractice Actions

All of the disciplines report an increase in malpractice claims against their members, which is reflected in the escalation of malpractice insurance policy costs in recent years. Malpractice insurance for psychologists, for example, has increased 800 percent since 1984 (Cummings and Sobel, 1985).

Psychology

Psychologists report escalating malpractice actions from forty-four annually in 1976 to 1981 to 153 per year in 1982 to 1984 (Cummings and Sobel, 1985; Fisher, 1985; Wright, 1981). This represents an increase of over 350 percent. An average of approximately 125 malpractice claims per year are currently filed against psychologists. The most frequent claims are based on sexual improprieties, other dual relations, fee collection problems, undue influence, breach of contract, abandonment, failure to care (and poor results), failure to refer, and failure to treat (Bennet et al., 1990).

Social Work

Malpractice claims against social workers escalated from one claim filed in 1970, to forty claims in 1980, to 126 claims in 1990 (Imbert, 1992, as cited in Reamer, 1995). Acts of commission (misfeasance or malfeasance) included incorrect treatment, sexual impropriety, breach of confidentiality, breach of contract, improper referral, and improper termination. Acts of omission (nonfeasance) included failures to diagnose properly, to prevent a client's suicide, to protect third parties from harm, to treat a client successfully, and to refer a client for consultation or treatment.

From 1969 to 1996, the two largest categories of malpractice suits, both in terms of monetary payout and numbers of cases, were incorrect treatment and dual relationships (*NASW News*, Jan. 1995; NASW Insurance Trust and The American Professional Agency, 1997). Patient suicide (or suicide attempt) accounted for 12 percent of monetary payout and 7 percent of frequency of cases. Other categories were reporting of abuse to authorities (4 percent of monetary payout), failure to diagnose or incorrect diagnosis (3 percent of monetary payout), and breach of confidentiality (10 percent of frequency of cases).

Although the pattern for both psychologists and social workers shows an increase in numbers of malpractice actions, the risk to the individual practitioner of getting sued is still low—for psychologists .5 percent (Pope, 1986) and for social workers even lower (Watkins and Watkins, 1989). And, as I shall discuss in Chapter 9, malpractice actions are generally more manageable for the accused therapist than are licensure board complaints.

FACTORS CONTRIBUTING TO THE LEGAL VULNERABILITY OF THERAPISTS

The context of litigiousness against therapists is fueled by many contributory factors. In addition to the loss of meaning; the emphasis on individualism, narcissism, and the marketplace; themes of victimhood and survivalism; the challenges to professional knowledge and expertise; and the problems with rule-based ethics, as discussed in Chapters 1 and 2, there are other contributing factors. These include: better educated consumers; the backlash against professionalism; the introduction of new and higher risk therapies; technician approaches to care; the expansion of pop psychology and its pathologizing jargon; professional infighting and turf-guarding; legal supervision; ill-defined, ambiguous standards; therapist naiveté; and declining resources in an increasingly complex social context.

Better Educated Consumers

Consumers know more about psychotherapy and its problems than ever before. They are aware of the overt harm done to some people in the name of mental health, such as when a therapist acts out sexually with a client or takes advantage of the professional relationship for unscrupulous financial gain. They are also more aware of the covert harm done when a clinician presents as true that which is only speculative and encourages his client to accept the treatment. Many unnecessary hysterectomies have been performed in response to such recommendations. Many psychotherapy clients have been convinced to cut off their families, divorce their spouses, view themselves as hopelessly schizophrenic, or take toxic medications that cause irreversible side effects.

Popular media articles, books, professional association and licensing board publications, victim self-help groups, and treatment centers for abused clients proliferate. In addition, the feminist movement and the growing awareness of violent crimes against women and children in our patriarchal culture have created a social context more vigilant about abuse of all kinds than in years past and more skeptical about the goodness of professionals.

Backlash Against Professionalism

The backlash against the professions and the sense that professionals are leeches living off the "real work" of other people contribute to a growing skepticism and mistrust of the mental health disciplines.

> Professions, as opposed to *jobs,* are understood to offer some measure of intrinsic satisfaction, some linkage of science and service, intellect and conscience, autonomy and responsibility. No one has such expectations of a mere *job,* and it is this, as much as anything, which defines the Middle Class advantage over the Working Class majority. The Working Class must work—often at uncomfortable or repetitive tasks—for money, and find its pleasures elsewhere. Only in the Middle Class (and among the working rich) is pleasure in work regarded, more or less, as a right. (Ehrenreich, 1989, pp. 260-261)

In a society in which the dollar is shrinking for the average American worker, the "secret hedonism" (Ehrenreich, 1989) of the professional middle class and its pursuits of pleasure and self-interest contribute to a growing cynicism and disillusionment with all professions. Those who used to be regarded as stewards of public well-being and custodians of the common good are now viewed as takers from an ever-dwindling public pot. Professionals have been exposed as profit-driven and self-interested rather than altruistic and service-oriented (Ansel, 1996; Austad, 1996). Even without this shift in perception, professions whose business is care and compassion are not likely to be supported in a cultural context that has abandoned an ethic of care for one of profit.

> From lawyer jokes to angry charges of "profscams" in the academy, to outrage at rising medical costs for declining services, professionals are finding their legitimacy threatened, their very professionalism trashed as a cloak of arrogant ascendancy. (Sullivan, 1996, p. 15)

An increasing antiauthority and antigovernment mentality in our society also contributes to the growing suspicion and distrust of *all* professions, not just those in mental health. This, combined with growing public expectations that government should compensate its citizens for the hazards of living, and an absence of channels through which to find such compensation with regard to professional services (except in litigation), pits consumers of services against providers (Charles and Kennedy, 1985).

The Introduction of New and Higher Risk Therapies

The credibility of the mental health professions is challenged by the introduction of new and higher risk therapies. Singer and Lalich (1996), for example, write about "crazy therapies" such as regression, rebirthing, and reparenting; past-life and future-life therapies; channeling; and the "alphabet soup" therapies of NLP (neurolinguistic programming), EMDR (eye movement desensitization and reprocessing), NOT (neural organization technique), and FC (facilitated communication). Each new therapy presents itself as a dramatic, quasi-miraculous mental health invention, offering everbriefer treatment to please managed care corporations' search for cheap cures. Each new therapy develops a school of followers and devotees to promulgate itself and carves out turf by emphasizing its differences from (rather than its similarities to) all other therapies (Miller, Duncan, and Hubble, 1997).

The crazy therapies open the door to public scrutiny of *all* therapy. Even more traditional therapeutic modalities are being challenged as bogus. The False Memory Syndrome Foundation, for example, has called into question the use of hypnosis and is actively lobbying to have it banned as an acceptable treatment modality. Any treatment that smacks of psychoanalytic orientation raises eyebrows in an environment increasingly dominated by managed care mandates. While hypnosis and psychoanalysis are not appropriate for all kinds of clients, their utility for some is jeopardized in such an environment.

Technician Approaches to Care

Professional knowledge and the power that goes with it are also being challenged as technology renders more and more professional services partialized, computerized, mechanized, and dehumanized (Gergen, 1991; Sullivan, 1996). The consumer is treated as an object whose body requires a laboratory test or a surgery, whose legal situation requires a document or a court action, whose mind and heart require "fixing" in six sessions.

Even in psychotherapy, the profession most dedicated to the whole person, there are computerized assessments of all kinds, ten-minute medication sessions to minimize the need for talk therapy, and a proliferation of books, brochures, games, gadgets, and audio- and videotapes to cut short the therapy process. A recent article in a widely circulated professional newsletter suggested filling the waiting room with such paraphernalia to make consumers feel they are getting more for their money and to impress managed care payers with the extras offered to clients.

In this kind of climate, the public is beginning to view all professionals more as technicians than as healers and helpers, as providers who dispense units of treatment in the proper dosage (Watts, 1996, p. 8). There is a suspicion of things that are "unquantifiable, unprovable, or lingering as probably being poor technique on the therapist's part, self-indulgence on the patient's, and a waste of money by both" (A. Gottlieb, 1997, p. 47). Increasingly, we are called on to justify what we do with "unprecedented precision and specificity" (Stern, 1990, p. 26).

The Expansion of Pop Psychology and Its Pathologizing Jargon

The expansion of pop psychology and its pathologizing jargon have provided a deviant label of some kind for just about everybody, a phenomenon bound to create resentment and angst for many people. The fact that much of this jargon is then used by some therapists as professional truth compounds the problem. In a spoof on the codependency label, Marianne Walters (1990) writes of "The Codependent Cinderella Who Loves Too Much. . . . " In a more serious discussion of the same label, Sandra Anderson (1994) addresses the ways in which it pathologizes characteristics associated with women in this culture, blurs responsibility for problematic behavior, and encourages separation from, rather than connection with, family of origin. Tavris (1990, p. 43) addresses the political implications of the codependency label which "obscure the real-life concerns that keep women entangled in bad relationships."

Professional co-opting of pop psychology jargon and the contributions mental health professionals have made to pop psychology are bound to put us in the line of fire as the public feels increasingly pathologized and questions the ludicrousness of some of our labels and concepts. Writes Gergen (1991, p. 15), "If immersions in exercise, religion, eating, work, and sex are questionable today, what will be left untouched tomorrow?" It seems as if we have pathologized every aspect of living.

Professional Infighting and Turf-Guarding

Jealous behaviors further jeopardize the credibility of the mental health professions. As each new school develops its own brand of truth and touts its theoretical and practice orientation as *the* cutting edge of psychotherapy, we look more and more ridiculous and our claims to knowledge become evermore shaky. The claims are often grandiose and have little substantiation other than personal opinion and anecdotal experience. The claims also seem intent on eliminating, rather than tolerating, ambiguity. Nowhere is this more apparent than in judicial proceedings pitting one therapist's truth against another's.

The fact that none of our truths have much scientific basis makes any claim to truth precarious (Dawes, 1994). The infighting within and between disciplines is based more on protection of economic privilege than on honest intellectual disagreements about theoretical orientation. It has further contributed to the image of the professions as conflicted and confused about their knowledge bases, tarnishing the image of professionals as benevolent and wise healers.

Professional Reactions to Therapist Abuse of Clients

Professional reactions to the knowledge that therapists *do* abuse clients often take the form of vigilant attempts to track down and punish perpetrators and to deny the possibility of their own potential as such. This countertransferential response creates a kind of witch-hunting atmosphere and a dichotomizing between us and them. In evaluating the behavior of colleagues, therapists may thus operate on the basis of hearsay, rumor, and partial information, further fueling the litigious forces currently in operation against the psychotherapy professions. Scapegoating is a poor substitute for honest self-examination and constitutes its own kind of evil as it seeks to destroy evil (Peck, 1983, p. 74).

In *every* situation in which I have been involved as supervisor or colleague in which a complaint has been filed against a therapist, there has been another therapist in the wings supporting the client's complaint without ever having talked with the accused. The presumption has been that, if the client accused the therapist, the therapist must be guilty. The standards we use for evaluating our clients' allegations against other people, such as in child abuse situations (American Psychological Association, 1994; Everson and Boat, 1989; Gardner, 1987; Jones and McGraw, 1987), get thrown to the winds when the allegation is against other therapists. Partial and often distorted access to information cannot substantiate abuse claims against *anybody*. This is especially true in alleged violations that are very ambiguous, such as dual roles and boundary violations.

Pejorative and punitive attitudes toward colleagues that deflect self-examination onto the excoriation of others interfere with honest acknowledgment and exploration of the mistakes that are part and parcel of being a therapist. There are many garden variety clinical mistakes that are unavoidable. What works with one client may not work with another. What works in one context may not work in another. We all, even on a good day, leave our offices thinking of something that we should have or could have done with a particular client that we did not think of at the time. And on a bad day, we may think of things we wish we had not done.

The freedom to discuss and learn from therapeutic errors is crucial to good psychotherapy. A spirit of condemnation prevents professionals not only from learning and growing from their mistakes, but also from being open to healing relationally the wounds with clients when they *do* make such mistakes (M. Peterson, 1992). Immediate concerns for self-survival predominate. This makes us more, not less, vulnerable to complaints.

Legal Supervision

The Primacy of Liability Concerns

Increasingly, the psychotherapy professions are allowing themselves to be supervised by the legal profession. In our anxiety about litigiousness, we are deferring to attorneys to advise and direct us. The clinical judgments we make on behalf of ourselves and our clients are filtered through the haze of legal liability concerns. This makes our responses to clients less genuine, creative, and ethical. A legal audience, indeed any audience, changes the focus of our concern.

> To sense that one's actions result from a belief, or an ideal held focally or passionately in mind, is to act sincerely. The belief is felt to be revealed immediately in action; the action is a transparent expression of self. However, to introduce an audience . . . brings a host of new factors to the fore. . . . [A]t this point the action is transformed. No longer is it a transparent reflection of a belief or ideal. Down to matters of facial expression and bodily posture, it is now a calculated, public performance—an attempt to *appear* sincere rather than sincerity itself. (Gergen, 1991, pp. 221-222)

The Different Language of Therapists and Lawyers

In addition to the lack of sincerity that performing for any audience elicits, performance specifically for a legal audience carries with it other problems. First, under the guise of client protection, therapist protection is the agenda. Lawyers, whether hired by the individual therapist for advice on a specific case situation or by a professional association for advice on ethics codes or standard of care issues, are obligated to advocate for their client. Their focus is on their client's, i.e., the *therapist's* or the *professional association's*, self-interest (Gabel, Rosenbaum, and Schorr, 1996).

Second, the very language of lawyers and the dualistic concepts of right and wrong, guilty and innocent do not lend themselves to the variable and ambiguous nature of client-therapist relationships. As already discussed, what is right varies from situation to situation, and guilty behavior, with some exceptions, also varies.

Third, lawyers frequently make unrealistic and untherapeutic demands of therapists in the service of their clients—demands that, if followed, would jeopardize the client's well-being. Therapists must, for the sake of their clients as well as themselves, not automatically respond to the demands from attorneys and must stay grounded in a therapeutic rather than a legal mind-set.

A prime example of such a demand is when a child's therapist is asked to make custody recommendations in divorce litigation. Another is when a therapist is asked to testify about damages in civil litigation in ways that might disempower the client and jeopardize confidentiality. I have known very competent therapists who succumbed to an attorney's demands out of their generalized anxiety about litigation and the atmosphere of increased power that attorneys now have to direct the overall functioning of the mental health professions. In succumbing, they made both themselves and their clients more, not less, vulnerable.

Fourth, lawyers are encouraged to ignore ethical considerations beyond the self-interest of their clients.

> [T]he "duty of zealous representation" . . . virtually requires the lawyer to not allow his or her own ethical concerns to interfere with the zealous legal pursuit of the clients' ends, irrespective of the impact of these ends on others. . . . (Gabel, Rosenbaum, and Schorr, 1996, p. 32)

This mentality, fostered in legal education, is not conducive to ethical functioning that takes the client-therapist *relationship* into account.

Ill-Defined, Ambiguous Standards

Not only have the mental health professions increasingly turned over to lawyers the supervision of their ethics codes and standards of care; they have done so in a legal context of ill-defined, ambiguous standards.

Some helping professionals . . . have been sued for confining patients in institutions. Others have been sued for not confining patients in institutions. . . . Sometimes professionals have lost court actions for not breaking confidentiality and failing to warn people who were subsequently endangered by the client. Other practitioners have been sued for divulging confidences. (Barker, 1992, p. 105)

In medicine, there has been a tendency to identify *any* bad outcome with medical negligence, a notion that " . . . moves well beyond the notion of fault . . . to an untoward incident of any kind, whether related to fault, chance, or fate" as justification for a tort action (Charles and Kennedy, 1985, p. 184). If adverse outcome is justification for malpractice action in medicine, a field that lends itself to concretization and specificity far better than the more ambiguous field of psychotherapy, how much more vulnerable are psychotherapists likely to be in litigation situations? Could adverse outcome be the therapist's failure to make someone happy? To facilitate the client's confrontation with painful memories? To help cure an alcoholic whose family then must change, perhaps with some struggle, to accommodate the client's sobriety?

In an atmosphere in which the expectation of a good and happy life is embraced by increasing numbers of people as their *right*, the ill-defined, ambiguous standards governing malpractice actions against therapists are potentially even more dangerous. Physicians have responded to increased litigation by withdrawing from high-risk specialties (such as obstetrics), decreasing experimental medical and surgical treatments, and practicing defensive medicine which mechanizes and bureaucratizes the physician-patient relationship (Charles and Kennedy, 1985). Even so, malpractice actions against them continue. These same trends (e.g., caution about working with high-risk clients and increased emphasis on mechanized risk management strategies) are already in place with psychotherapists and also seem ineffectual in reducing the rates of malpractice actions and licensing board complaints.

Incongruent Standards

Ethics rules and standards are often incongruent with the realities of treatment situations. In a review of relevant research, Miller, Duncan, and Hubble (1997) found that most clients both expect and participate in short-term therapy (less than ten sessions). Yet, many of the standards of care promulgated by the mental health professions for risk management purposes incorporate recommendations for procedures requiring longer-term therapy for their implementation. NASW's recent publication, *Prudent Practice* (Houston-Vega and Nuehring with Daguio, 1997), for example, discusses the necessity to orient clients to the assessment and service process; secure working agreements, service contracts, and releases of information; make adequate assessments; and formulate treatment plans consistent with diagnoses. Each of these requirements involves lengthy forms, some of which necessitate the use of additional forms. The informed consent document, for example, includes the following forms: fee agreement, instructions on how to file a complaint in the treatment setting, termination policies, follow-up procedures, appointment information, a description of "the special nature of the treatment relationship," and information about the setting and the therapist.

The presumption in such forms is that the client will be with the therapist long enough for all of the forms to be relevant and useful. In long-term therapy, this is realistic, since such documents require adequate numbers of sessions to fulfill. They cannot be completed in a one- or two-session client contact. With most short-term clients, a full-service contract with adequate diagnoses, informed consent, and treatment plan is thus required, but not possible. This inability to comply renders the practitioner vulnerable to complaint procedure.

Likewise, in a recent publication by the American Psychological Association (Bersoff, 1995), contributing authors recommend similar formulas and procedures for assuring that clients make informed choices. For clients who come in in crisis (a vast majority), several authors suggest that it may take several sessions for an examination of therapy and its alternatives, but recommend that, even if it "is postponed for several sessions, it should not be foregone" (Hare-Mustin et al., 1995, p. 307). Again, this recommendation is relevant when clients remain with the therapist long enough to adequately address the issues in fully informed consent, but irrelevant in many short-term treatment situations. In a managed care era of shrinking sessions, the models being promulgated by the mental health professions are increasingly unrealistic.

Therapist Naiveté

Changing Client Populations

The professions, even as they try to protect themselves with legal advice, are naive about their legal vulnerability. Before managed care made psychotherapy more available, the typical consumer of mental health services was middle or upper-middle class. Except for services provided in the public sector to clients who were too poor to bother with complaints against their therapists and whose voices would not have had much credibility anyway, the bulk of the psychotherapy population previously consisted of the so-called "worried well."

With the advent of managed care and the burgeoning child sexual abuse and adult survivor movements, client profiles expanded to include more seriously disturbed people—people who, in a climate of ever-increasing litigiousness, *can* and *do* file complaints. The professions were not prepared for the change and their ethics codes and standards of care reflect this (Marine, 1997). The tendency, for example, to hold the therapist totally responsible for setting boundaries, as discussed in Chapter 7, does not take into account the difficulties encountered with many very disturbed clients who routinely push against such boundaries. The professions' emphasis on empathy, caring, and compassion (and, increasingly in feminist theory, on mutuality and collegiality) without an equal emphasis on strength of character and capacity to set limits, does not take into account the kinds of clients who cannot enter into mutual, collegial relationships and who are threatened by empathic and compassionate connection with the therapist.

Therapist Surprise at Predictable Behaviors of Some Clients

The DSM-IV (American Psychiatric Association, 1994) specifically mentions vengeful, rageful, and out-of-control behaviors in some Axis II diagnostic categories. However, there is still usually a sense of surprise when an individual therapist actually becomes the *target* of such behaviors, particularly when she has expended great amounts of time and energy in working with the client (Hedges, 1996).

More and more publications are hitting the market describing the dynamics of such clients in relation to their therapists (Comstock and Vickery, 1992; Maltsberger, 1993; Pearlman and Saakvitne, 1995; Stark, 1995; Wilson and Lindy, 1994b). Ethics codes and standards of care typically lag behind in changing to accommodate such cutting edge information, although there is some indication that they are beginning to shift. The new *Code of Ethics* of the National Association of Social Workers (1996), for example, now includes "Social workers should defend and assist colleagues who are unjustly charged with unethical conduct" (2.11[e]). The American Psychological Association's *Ethical Principles of Psychologists and Code of Ethics* (1992) recently added to its code "Psychologists do not file or encourage the filing of ethics complaints that are frivolous and are intended to harm the respondent rather than to protect the public" (8.07, 15). Such provisions reflect the growing awareness that clients sometimes do target their therapists with vengeful and/or frivolous complaints.

The Absence of Ethical Standards to Protect Therapists from Dangerous Clients

While the above two examples are some acknowledgment that unjust, frivolous complaints *do* occur, none of the codes address the potential risk to the therapist caused by the behaviors of some clients. For example, in the termination standards of The American Psychological Association, The National Association of Social Workers, and The American Association for Marriage and Family Therapy, specified reasons for termination are all couched in terms of *client* need. *Therapist* need—to be protected from physical violence or the emotional violence of litigation threats—is not addressed. Proper referral (necessitating contact with the client, no matter how dangerous it may be to the therapist) must still occur or the therapist is open to charges of abandonment—a grave ethical violation.

The American Psychological Association's *Ethical Principles of Psychologists and Code of Conduct* (1992) does allude to situations of "client conduct" that may preclude normal referral procedures (4.09[c]). NASW's *Code of Ethics* (1996) also allows for a "precipitous withdrawal" of services under "unusual circumstances" (1.16[b]). Yet neither code specifically addresses what kinds of client conduct or unusual circumstances might allow the therapist to withdraw services immediately without being required to remain in contact with a dangerous client for referral purposes. The American Association for Marriage and Family Therapy (1991) has no provisory guidelines for exceptions to its termination procedures.

Likewise, the *NASW Standards for the Practice of Clinical Social Work* (NASW, 1989) addresses premature termination of clients only in those circumstances when the client decides to terminate and makes no provision for situations in which the *therapist* makes such a decision. And the American Psychological Association's *General Guidelines for Providers of Psychological Services* (1987), while specifying conditions in which a psychologist may withhold professional services (based on practitioner competence, appropriate applicability of assessment procedures, therapist limitations, and client characteristics), still exhorts psychologists to assist clients in obtaining services from another source (3.1).

Only in the *NASW Guidelines on the Private Practice of Clinical Social Work* (NASW, 1991) is premature termination based on client behavior addressed in any depth. Ethical termination may occur when the client injures or threatens to injure the social worker physically, harrasses him, or files an official complaint against him or a person practicing with him. It may also occur when the client seriously violates the fee agreement, requires expertise different from what the social worker can offer, or is chronically noncompliant; or when the social worker becomes ill or incapacitated, moves, or sells his practice.

Yet even in such specified circumstances, there is no clear-cut right for the therapist to terminate immediately, without contact, to facilitate client referral. The combining of such circumstances as fee agreement violations, noncompliance, and therapist illness with client violence or malpractice action against the social worker implies that all require appropriate transfer and referral. In addition, the fact that the guidelines are solely for private practitioners calls into question the rights of social workers in other clinical settings to terminate clients prematurely under similar circumstances of dangerousness.

The publication's availability is also a problem. Unlike all of the standards, guidelines, and ethics codes, which are available free of charge to members and to the public from all of the professional association national offices, the *NASW Guidelines on the Private Practice of Clinical Social Work* is a special publication that is sold—at a hefty cost—through the NASW Distribution Center. It is thus not available either to the public or to members as an association office service. Its obscureness and lack of availability make it less credible.

The ambiguity about therapist protection in the codes and standards of the mental health professions is puzzling in light of data substantiating the problem of violence against therapists. In a study done by the Massachusetts Chapter of the National Association of Social Workers (NASW, n. d.), for example, more than half of 1,000 surveyed social workers had been physically assaulted in a work-related incident and three-quarters verbally abused. Another third had had a weapon brought into the workplace and over three-quarters had experienced fear in the presence of clients. Kipper (1986) states that social workers are second only to police officers in the risk of work-related violence. Others (Hiratsuka, 1988; Littlechild, 1995; Newhill, 1995; Norris, 1990; Rowett, 1986; Schultz, 1987, 1989) also substantiate the problem of violence against social workers. Although such publications do not generally differentiate between clinical social workers and others, the problem of violence directed toward therapists in all disciplines is also well documented in the literature (Bernstein, 1981; Craig, 1982; Hatti, Dubin, and Weiss, 1982; Lion and Reid, 1983; Madden, Lion, and Penna, 1976; Star, 1984; Whitman, Armao, and Dent, 1976).

The subject of violence against therapists seems to be addressed as a topic unto itself and is not included in books and publications dealing with the general stresses and strains of being a psychotherapist (e.g., Figley, 1995b; Pearlman and Saakvitne, 1995; Sussman, 1995). It is as if violence is a nondominant discourse that is peripheral to psychotherapist awareness—present but not very visible, a suppressed possibility in the realities of everyday practice.

Perhaps therapists are reluctant to admit that they are ill-equipped or unable to help some people and that they can, in fact, place themselves in danger by trying to do so. Newhill (1995) believes that many violent incidents occur because practitioners believe they are inadequate if they cannot handle situations alone. The traditional grandiosity of the mental health professions supports such thinking as it holds the therapist responsible for everything that occurs in the therapy relationship. Failure is a bad word. This attitude may blind the the therapist to the grave danger encountered with some kinds of clients and the need to consider self as well as client protection.

Perhaps therapists must deny the dangers of their work if they are to perform effectively—just as parents must deny the dangers their children encounter in the world if they are to function calmly. Putting aside conscious awareness that the person he is trying to help could harm him, the psychotherapist concentrates on the healing process rather than on self-defensive maneuvers. In the process, he is vulnerable—and made more so by the ways in which the professions also put such considerations aside in their ethics codes.

Ill-Preparedness for Complaints and Lawsuits

Therapists are naive about their vulnerability to complaints (Besharov and Besharov, 1987). They are also naive about licensing boards whose purpose, many believe, is to protect them as well as the client. It is a cold shock when they learn of the licensing board's presumption in favor of the client. Since boards are *business* entities set up to *protect the consumer,* they generally proceed without taking into account that the client may be "crazy."

Therapists are also typically ill-prepared for litigation. Their professional functioning requires that they hold secrets, so disclosing them in a court of law (even for their own protection) can be difficult. Therapist tendencies toward empathy, tolerance for ambiguity, self-examination, collegiality, expectation of fairness, withholding of feelings, and grandiosity are not conducive to functioning in a legal environment that is anything but empathic or collegial and where certainty, rather than ambiguity, is required. In addition, the subtleties of psychotherapy practice are difficult to convey to a jury consisting generally of nonprofessional people. Expert witnesses to support the accused therapist are not only hard to find, but are also seen by many jurors as biased and self-serving (Marine, 1997).

Declining Resources in an Increasingly Complex Social Context

Finally, declining resources in an increasingly complex social context are reflected in the kinds of clients we see and the therapeutic dilemmas with which we are faced. Gone are the days when unlimited insurance reimbursement allowed us to prolong the treatment of middle-class clients while community mental health staffing grants provided relatively generous services to the poor. We are now faced, as never before, with difficult decisions about resource allocation. Managed care gatekeepers may allow only limited sessions for clients with major depressions, post-traumatic stress disorders, and chronic mental illness. Community mental health centers may not be able to pick up the slack when managed care benefits are exhausted.

Every day, we are faced with decisions about how to be ethical when what we think a client needs is not available to her. Do we continue on a pro bono basis? Are we responsible for finding a referral source even though one is not available to meet the client's needs? Do we challenge the managed care gatekeeper even if it means we risk our place on the managed care company's panel? Do we have an obligation to consider the good of the entire community as well as the good of a particular client in the way in which limited mental health care dollars are allocated?

These and other increasingly sticky ethical questions surface daily in every service provider's office. They pose dilemmas not readily addressed in our ethics codes and standards of care, and subject practitioners to potential ethical violations simply because our standards are not congruent with the harsh realities of such questions. What are the guidelines, for example, when a therapist is required by a managed care company to refer a client for medication before further therapy sessions are authorized, even if both the therapist and the client do not think medication is warranted? What are the guidelines about confidentiality when submitting outpatient treatment reports that will be seen by multiple sets of eyes in the managed care office?

Bentley suggests that

> [s]ocial workers must stand with the right of patients to refuse medication—even though they as individuals or the profession as a whole may experience some negative professional consequences for their advocacy. . . . (1993, p. 104)

Newman and Bricklin (1991) caution therapists to balance cost containment with quality of care in managed care arrangements that give financial incentives to providers who hold down costs of service delivery. Haas and Cummings (1995) advise therapists to consider their duty to treat clients until their problem is resolved, an appropriate referral is made, or the client discontinues treatment. " . . . [A] key question before joining a plan that limits benefits may well become, How do practitioners avoid abandoning patients without going bankrupt?" (p. 510).

At this point, there are few clear guidelines regarding how to deal with the splits between the current ethics codes and the realities of managed care practice. Applebaum (1993) suggests that managed care has already led to modifications in mental health standards and that it will continue to affect the shaping of such standards as clinicians and the courts deal with such questions. In the meantime, it is incumbent on individual practitioners to wrestle with the incongruence between current standards and the realities of practice in a managed care era.

SUMMARY

The incidence of licensing board complaints and malpractice actions against therapists of all disciplines is escalating. Factors contributing to the legal vulnerability of therapists include better educated consumers; a backlash against professionalism; the introduction of new and higher risk therapies; technician approaches to care; the expansion of pop psychology and its pathologizing jargon; professional infighting and turf-guarding; professional reactions of denial or punitiveness to colleagues accused of abusing clients; the legal profession's supervision of psychotherapy; ill-defined, ambiguous standards in mental health; therapist naiveté; and declining resources in an increasingly complex social context.

In addition, some special problems with licensing boards and malpractice actions contribute to the legal vulnerability of therapists. The following chapter discusses these problems and details more specifically profiles of high-risk clients, contexts, and therapists.

Chapter 9

Licensing Boards, Malpractice Actions, and Profiles of Complaints

Following is a discussion of the ways in which licensing boards exacerbate therapist vulnerability. The administrative law governing licensing board investigations is contrasted with the court procedures of malpractice actions. Therapist, client, and context profiles with high-risk components are assessed.

LICENSING BOARDS

The proliferation of licensing boards is a relatively recent phenomenon. The oldest state board of examiners of psychologists has been in existence since 1945 (Connecticut) and it was not until 1977 that licensing boards for psychology appeared in all fifty states and the District of Columbia (Smith, 1978). Licensing boards in social work and marriage and family therapy are even more recent and do not yet exist in every state.

Their Purpose and Character

Every mental health profession advocated for inclusion in licensing and for the creation of licensing boards. With the advent of managed care, licensing became a major prerequisite for inclusion on provider panels. To eliminate licensure now is tantamount to economic death for most mental health professionals. Many therapists thus think of licensure as a positive thing and naively assume that licensing boards are beneficial to practitioners. In some respects, they are. They do provide the mental health professions with enhanced professional status and economic well-being, so much so that they have been criticized by some as more attentive to professional economic self-interest and elimination of competition than to the protection of the public from incompetence (Davis, 1981; Dawes, 1994; Hogan, 1983; Lambert and McGuire, 1991).

Licensing boards are consumer protection entities. Once in operation, they have to maintain their credibility and justify their continued existence by weeding out bad apples in the professional barrel (Marine, 1997). Their stated mission is to protect the consumer and, in order to do this, they must find and sanction offending practitioners. While on the surface this makes sense, upon further investigation, the methods and mentality with which they do this can be dangerous to the practitioner, especially in the litigious context comprising all of the factors described in Chapter 8.

The licensing board that searches out and punishes offenders is seen as a good board. Recently, there have even been awards given to boards that sanction the most offenders, encouraging competition among boards to increase their number of adjudicated complaints and thus prove their effectiveness in protecting the consumer (Steinberg, 1997).

Since each state has its own licensing boards, there is variation in procedure. Because most boards belong to a national association of boards, however, there is also a great deal of uniformity (Steinberg, 1997). The patterns of most boards reveal some frightening realities.

Licensing boards are administrative in nature, many of them politically appointed. They are governed by administrative law, which does not offer the accused the same protections as civil and criminal law. Although there is a trend for boards to be subjected to legal challenges of their decisions when they do not adhere to due process principles (Smith, 1978), in actuality they provide very few due process protections to accused therapists (Barnett and Morris, 1996; Caudill, 1991; LaSala, 1994). One reason for this is that many boards, especially for the masters level disciplines, are relatively new, may not yet have adopted and/or published formal rules, and have little experience to guide their decisions. In addition, boards do not always abide by the rules they do adopt (Smith, 1978).

Problems with Licensing Boards

[T]he lowest criminal defendant has more rights under the law than a professional who is accused of malpractice or misconduct before the Board. (Caudill, 1991, p. 11)

The following discussion outlines commonly experienced problems with licensing boards (Barnett and Morris, 1996; Bergantino, 1996; Caudill, 1991; Hedges, 1996; LaSala, 1994; Marine, 1997; *PAN Observer,* 1994; Professional Advocacy Network, n.d.; Sherven, 1994; Steinberg, 1997).

The accused therapist is presumed guilty until proven innocent. In some jurisdictions, he is called a perpetrator and the client a victim from the initiation of the investigation. The therapist has no right to face his accuser and may not even be told the accuser's identity or the specifics of the charges. There is no statute of limitations. Charges can be added at any time, making the therapist vulnerable to complaints in perpetuity. Therapists can be investigated multiple times as new information comes to the board's attention from the same complainant. There have also been situations in which the board finds "new" violations as a way of reopening a case in which the Superior Court (the final court of appeals in licensure board investigations) has exonerated the defendant.

The therapist has no right to a jury of her peers. The boards have total control over whom they call as witnesses. Because the therapist has no right to a speedy process, investigations can stretch on for years. There is no requirement for proof beyond a reasonable doubt. The board is not required to reveal evidence favorable to the defense if such information comes to its attention during the investigation.

Charges can be evaluated in light of current ethical standards, even though the alleged infractions may have occurred years ago in the context of very different standards. Charges can be evaluated according to a specific theoretical orientation that may not be applicable to the accused therapist's practice. (A humanistic psychologist, for example, held to a psychoanalytic standard, might be cited for an ethics violation because he did not adhere to psychoanalytic standards.)

There are no uniform standards for assessing damages (Bergantino, 1996). In actuality, damages do not have to be proven, only the fact that a therapist has committed an ethics violation. In addition, the violation the board finds may not even be the one about which the client complained. There have been incidents in which both the client *and* the therapist denied that a specific ethics violation occurred and the board still cited the therapist for the violation (Sherven, 1994). There have even been situations in which boards have demanded the records of the therapist's other clients and/or interviewed other clients to aid them in their investigation (Steinberg, 1997). The basis of such actions is that since the boards are established by law, they have the right to investigate *any* perceived infraction of the law that comes to their attention, whether it is in the complaint or not.

Licensing board investigators often are police investigators or criminologists with no training in psychotherapy and little, if any, awareness of the "craziness" of some clients and their complaints. For example, the working knowledge of board investigators probably does not include an awareness that clients can project their own inner pain and terror from past abuse experiences onto their therapists, truly believing that their therapists are, in fact, perpetrators. In some jurisdictions, paid undercover informants have been known to fake symptoms to entrap therapists (Sherven, 1994). Again, the presumption is that the therapist is probably guilty of whatever the client alleges.

Experts paid to consult with licensing boards may or may not have expertise in the particular area required by the nature of the complaint. Since they are paid by the board, their neutrality is jeopardized. In addition, licensing boards are not generally required to adhere to the opinion of an administrative law judge, the next level of review after board deliberation. The judge may be the only reviewer who actually sees and listens to all parties, whereas the board may have access only to written materials and the reports of investigators. Even without access to the actual people, however, the board can make the final decision. A new law in California effective in 1997 made the administrative law judge's decision binding if he finds that the prosecutor's witness is not credible (Barnett and Morris, 1996; Steinberg, 1997).

Until very recently, no malpractice insurance policies offered any coverage whatsoever for licensing board actions against therapists.

The defense costs of licensing board complaints, therefore, came totally out of the therapist's pocket. In some jurisdictions, the therapist pays the entire cost of the investigation if found guilty, a fact which is bound to slant the board's findings against the therapist.

Sanctions can involve a peremptory and immediate loss of license to practice as well as publication of the therapist's name and loss of license in official publications and the media. Sanctions can also involve continuing education, supervision, and personal psychotherapy, all of which must be paid for by the therapist. Periodic reports to the licensing board of the therapist's progress are usually required. The fact that such reports violate the confidential nature of psychotherapy is a serious problem (*NASW News*, March 1997, p. 14).

In many jurisdictions, sanctions are punitive and extreme. Sherven (1994), for example, describes a California case in which an unblemished career of fifteen years was ruined by a dispute regarding psychotherapeutic modalities. The therapist's license was revoked and (s)he was put on five years probation with required ongoing supervision, continuing education, and psychotherapy. (S)he was required to have a diagnostic evaluation and DSM-III-R diagnosis by a board-appointed clinician and to retake both the written and oral licensing exams. All clients had to be notified of the probationary status and (s)he had to make client records *and* the clients themselves available to the supervisor upon request. (S)he also had to pay for the entire cost of the board investigation.

The Need for Reform

Because of the grave due process problems in licensing board complaints and the variability of professional knowledge and standards upon which practitioners are licensed, many think that the boards' scope of authority should be sharply curtailed. Serious violations, such as sexual misconduct or insurance fraud, should be a violation of criminal law, not administrative law, and should be turned over to criminal courts for prosecution just as are domestic violence and child abuse. Many states have already moved in this direction (Strasburger, Jorgenson, and Randles, 1991). The more garden variety complaints should go through some kind of mandated mediation, such as a professional association committee, before they ever reach the level of a licensing board investigation.

In the adjudication process, all complaints should be subject to a thorough assessment of *all* information, not just the content of the client's allegations. Therapists should have access to the particulars of clients' complaints with reasonable and timely opportunities to respond. They should be interviewed in the initial phase of the investigation so that their response is weighed equally with the complainant's allegations.

Currently, therapists are often not even interviewed until a long time after the investigator has interviewed the client, the client's family members, the client's new therapist, and others whose role it is to substantiate the complaint. In such a process, the therapist's "guilt" is thus entrenched in the investigator's mind before he even meets him and hears his side of the story. All of the other due process problems, as previously described, should be corrected so that the therapist has at least the same protections as he would have in judicial proceedings.

Some question the need for licensure in any contexts except those in which there is a high degree of social control and client vulnerability, such as psychiatric hospitals, prisons, residential treatment facilities, juvenile detention centers, and facilities for children (Dawes, 1994). Even in such settings, licensure as a valid quality control mechanism is questionable. Johnson and Huff (1987), for example, in a study of social workers in Idaho, found that the licensing exam for social work practice fell short in measuring knowledge unique to the practice of social work and demonstrated no relationship between passing a written exam and practice competence. The mentality that *all* consumers must be protected from psychotherapists through (invalid) licensure requirements is problematic. Not only does it not produce the practice competence it promises; it also implies that all therapists are potentially harmful and that all clients potentially stupid. In reality, most therapists are helpful and most clients wise.

MALPRACTICE ACTIONS

Malpractice actions take place in civil court as tort actions. Torts are wrongful actions that harm another in some legally recognized way for which the plaintiff seeks monetary compensation. Thus, a malpractice suit against a psychotherapist is an allegation that the therapist has damaged his client, who deserves compensation for such. As the following discussion shows, the rules and standards governing civil malpractice actions are very different from the rules and standards governing licensing board investigations.

The Protections of Court Procedures

In contrast to licensing board investigations, malpractice litigation requires the plaintiff to prove, with a preponderance of evidence, that the therapist had a legal duty, was derelict in that duty, and that the client suffered harm caused by the professional's dereliction. The therapist is innocent until proven guilty, has a right to know the charges and face his accuser, is protected from unending litigation by statutes of limitations, and is generally assisted in his defense financially via malpractice insurance coverage. All of his due process rights are protected and standards of care and of damage are more defined, although the ambiguity of mental health practice still lends itself to great variability.

Appeal procedures are clearer in court litigation than in licensing board investigations. If found guilty, the damages are generally monetary and do not involve endless sanctions of supervision, personal psychotherapy, continuing education, and other financially costly requirements. The process is finite—not forever open to additional charges in the future. Furthermore, because a malpractice case takes place in a public arena (when it is not settled), the therapist is in a position to accept and use colleague support *after the trial is over* in ways that may not be available to him in a licensing board complaint in which *all* of the particulars of the investigation remain confidential forever.

Difficult for Plaintiff to Win

Malpractice cases are difficult for a plaintiff to win. There are few reported court decisions in which clients have successfully claimed harm from negligently provided psychotherapy (Otto and Schmidt, 1991). The plaintiff must prove that there was a breach of duty that was the *proximate cause* of substantial damages and must produce competent testimony by expert witnesses to prove her case

(Greenburg and Greenburg, 1988). Because most lawyers are retained on a contingency basis, they are not likely to take a case unless there are substantial damages at stake, particularly as insurance companies have stopped settling cases at a "nuisance level" and states are increasingly legislating caps on damage payments and attorney fees (Greenburg and Greenburg, 1988).

The Role of Money

Malpractice suits are about money, not about protection of the public. They are a way to compensate a client for damages caused by acts of omission or commission on the part of the therapist. Money involves malpractice insurance carriers whose role is to carry the financial risk for the insured. By paying a premium, the insured transfers the unknown expense of a possible malpractice suit to the insurance company (Nolan and Marine, 1997).

Because settlement is usually cheaper for insurance companies, which have the realistic perspective on win/loss odds in thousands of cases, most malpractice cases settle and never go to court (Marine, 1997). A study done by the American Psychological Insurance Trust (cited in Pope, 1986) reported that 850 claims out of a total of 1,000 were settled from 1976 to 1986.

If the therapist refuses to settle and then loses the case, the insurance company typically only pays what it would have for *settlement* regardless of what the policy's limits of liability coverage are. This is because most policies have a consent-to-settle clause that the insured agrees to honor (Marine, 1997). If the limits of liability are $3 million for example, and the case could have been settled for $300,000, the therapist who refuses to settle can find himself paying the balance between $300,000 and the amount of damages awarded to the plaintiff by the jury. Many therapists thus are forced to settle regardless of their own convictions about their guilt or innocence (Steinberg, 1997).

Judith Peterson, a psychologist in Houston, has been sued eight times for charges relating to her work with dissociative disordered clients. In every case, she had to settle. No judgments were ever made against her. This was after an unblemished career of thirty years (Peterson, 1997).

PROFILES OF COMPLAINTS

The literature describing therapist risk for malpractice claims and licensing board complaints parallels the development of the literature on child sexual abuse. Initially, there was very little acknowledgment that child sexual abuse ever occurred. Thanks primarily to the women's movement, society's denial (and the denial of therapists) was broken and many articles and books surfaced outlining profiles of child sexual abusers, their partners, and their families. Initially, the assumption was that if a child reported sexual abuse, her story was true. Soon thereafter, more complex studies on children's memory and on contextual factors, such as child custody battles, brought into question the assumption that children's reports were always reliable. Profiles of false allegations and the contexts in which they occurred began to appear in the literature (Ehrenberg and Elterman, 1995; Gardner, 1987; Ney, 1995; Yuille, Tymofievich, and Marxsen, 1995).

The mental health professions did not begin acknowledging the problem of therapist perpetrators until the 1970s, when the women's movement and better consumer education brought the problem of sexually abusing therapists to public attention. Numerous articles began to appear describing impaired therapists who preyed on their clients. Once such therapists had been described, profiles of complainants started surfacing and, very recently, a skimpy body of literature has appeared outlining situations in which some clients make false complaints against their therapists. The following discussion outlines perpetrator profiles, complainant profiles, and context profiles.

Perpetrator Profiles

Sexual Perpetrators

Gabbard (1995) alleges that 80 percent of therapist sexual abuse of clients is males abusing females, 11 percent females abusing females, 6 percent males abusing males, and 3 percent females abusing males. Profiles of perpetrators include those with psychotic disorders, those with character disorders (including predatory, psychopathic, and paraphilic problems), those who succumb to "lovesickness" in an eroticized countertransferance, and those who give in to a client's abusiveness in masochistic surrender.

Lovesickness is the category to which most therapists are vulnerable. Included here are therapists who unconsciously reenact their own incestuous longings, engage in interlocking enactments of rescue fantasies, become confused about the client's needs and their own, have the fantasy that love in and of itself is curative, repress their rage at the client's persistent thwarting of their efforts, are angry at someone or something in their professional context, view the client as an idealized version of themselves, misperceive as sexual the client's wish for nurturance, delude themselves into thinking that this case is an exception, use the client as a transformational object, or have conflicts around their own sexual orientation (Gabbard, 1995).

Gonsiorek (1995) schematizes perpetrators a little differently, describing them as ranging from the naive and untrained to the normal and/or mildly neurotic, from the severely neurotic and/or socially isolated to the more seriously impaired (e.g., impulsive, sociopathic, or narcissistic character disorders; psychotics; classic sex offenders; medically disabled; and masochistic/self-defeating individuals).

Absence of Profiles of Nonsexual Perpetrators

Profiles of therapist perpetrators are of sexual offenders only. There are no profiles of perpetrators in other categories of ethical violation. What kind of therapist, for example, is most likely to commit insurance fraud? Reverse emotional roles in which the client becomes the therapist's caretaker? Improperly diagnose or treat the client? Fail to take adequate precautions with a suicidal client? Make judgment errors about simultaneous dual roles? There are resources that outline the processes involved in such ethical violations (Gonsiorek, 1995), but none that detail the specific characteristics of violators with anything nearing the descriptions available about sexually offending therapists.

The absence of such profiles in the literature is probably because these other violations are so vague and context-driven that it is impossible to isolate therapist characteristics from the whole picture which includes therapist, client, family, agency, and so forth. Sexual violations can be (although not always) more clear-cut.

I suspect that the absence of such profiles is also related to the fact that *any* therapist is susceptible to such violations and any profile, therefore, would be a description of *all* of us at various moments in our professional lives. How many of us have *not* made mistakes in filing insurance? Have *not* had clients in which roles became blurred? Have *not* made errors in decisions about providing both individual and marital therapy to the same client? Have *not* lost a client to suicide and realized that we missed a warning sign? Profiles of sexual perpetrators support an us-them dichotomy; profiles of other kinds of ethical violators collapse this dichotomy and make it evident that we *all* make mistakes. Chapter 10 discusses psychological and situational factors that increase therapist vulnerability to such mistakes.

The absence of therapist profiles for nonsexual ethics violators is also due to the variability and complexity of human situations and how they are perceived by both participants and observers. Theoretical orientation is a huge variable in any description of therapist error. A Haley-trained family therapist, for example, might respond to a suicidal client by setting up a suicide watch, utilizing the client's family rather than an institution as her protector (Haley, 1981). A psychodynamic therapist might refer immediately for hospitalization or request a suicide contract with the client. In either situation, the client can still commit suicide and the postmortem observers can retrospectively critique the therapist's thoroughness in attempting to prevent it. In any situation, there is always another point of view about what *could have* been done to prevent the client's death.

Similarly, a Bowen-trained family systems therapist might provide both individual and couples therapy to some clients, based on beliefs that both the couple's marital problems and the individuals' levels of emotional differentiation will be helped by individual family-of-origin work as well as by couple's sessions (Bowen, 1978). An individual therapist with a different theoretical orientation might consider a combination of individual and couples work a dual role and require that the individual see one therapist and the couple another. If the couple gets a divorce, the individual therapist might question the ethics of the dual roles the family therapist has maintained. In the same circumstances, the family therapist might question the role of the individual therapist in enhancing the chances that the couple would divorce by not tempering his understanding of the client's story with an equal understanding of the spouse's story. Each would view her ethical responsibilities differently because of her different theoretical orientation. An ethical mistake from one theoretical orientation can be a justifiable clinical decision from another.

A survey of six hundred randomly selected members of Division 29 of the American Psychological Association (Haas, Malouf, and Mayerson, 1986) revealed practitioner variability in perception of ethical issues. Ten vignettes, each describing a dilemma of professional ethics, were presented to the subjects. The vignettes contained seventeen areas of potential ethical difficulty. There was high agreement (75 percent) among the respondents on only three out of the ten vignettes. Consensus was reached regarding the inappropriateness of referring a client to a therapist whom they did not respect, the inappropriateness of trading psychological services for other professional services, and the duty to warn in cases of threatened violence or the sexual abuse of children.

Some of the problematic issues in the vignettes to which the subjects responded with greater variability included how to manage confidentiality within families or couples, how to respond to the unethical behavior of colleagues, what constitutes practicing outside of one's area of competence, and how to deal with the multifaceted aspects of diagnosis.

Similarly, a study examining professional social work behavior and beliefs with regard to intimate relationships, dual relationships, mixed modalities, advice-giving, boundary behaviors, and financial transactions showed much confusion and disagreement among social workers regarding what constitutes appropriate professional conduct. In addition, there was a disconnection between social work education and practice standards from the current realities of practice (Jayaratne, Croxton, and Mattison, 1997). The fact that many of our ethics codes and standards are written by academicians and professional association officials probably intensifies this disconnection.

Client Profiles

Sexually Abused Clients

The absence of profiles of therapist ethics violators (except for sexual infractions) is matched by an absence of client victim profiles. Even in the arena of sexual violations, there is no clear agreement on any client profiles except by gender; women are overrepresented in the victim population in comparison to men (Bouhoutsos et al., 1983). Stone (1980) reported on a study of forty-six women who had been in therapy with male therapists. No difference was found in ego strength or in levels of anxious attachment among women who had been sexually intimate with their therapists, those who had been propositioned by their therapists, those who had terminated therapy prematurely, and those who had successfully completed therapy. Likewise, Feldman-Summers and Jones (1984) found little difference between clients who had had sexual contact with therapists and those who had not, except that the former showed a greater mistrust and anger toward men in general.

Schoener (1989a,b), based on a thorough review of the literature and on his experience with the Walk-In Counseling Center in Minneapolis (a leading program both in the treatment of clients who have been abused by their therapists and in the rehabilitation of professionals) categorically dismisses the notion of a profile of victims. Characteristics that have been identified as common among victims of therapist sexual violations are also present in nonvictims. In addition, there is great variability among victims.

William White (1995) discusses reductionistic models in professional thinking that attribute responsibility for sexual violations to clients, including the "victim morality" model, which attributes sexual violations to the maliciousness of the client's character, and the "clinical model," which attributes them to the client's psychopathology. These views are generally seen as the professions' historic denial of the problem of therapist-client sexual relationships and as a projection of blame onto the victim. Attempts to profile client victims thus are risky; they could be interpreted as an attempt to attribute responsibility to the client for the behavior of therapists. Even the gender profile of predominantly female victims of sexual perpetration risks masking the problem of male victims and female perpetrators and same-sex encounters.

Profiles of Clients Most Likely to File Complaints Against Therapists

Profiles of victims of nonsexual ethical violations are as varied, complex, and undefined as are profiles of therapist violators, for all of the reasons just discussed. There is, however, a growing body of literature on the kinds of clients who are more likely to become enraged with their therapists, either magnifying the garden variety of clinical errors their therapists may have committed and/or falsely accusing them of ethical violations.

Just as in the arena of child sexual abuse, once the problem of therapist sexual abuse of clients was named and responded to by professional complaint channels, it could be expected that some false complaints would begin to filter in along with legitimate ones. False complaints may actually be less traumatic to make than legitimate complaints (Schoener and Milgrom, 1989). Indeed, the ease in making a complaint as a red flag of a potentially false complaint is documented in the child sexual abuse literature (Gardner, 1987).

In the Minneapolis Walk-In Counseling Center, some aspects of false complaints have been identified, including the following: misunderstanding by a follow-up helper; misinterpretation of looks, words, or touch; mistaken identity; exaggeration or distortion by the client; personal relationship rather than professional relationship complaints; fabrication; and revenge (Schoener and Milgrom, 1989).

It is in the literature on work with adult abuse survivors that the problem of vengeful complaints has perhaps received the most attention. Clients who have been raised in abusive families are familiar with the victim-perpetrator polarity and often try to replicate it in the therapist-client relationship (Adler, 1985; Gabbard and Wilkinson, 1994; Grotstein, 1981; Kernberg, [1975] 1985). They may gain temporary relief through cathartic explosions and narcissistic demands, become confused in flashback experiences of past abuse, and act out sociopathically in their attempts to deal with early attachment disturbances (Comstock and Vickery, 1992). Through splitting and externalizing the good and the bad, the therapist can flip from one position to the other in the client's mind. One moment, she is idolized, the next moment, hated. Therapists are often stunned by the sudden shift.

Difficult Clients

For some therapists, experiencing a client's vitriol and rage, frequently accompanied by accusations that the therapist is abusive, leads to what Pearlman and Saakvitne (1995, 31-32) call "vicarious traumatization." This is a "transformation in the inner experience of the therapist that comes about as a result of empathic engagement with clients' trauma material . . . [making the therapist] a helpless witness to past events and present re-enactments" of the trauma in ways which are especially stressful to the therapist.

It is difficult enough to listen to stories of past atrocities and abuse. When the client turns on the therapist and accuses him of being a perpetrator in the present, the therapist may experience traumatization at multiple levels. His ability to tolerate affect, maintain a positive sense of self, and feel safe, trustful and trustworthy, intimate, in control, and valued may be jeopardized. This affects how he then is able to relate to the client (Pearlman and Saakvitne, 1995). For some therapists, the rage they feel in response to client distortions can contribute to their own negative countertransference behaviors and feelings, giving the clients more ammunition for their beliefs that the therapist is abusive. Hedges (1996) attributes most false accusations against therapists to problems of transference, resistance, and countertransference between client and therapist.

There is a certain consensus in the field that some kinds of clients are more difficult and stressful for therapists than others. These include suicidal clients and borderline, sociopathic, narcissistic, and other character-disordered clients whose manipulation, dramatic and painful transference, and projective identification onto the therapist make the therapy relationship trying (Farber and Heifetz, 1982; Guy, 1987; Guy and Liaboe, 1985; Jobes and Maltsberger, 1995; Kottler, 1993; Stark, 1995).

Traumatized children are also a difficult group because of their extreme vulnerability, the therapist's tendency to overidentify, and the limited power the therapist has to protect them. In addition, anxiety about society's lack of protection of children often gets projected onto the therapists who work with them. During the 1980s, the fastest growing malpractice claims against social workers were in the child welfare arena, where social workers were increasingly being held accountable for our society's abysmal treatment of children (Besharov, 1985).

Other difficult and high-risk groups of clients cited in the literature include the following: clients with physiological disorders (strokes, closed head injuries), clients with hidden agendas, clients who ignore boundaries, clients who take no responsibility for their own healing, clients who are argumentative, clients who fear inti-

macy, clients who make demands the therapist cannot accommodate, clients who push the therapist's buttons, clients who are countertransference objects for the therapist, clients who are impatient,
clients who are literal and concrete, clients who feel hopeless, and
clients with poor impulse control (Kottler, 1993).

Other problematic client characteristics cited in the literature
include: a history of multiple failed therapies, previous filing of
complaints against therapists, a sense of entitlement and wanting to
be special, an insistence on the right to self-abuse, illegal behavior,
lying to the therapist, a victim mentality, and a need to be 100
percent right. In addition, situations in which a client's agenda is not
about healing but about winning (e.g., child custody disputes, disability benefits applications, vengeful marital disputes) are also
difficult and can enhance legal and psychological vulnerability.

Obviously, reality is in the eye of the beholder and many of the
characteristics described above would be more or less problematic
depending on the unique vulnerability of each particular therapist.
Clients who are most likely to bring out the therapist's own intense
countertransference feelings are clearly the most difficult and
potentially the most dangerous. Regardless of the individual therapist, however, the kinds of clients who are most likely to file lawsuits and ethics complaints are:

- clients with a primary diagnosis on Axis II and/or who have
  been a victim of serious trauma
- violent or suicidal clients
- clients involved in contested divorce or child custody cases
- clients in which rapid and intense transference occurs (Harris,
  1995)

Context Profiles

In addition to the person of the therapist and the person of the
client, the context in which their relationship occurs can have significant impact on what happens in the relationship between them.
Whether the context is a small private practice or a large family
service agency, it affects the therapist-client relationship. This is
discussed further in Chapter 10.

William White (1995) describes systems in which potential
power abuse is magnified because of incestuous qualities such as

the following: blurred boundaries between work and personal life; immersion in work to the exclusion of outside sources of personal, professional, social, and sexual replenishment; personal depletion resulting from excessive work demands; and distortion of organizational values resulting from isolation from external feedback.

Such incestuous systems typically have a rigid organizational dogma, centralized and charismatic leadership, an isolated position with respect to the outside social and professional world, a homogenized work force, an intense focus on the personal and interpersonal problems of staff, disruptions in work functioning because of social and sexual relationships among staff, projection of organizational problems onto some external target, and a punitive, abusive organizational culture. All of these characteristics contribute to a myopic view of the world, constraining flexibility of therapist thought and action. While White is specifically writing about high-risk contexts for sexual abuse, the characteristics he discusses could certainly also increase the possibilities for other kinds of ethics violations and/or allegations of such.

THE MENTAL HEALTH PROFESSIONS AS INCESTUOUS SYSTEMS

Interestingly, some of the characteristics that White describes in incestuous systems appear similar to the characteristics of our professional systems. As we become more rigid and rule-based in our ethics codes, we are also becoming more dogmatic. Our ethics leadership is centralized in a handful of professionals who staff our ethics and disciplinary committees within the professional associations and the licensing boards.

Our lack of significant consumer input isolates us from outside social forces. Our legislated dos and don'ts rest on assumptions of both client and therapist uniformity (that the same rules should work in all variations of client, therapist, and context profiles). We project responsibility for the problems encountered in ethical functioning in such an environment onto individual practitioners and individual clients rather than looking to the inherent problems within the professions and the current social context as major contributors to the rising incidence of client complaints against therapists. And, finally, we have become more punitive and abusive in the treatment given to accused therapists, especially by licensing boards.

All of these incestuous characteristics interfere with ethical thinking. In such an environment, individual practitioners and their clients are less able to take creative risks in the healing process because such risks may not fit dogmatic ethics codes and may subject the practitioner to grave professional danger. Like White's incestuous systems, our ethics codes constrain, rather than facilitate, ethical functioning.

SUMMARY

Licensing boards are administrative entities that do not provide the accused therapist with the due process protections of court procedures. In the name of consumer protection, their job is to search out and punish violators of the law.

Malpractice actions, by comparison, provide the therapist with due process protections. But even with malpractice actions, the ambiguity of mental health practice lends itself to great variability. In addition, malpractice cases almost always involve professional liability insurers whose agenda is to conserve money. Many therapists, therefore, must settle in malpractice situations in which they are not guilty.

Other than for sexual offenses, there are no profiles of therapists who violate ethics principles, probably because the nature of most other offenses is variable, ambiguous, and open to multiple interpretations. The lack of profiles also reflects the fact that *all* therapists make mistakes.

There are also no profiles of abused clients that differentiate them from all other clients. There is a growing body of literature, however, that addresses the kinds of clients most likely to make false complaints against their therapists, including trauma survivors, clients with an Axis II diagnosis, those involved in contested divorce and child custody situations, and suicidal clients (Harris, 1995). In addition, there is some descriptive reference to the kinds of contexts in which ethics violations might be most likely to occur (W. White, 1995).

The next chapter discusses the psychological vulnerability of therapists in general and the particular vulnerability of therapists in today's litigious, anxiety-based, and dogmatic professional context.

Chapter 10

Psychological Vulnerability

Within the last several years, three major publications on the risks of psychotherapy practice have emerged (Figley, 1995b; Pearlman and Saakvitne, 1995; Sussman, 1995), as well as an increasing number of articles on the risks of victimization of therapists by clients (Comstock and Vickery, 1992; Hedges, 1996; Maltsberger, 1993; McCann and Pearlman, 1990; Sherven, 1994). Although previous publications outlined some of the psychological consequences of being a psychotherapist (Edelwich and Brodsky, 1980; English, 1976; Farber, 1983a,b; Farber and Heifetz, 1981, 1982; Freudenberger, 1983; Guy, 1987; Guy and Liaboe, 1985; Guy, Poelstra, and Stark, 1989; Jayaratne and Chess, 1983; Maslach, 1976), such discussions did not acknowledge the additional psychological consequences fueled by an environment of litigiousness and fear. With few exceptions, this awareness seems to have surfaced primarily in the 1990s.

Different theoretical orientations have different views on the importance and use of self in therapy, ranging from extreme importance in psychodynamic and relationship oriented therapies to modest importance in strategic, cognitive, and solution oriented therapies. Whatever the theoretical orientation, however, it is indisputable that the main tool of the therapist is his or her self. Psychological vulnerability is always an aspect of self and, as such, affects the client-therapist relationship.

Psychological vulnerability is present because of the values, beliefs, and practices promulgated by the mental health professions; specific aspects of practice contexts; life cycle issues of the therapist; sudden and unpredictable crises in the therapist's life; and unique and particular aspects of the therapist's character, history, and emotional life. Following is a discussion of each of these factors and an exploration of how the litigiousness and anxiety in today's professional context exacerbate the psychological vulnerability of therapists.

VALUES, BELIEFS, AND PRACTICES

Guy (1987), Kottler (1993), and Kottler, Sexton, and Whiston (1994) have some of the most thorough and thought-provoking discussions of the ways in which the values, beliefs, and practices of the mental health professions affect the therapist. Much of the following discussion is based on their writings.

Isolation

The therapist is not only isolated from colleagues, as she sits hour after hour with clients, but also from the outside world (informationally as well as physically), family, and friends. During a typical day, the therapist does not listen to the radio, watch television, receive calls from family or friends, or spend time with "normal" people. Reality can get skewed. In addition, there is the isolation of confidentiality—having to hold secrets that cannot be shared with family and friends. There is a kind of psychic isolation too, resulting from abstaining from disclosing personal information; setting aside personal needs and concerns; controlling emotions; participating in one-way intimacy; experiencing devaluation, attack, and/or idealization and admiration; and constantly being required to say good-bye to those with whom we have shared an intimate relationship.

Some of the risks of isolation are that the therapist may carry emotional neutrality and control too far and detach from his own feelings. Or he may go to the other extreme—getting too involved emotionally, becoming drained. He can also have difficulty setting aside the therapeutic role and become detached, secretive and withholding, less empathic, empty, and numb to or anxious about abandonment in personal relationships. Isolation can lead the therapist to take his power too seriously in other relationships; becoming too analytical and/or dogmatic; burdening other relationships with ideal, unrealistic expectations; and measuring all time in terms of money (Guy, 1987).

While the therapist is isolated, he is also on constant display.

> All over the city there are restaurants and bars we cannot feel comfortable visiting because clients or ex-clients work there. At parties we have to monitor closely how much we drink, knowing that losing control would sully our reputation. Neighbors watch our children for signs of emotional disturbance so they can substantiate the myth of the crazy shrink down the block. People constantly ask for advice on what to do about their jobs. Others feel intimidated by their own perceptions of therapists as mind readers. They will not get too close for fear we will disrobe their insecurities with a casual glance. "Oh, you're a therapist. I suppose I should be careful around you [giggle]." (Kottler, 1993, pp. 104-105)

Living in a glass house also affects therapists' partners and children who are also on display and have to deal with the intrusions of clients into their private lives.

Intensity

Being in the presence of conflict and intense feelings is stressful. The client's feelings are often not just expressed *with* the therapist but also can be targeted *at* the therapist. In addition, the therapist is privy to stories of horror and human cruelty that pose existential and spiritual crises as well as emotional responses.

> The risks that come with the territory of being a therapist emanate primarily from getting so close to the flame that burns deep within the sorrow of each client we see. (Kottler, 1993, p. 46)

Griffin (1992), in her poetic descriptions of war, graphically depicts the risks of being close to pain on the battlefield:

> [O]ne can see a young German stretcher-bearer. The man he is carrying has a gaping wound in his stomach. Just as the stretcher-bearer begins to find the cries of the man unbearable, the man calls out that he can no longer bear his pain. The stretcher-bearer stops and, laying the stretcher down, begins to

> stroke the wounded man all over his body, as if he were a
> mother, moved now not only past the boundaries of separation
> but also beyond any circumscribed idea of self. The voices of
> dying and wounded men will never leave him. Later, in his
> most vulnerable moments, these voices will haunt him as
> nightmare and hallucination. (p. 209)

While as psychotherapists we do not usually witness or participate
in such life-threatening events as war, we do hear stories of trauma
and experience with our clients the psychic and spiritual residue of
pain that drives them to our offices for relief. The effects of being in
the presence of such stories have begun to collect various labels, e.g.,
compassion fatigue (Figley, 1995a,b), *secondary traumatic stress
disorder* (Dutton and Rubenstein, 1995; Figley, 1995a,b), *empathic
strain* (Wilson and Lindy, 1994a), and *vicarious traumatization*
(McCann and Pearlman, 1990; Pearlman and Saakvitne, 1995).

Maintaining empathy and connection with a client whose pain is
overwhelming takes its toll on the therapist, especially when the
therapy does not seem to help the client or when he abruptly termi-
nates. "Every time the wounds cannot be healed or the suffering
alleviated, it becomes harder to open oneself to another's pain"
(Edelwich and Brodsky, 1980, p. 35). The intensity of our work can
often lead to feelings of emptiness, hopelessness, and exhaustion—
a clinical state described as burnout.

Burnout is not just stress but rather a state of "utter despair and
exhaustion resulting from the cumulative impact of a host of stressors and aversive aspects related to therapeutic practice" (Guy, 1987,
p. 253), an "erosion of the spirit" (Grosch and Olsen, 1994, p. 4). A
growing body of literature on the prevention and rehabilitation of
burned-out therapists has been steadily growing during the last two
decades.

Believing We Are Special

"Therapists in our society are treated *as if* we have special powers that allow us to see inside people's hearts and souls, predict the
future, and heal suffering" (Kottler, 1993, p. 94). This special treatment may lead us to believe that we are special and that we are
therefore *entitled* to certain things because of the drain and strain of

being a therapist. This not only can jeopardize our relationships with clients, but can also stress personal relationships. We may place demands on spouses and children for nurturance (or distance), care, and good behavior, expecting the same idealization from family members as we receive from clients, while masking our own vulnerabilities and hostilities behind "objective" diagnosing and/or intrusive and controlling labeling of family members' behaviors (Guy, 1987). This does not go over well with most family members and, if the therapist continues to approach them in these ways and meets with frustration, he may then be at risk for putting all of his energy into the one-way intimacy of his relationships with clients.

A sense of entitlement can also fuel overspending and the complications and risks of living on the edge financially. Perhaps a new car, a trip to Hawaii, or a gold bracelet will help compensate for the emotional drain the therapist feels in his one-sided giving. Overspending heightens the pressures on the therapist to work harder, creating a vicious cycle of escalating work demands to support his lifestyle requirements.

Ambiguity

Our work is ambiguous and full of seeming contradictions. Psychotherapy is equal and democratic yet unequal and authoritarian, intimate and personal yet professional and distant, real and genuine yet manipulative and projective, independent yet dependent, spontaneous yet prescribed, natural yet requiring professional training, technological and scientific yet human, safe and predictable yet dangerous and changing (Kottler, Sexton, and Whiston, 1994). Our work requires that we hold dichotomous and ambiguous realities without disavowing the presence of any of them.

There are no clear criteria for success. We often have no idea what happens to clients after they terminate the treatment relationship, especially with short-term clients. There are clients with whom we think we have succeeded when they think we have not. We have clients we think we have failed, yet they feel the therapy was successful. The more isolated we are, the more skewed our perceptions can become.

Farber (1983a) describes what he calls the dysfunctional aspects of the psychotherapeutic role in terms of role ambiguity, role con-

flict, role overload, and feelings of inconsequentiality. Role ambiguity relates to the lack of clarity about what constitutes success.
Role conflict refers to the inevitable clashes between the needs of
clients and the needs of self and family, as well as to the unavoidable dualities that arise in the therapy relationship. Role overload
refers not only to the number of hours and/or clients that the therapist is expected to maintain, but also to the constant need to upgrade
knowledge as new standards of care and new treatment modalities
evolve. Feelings of inconsequentiality are a sense that what we do is
not, in the overall scope of things, really that important in a society
that is increasingly suspicious of psychotherapy.

Quick Fix and Other Magical Expectations

Economic resources to pay for psychotherapy have dwindled. As
managed care asserts a supervisory role in most psychotherapy practices, there is an ever-growing pressure for the quick fix. While
single-session, brief, and intermittent brief therapies are effective
with many clients, they do not work with many others. This puts
tremendous pressure on the psychotherapist, not only in terms of
increased paperwork and time spent in negotiating extra sessions
with the managed care gatekeepers, but also in terms of psychological vulnerability. The therapist may question her own competence,
feel anxious that she will be eliminated from a managed care panel
for asking for too many sessions too many times, and feel the strain
of being caught between the client's need for services and the managed care company's need for brevity. She may become frustrated
both with herself and the client if the client does not get better
quickly enough.

The fact that brief therapy workshops have sprung up like mush-
rooms in the face of managed care demands may exacerbate her
vulnerability as more and more professionals tout treatment interventions that seem magically effective in the protected space of a
training room, without the voice of the client to correct presenter
distortions. Brief videotape clips used to demonstrate such interventions are presented with little or no follow-up data or discussion of
the tedious, hard work that both preceded and followed the interventions. Outcomes are typically presented as positive and the

theoretical frame of the presenter as efficacious, often with little or no substantiation.

How many therapists leave such presentations feeling incompetent or embarrassed that they cannot produce the same results? Many therapists are reluctant to admit that they do long-term therapy, feel pressured to "fix" clients quickly, question their own competence if they cannot, and tend to screen out of their practices clients who have intractable problems requiring longer-term work.

Many therapists feel defensive in responding to managed care reviewers' questions about *why* the client has not gotten better in a short period of time and *why* the therapist is asking for additional sessions. In the brief therapy mentality of the 1990s, therapists are being held accountable (and often hold themselves accountable) to unrealistic standards for success, and then suffer psychologically when confronted with their failure to measure up.

Empathy

A major requirement of being a therapist is empathy—"the ability to project oneself into the phenomenological world being experienced by another person" (Wilson and Lindy, 1994a, p. 7). The degree of psychological stress that this entails varies from therapist to therapist and from client to client, but sustained empathy with trauma survivors can be particularly demanding. Tendencies to over-empathize can lead the therapist down the trail of overinvolvement and burnout. Underempathizing as a defense against the pain of the client's phenomenological world can cause withdrawal and distance.

Balanced, sustained, optimal empathy with some clients is psychologically demanding and potentially damaging to the therapist. Kluft (1994), for example, describes the psychological strains of working with clients with dissociative disorders:

> [T]hose who work with MPD report a sense of a loss of innocence and a challenge to the benign and optimistic assumptions that had guided their lives and given them a sense of security. They become sensitized to the darker side of life. . . . (pp. 146-147)

Even with less serious client problems, the challenge of maintaining sustained empathy is draining. Emotional depletion caused by the focused and one-sided entering of another's emotional experience can, in addition, affect the therapist's family as well as the therapist. Spouses of therapists frequently say that they wish their husband or wife could listen to them with half the empathy and attentiveness given to their clients. Children sometimes wonder why Mommy is too tired to play with them when she has been with other people's children all day.

PRACTICE CONTEXT

Considering any of the dimensions described above, it is easy to see how the interlocking professional selves in any practice context can affect one another as well as the lives of the therapist and his family. If one therapist is pouring himself into work as a way of avoiding family problems, another therapist in the same practice (especially with the workaholic mentality of the therapy professions) might feel compelled to do the same, particularly if referrals for the entire practice are low. The second therapist's family may then begin to protest, a situation that gives her either an opportunity to address the issue or to withdraw from her family's complaints by concentrating most of her energy on her practice. What starts as one therapist's family problems thus spreads to the second therapist's family.

Or perhaps, one therapist in a practice setting becomes disillusioned and burned out in the face of the emotional and spiritual pain of listening hour after hour to survivor stories and experiencing intense negative transference from her clients. Her emotional numbing may make her insensitive to the normal relationship demands of a colleague in her office, causing the colleague's withdrawal, and alienating a source of support needed to ameliorate her burnout.

Friedman (1985) discusses interdependence in work systems, describing the higher-risk situations as those in which there is an intense degree of emotional interdependence in the system *and* the business of the system is "life" and its stresses. Thus, in practice settings in which there is a high degree of interdependence, there is more likely to be contagion from one therapist's work or family problems to another's. Even with less interdependence, the risk of contagion is present because of the intensity of the life-and-death issues with which therapists routinely deal. This makes therapists psychologically vulnerable, not just to the impact of clients, but also to the impact of colleagues and the clients and family members of colleagues in their practice settings

I once became involved in a chain of referrals for supervision. Several therapists from the same practice setting independently presented to me the negative effects of working with one particular colleague whose narcissistic entitlement had burdened them. The particular psychological vulnerability of each therapist shaped the unique effects of the colleague's narcissism on them, but all reported symptoms of exhaustion, anger, and self-doubt. One had overfunctioned to assist the colleague in the management of practice details he had allowed to deteriorate in ways that jeopardized the entire practice. Another found himself picking up the pieces when disgruntled clients complained of the colleague's forgetfulness about appointment times and telephone calls. Another was the target of the colleague's accusations of ethics violations that he himself had actually committed. Another found himself running personal errands for the colleague and loaning him money. And still another became stage manager for the colleague's training and workshop presentations.

As each one struggled to disentangle from these enabling positions, the pressure on those remaining became more intense. Gradually, all of the therapists in the practice system withdrew their support sufficiently to create a crisis that necessitated the narcissistic colleague's separation from the practice. This took tremendous expenditures of energy, jeopardized personal and professional relationships, and put the entire practice in danger because of disgruntled clients, record keeping chaos, and general public relations snafus caused by the narcissistic colleague.

Most practice settings may not have to deal with such an extreme problem, but all are subject to the vagaries of the lives of the therapists within them. Life-cycle issues, illnesses, and catastrophic occurrences in the lives of therapists impact not just the therapist but all of her colleagues. The following two sections discuss these issues.

LIFE-CYCLE ISSUES

The life-cycle issues of the therapist affect the particular kinds of psychological vulnerability she experiences. MacNab (1995), for example, describes the dilemma of being a mother and realizing that she is not any better at it than some of her clients, viewing her own children through skewed eyes based on a distorted sample from her practice, overempathizing with her own children and having difficulty setting limits, and worrying that the same traumas that have happened to clients could also happen to her own children. Many therapists who treat survivors of child sexual abuse talk about the difficulties they have in being parents of young children and simultaneously working with clients who have been traumatized and abused as children. The demands of parenthood require some denial that bad things happen to children; abused clients penetrate this denial.

Many life-cycle issues are obvious and cannot be hidden from clients by the therapist. Divorces, remarriages, deaths of family members, and illnesses are examples of these. While the therapist may want to preserve privacy in her own life, she often has no choice about self-disclosure. The sudden absence of a wedding ring, the change of a last name, the acquisition of stepchildren through remarriage, and the cancellation of appointments for funerals or medical problems occur in the presence of a client audience. While most clients may be respectful of the therapist's privacy, they are still privy to changes in the therapist's personal life, whether she wants them to be or not.

Client Responses and Needs

Some clients require more information concerning changes in the therapist's life than others. Survivor clients, for example, are often exquisitely tuned in to *any* perceived change in the therapist's demeanor, affect, attentiveness, and responsiveness to them. They tend to take it personally if they perceive any variation and therefore require more self-disclosure on the part of the therapist than do other clients, particularly if the therapist's distress is unrelated to them. Unnamed distress can be frightening (Pearlman and Saakvitne, 1995).

Even less fragile clients may have intense reactions to events in the therapist's life. Divorce stirs up anxieties about the permanence of the client's marriage, raises fears that the divorced therapist may no longer be able to provide effective couples therapy, and arouses curiosity and perhaps discomfort about the therapist's sexual availability. Deaths of family members highlight the finiteness of life, intensify grief about past losses or anxiety about future losses, and stimulate confusion about caretaking roles (How can I talk about my petty problems when my therapist has just lost her mother?) Therapist illness may elevate feelings of client vulnerability, compromise client faith in the power of the therapist to be a healer, and require adaptations to sudden shifts in scheduling, long intervals between appointment times, and changes in therapist appearance and demeanor.

The therapist has to frame how she talks about her distress for the benefit of the client. This is a difficult task when she herself may be overwhelmed, and one that requires that she put her own needs aside at a time when this may be detrimental to her health and well-being. This enhances psychological vulnerability as her emotional space to grieve, feel afraid and anxious, and absorb the realities of changes in her own life must be constrained by client need. Most other work settings allow more fluidity of feeling expression across contexts and are thus (potentially, at any rate) more supportive of life-cycle crises.

Therapist Vulnerability

In addition to the strains of the client as audience and the requirement for careful self-disclosure for client—not therapist—need such life-cycle crises remind the therapist of his own vulnerability. They penetrate his denial, challenge the built-in grandiosity and one-sidedness of the caretaking role, call into question his competence, and confront him with the unknown. Munn (1995) addresses some of these vulnerabilities with regard to physical illness in her description of how her multiple sclerosis makes her constantly challenge her competence.

> I judged throughout that I was a "good enough" therapist, but I felt I was not as good as I had been, so the question of competence seemed always in front of me, and always needing reassessment. (p. 107)

She goes on to describe how, as her life narrows during periods of illness, she becomes isolated and more immersed in the material her clients bring, thereby removing herself further from the "anchors of reality" generally available through contact with the outside world (pp. 109-110).

I have struggled with chronic degenerative disc disease for over ten years, necessitating periods of time in which I have to lie on the floor to see my clients because of the severe pain involved in sitting up. The first two or three rounds of pain seemed manageable to me. I was able to joke with my clients about "lying down on the job" or taking a (literal) "one down" position with them. I felt balanced in managing the many solicitous attempts at role reversal, allowing some of my clients to carry my coffee cup or offer me a hoist from the floor, reassuring them that I was getting good physical care and had lots of emotional support from family and friends so that they would not feel compelled to provide it. I shared only limited snippets of my own emotional pain as they were relevant to the therapy relationship. I stayed optimistic and focused on the benefits to my clients of my increased vulnerability.

By round four I began to recognize the cost to myself of having to filter so much of my pain and vulnerability through the lens of client benefit. I found myself transferring to other therapists clients who were especially demanding, taking more time off from my office to deal with my pain in private, and modifying my office furniture and routines to accommodate my increased vulnerability. As I protected myself more, I felt less vulnerable. I was gradually able to feel healed enough from the psychic stress of dealing with constant chronic pain to once again use my own vulnerability in the service of my clients.

While there may be very positive outcomes for both client and therapist in the presence of the therapist's increased vulnerability (the so-called wounded healer benefit), the therapist's vulnerability can be magnified and complicated by the unique demands of clinical practice. The therapist cannot wait until her vulnerability is manageable, is somewhat healed, and has scar tissue to protect it. She is forced to deal with it immediately with clients as she struggles to adjust to all of its implications. She also may have very real physical limitations that compound her psychological vulnerability, requiring her to modify not only the ways in which she relates to physically aggressive child clients or unpredictably volatile and potentially violent adult clients, but also the ways in which she runs her entire practice.

SUDDEN AND UNPREDICTABLE CRISES AND EVENTS

Therapists sometimes have unpredictable and public crises that are impossible to hide from their clients. Lewis and Stokes (1996), for example, describe how one therapist handled the public disclosure of her husband's murder. As with life-cycle crises, such situational vulnerabilities challenge all aspects of the client-therapist relationship and require the therapist to deal with client reactions while she herself is struggling to absorb the implications and feelings engendered by the crisis.

On a less tragic scale, there is probably no therapist who does not eventually have some aspect of his own vulnerability made public to a client without his choice and who must then deal with the consequences. I remember one time when I was standing in the locker room of my exercise club, totally nude, and I heard a voice greeting me. As I looked up, there was one of my clients, also nude. I was totally revealed—all of my physical imperfections glaringly apparent. As it turned out, this encounter was useful in the client's therapy since one of her issues was a preoccupation with and dislike of her body. Seeing me au naturel facilitated some very healing conversations with her about body image and the tyranny of perfectionist beliefs in this culture about ideal female shapes.

While the encounter was therapeutic for my client, I must admit that the intrusion into my own personal space was not without some psychic cost to me. From that point on, I was always aware of the possibility of running into her or other clients at my exercise club. Its meaning as a sacred refuge for me was lost and I eventually changed clubs.

UNIQUE ASPECTS OF THERAPIST HISTORY,
CHARACTER, AND EMOTIONAL LIFE

While all of us have unique areas of vulnerability based on character, history, and emotional life issues, some are more vulnerable than others. Therapists who are at high risk for burnout include:

those who are emotionally and spiritually depleted and exhausted; lonely therapists; overly idealistic, dedicated, and people-oriented therapists who are at risk for losing their identity in their service to others; therapists with excessively high, perfectionistic expectations; therapists who are authoritarian and controlling and who get frustrated when clients do not comply; therapists who give to others to meet their own intimacy needs; and those with unresolved conflicts and issues from childhood (Farber and Heifetz, 1981; Grosch and Olsen, 1994). People who have been traumatized as children are also more susceptible to burnout (Figley, 1995a). Since psychotherapists are more likely than professionals in other fields to have been maltreated as children (Briere, 1989), this aspect of burnout susceptibility is particularly significant.

Other problematic characteristics include: the desire to be relieved of pain and emotional distress; vicarious, voyeuristic coping; isolation and the need to get intimacy behind the safety of the therapy relationship; desire for power; vicarious rebellion; and the need to be loved and needed (Guy, 1987).

Obviously, any of these characteristics can both compromise client protection and care and increase therapist vulnerability. However, some are more likely to exacerbate client vulnerability. Certain characterological problems, for example, may serve as defenses against therapist vulnerability at the expense of the client. Character disordered therapists, especially those who are narcissistic, antisocial, or borderline, are at high risk for doing harm to clients out of their tendencies to view them as objects and extensions of themselves. Others may have only a vague notion that something is wrong with them and little or no idea about how to struggle with specific destructive behaviors (Shub, 1995).

Some characteristics are more likely to heighten the therapist's sense of vulnerability without substantial threat to client well-being unless carried to the extreme. Therapists who, for example, tend to overfunction on behalf of their clients and lose themselves in sacrificial caretaking are more vulnerable psychologically than those who recognize their own needs and set limits on the extent to which they accommodate client need.

Any of us is vulnerable to particular kinds of clients at times of crisis or stress in our own lives. But even in nonstressful periods, the unique psychological demands of being a psychotherapist, combined with the current anxious, litigious nature of clinical practice, can exacerbate psychological vulnerability.

INCREASED PSYCHOLOGICAL VULNERABILITY IN A CONTEXT OF ANXIETY AND LITIGIOUSNESS

The following discussion is informed by my own clinical experience in treating therapist offenders, supervisory experience with many therapists who have gone through the ordeal of lawsuits and licensing board and professional association ethics committee complaints, as well as the reported experiences of others (Charles and Kennedy, 1985; Hedges, 1996; Maltsberger, 1993; Marine, 1997; *Seattle Times*, Dec. 29, 1993; Sherven, 1994; Steinberg, 1997).

Therapist Denial

One of the primary responses by therapists to today's anxious and litigious atmosphere is denial. "It couldn't happen to me." Sometimes, this is paired with the dichotomizing of therapists into good and bad categories (discussed in Chapter 8), the projection of all problematic behaviors onto bad therapists, and the self-reassuring attitude that nothing bad can happen to good therapists. Such denial, projection, and self-reassurance can interfere with the therapist's ethical decision making, rendering her less likely to see potentially problematic aspects of her own professional behavior.

Therapist Reactions to Being Complained Against

Shock and Naiveté

When denial, projection, and self-reassurance are punctured because the therapist or a close colleague is the subject of a complaint, the reaction is one of shock, indignation, fear, outrage, and often panic. How could this possibly happen to me (or to my friend) because I have always been a good therapist? Self-reassurance may then follow in the form of a naive assumption that the complaint body surely will vindicate her.

Self-Examination

Soon she begins to realize that no matter how innocent she believes herself to be, she is still in for a critical and often punitive investigation into her professional behavior. She begins to question every clinical decision she ever made and every possible mistake that could be misinterpreted as an ethics violation. The three ethical buzzwords discussed in Chapter 7 and others like them may loom large at this point. Could her calling the client on a Sunday to reschedule an appointment be misconstrued as a dual role? Could her hug at the end of a session be misinterpreted as erotic touch? Could her self-disclosure about her divorce be interpreted as a boundary violation of some kind?

Hypercriticalness and Hypervigilance

Depending on the therapist's own personal issues, she may become hypercritical of herself, obsessing over a retrospective analysis of what went wrong in the therapy relationship with the complainant. Isolated from colleagues and friends out of her shame at being an alleged perpetrator, she may have difficulties sleeping, functioning adequately at work, being fully present with clients and family, and pursuing normal life interests. She also may become wary of new clients, refrain from seeing anyone who smacks of similarity to the complainant, and replace her former naiveté and trusting attitude with cynicism and suspiciousness.

The Price of Confidentiality

Because of the confidentiality she must maintain, she cannot talk freely about her distress with anyone. Her spouse and children cannot be privy to the details of her worst nightmare and may feel helpless and confused about what to do. Her most important support system is thus rendered ineffectual. The shadow of the accusation permeates all aspects of her life.

Connection with Others

After a time, she may begin to read more and network with others who have been through similar experiences. She no longer has naive expectations that she will automatically be exonerated in the investigatory process and begins to prepare herself for the ordeal ahead, garnering support where she can, and gradually coming to a more thorough and complex understanding of how this could have happened to her.

Following completion of the investigation, she may become more outspoken in professional circles about the hazards of psychotherapy practice and may devote time and energy to mentoring colleagues through the investigatory process. Whether she is exonerated or found guilty, she reports that both personally and professionally she has been permanently changed by the experience and that her family also has been changed.

Disconnection from Others

Other therapists, faced with the same trauma, go underground, becoming ever-more secretive about their experience, sharing it with no one, and nursing in silence their own private shame and embarrassment. Some therapists are advised by attorneys to wall off from all colleagues with whom they might possibly be accused of discussing the case, a precaution with great psychological expense to the therapist.

Heightened Awareness and Fearfulness

For therapists who have not been touched either directly or vicariously by a complaint process, denial of vulnerability is still possible. The fact that complaints are rising in numbers, combined with the complex and ambiguous nature of all but the most flagrant violations (such as substance abuse, sexual improprieties, and financial exploitation), make it more difficult for the average therapist to keep her head in the sand. Most practitioners these days have a heightened awareness of their vulnerability.

This awareness exacerbates the psychological vulnerability of being a therapist, complicating the isolation, intensity, ambiguity, and unrealistic expectations that are part and parcel of the psychotherapy professions. It also makes many therapists go overboard in trying to go by the book as a means of self-protection. They take progress notes—not in the interest of good client treatment, but as future protection in a malpractice action. They inform the client of the treatment modality they are using—not for the sake of collegial treatment planning, but to follow legalistic standards of care. They avoid all touch—not because it would be intrusive for the client, but because they are afraid of its implications in a licensing board complaint. Such self-protective measures can only enhance, not decrease, vulnerability as clients feel unseen, unheard, and misunderstood by their therapists.

SUMMARY

Psychological vulnerability is part of being a psychotherapist. It inheres in the values, beliefs, and practices promulgated by the mental health professions. It is compounded by the nature of some practice contexts, life-cycle issues in the therapist's life, sudden and unpredictable crises and events, and unique aspects of the therapist's history, character, and emotional life. The cultural context of anxiety and litigiousness further compounds psychological vulnerability.

Chapter 11

Alternatives to Traditional Models

> Aspiration is elusive without models to aspire to, but following a single model has its own dangers.
>
> —M. C. Bateson, *Composing a Life*

> [S]o many things are possible just as long as you don't know they're impossible.
>
> —N. Juster, *The Phantom Tollbooth*

Obviously, something has to change. Psychotherapists cannot continue functioning on behalf of their clients with some of the anachronistic, outmoded objectivist concepts that have traditionally informed them. Nor can they continue functioning in a rule-based context of ethics that threatens both their legal and psychological well-being and subjects them to increased risks of client complaint and emotional malaise.

Even as ethics standards and rules proliferate, other voices are calling for non–rule-based models of ethical functioning—ethics that inform and are an integral part of clinical thinking and not just an addendum to it. Such voices include those of feminist theorists and ethicists, social constructionists, advocates for the morality of communal as well as individual welfare, and those who see ethical functioning as inherent in the character of the therapist. Without exception, all of these models are contextual, process- and meaning-based, and challenging of traditional psychotherapy practices and ethics.

FEMINIST ETHICS

The moral problem [for women] arises from conflicting responsibilities rather than from competing rights and requires for its resolution a mode of thinking that is contextual and narrative rather than formal and abstract. This conception of morality as concerned with the activity of care centers moral development around the understanding of responsibility and relationships, just as the conception of morality as fairness ties moral development to the understanding of rights and rules. . . . The morality of rights differs from the morality of responsibility in its emphasis on separation rather than connection, in its consideration of the individual rather than the relationship as primary. (Gilligan, 1982, p. 19)

The following discussion addresses the basic tenets of feminist ethics and the criticisms of such. Two case illustrations demonstrate circumstances in which they are helpful and circumstances in which they are not.

Feminist Ethics and the Feminist Therapy Institute

The Feminist Therapy Institute was developed in the second wave of the women's movement. A grassroots organization characterized by the absence of any one major designated leader, the Institute was formally established in 1982 and published its first code of ethics in 1987. The code is based on feminist principles of collegiality, cultural diversity, and the minimization of power differentials, not only between therapists and clients but in society in general. It embraces the correction of social oppression, the complexity of and therapist responsibility for overlapping relationships, and therapist accountability for professional and personal competence. Its emphasis is on self-in-relation and on the responsibilities of the therapist to take not only the therapeutic relationship but the entire context of meaning into consideration in making ethical decisions. As such, it is more variable and diffuse than traditional (more male) models based on individual rights and separated selves.

The Feminist Therapy Code of Ethics (1987) deconstructs many traditional psychotherapy beliefs and traditions. It insists that the personal is political and that the individual problems that clients (both men and women) bring to therapists are caused by a patriarchal society that privileges white male realities over those of women and other minorities. It suggests that the feminist informed therapist must therefore constantly listen to the individual stories of clients as reflections of social and cultural inequities and biases, and work to change social as well as individual conditions.

Power imbalances are addressed, both in society and in the therapist-client relationship, with emphasis on collegial ways of acknowledging and dealing with the lack of equal power between therapist and client. Emphasis is on the admission of power imbalances and the dangers of denying them. The traditional view of the client as a helpless recipient of therapist services is tempered by an understanding that clients *do* have power to cocreate with their therapists their experiences in the therapy process, and that the therapist-client *relationship* rather than the individual client is the focus of concern.

The existence and inevitability of overlapping relationships are acknowledged rather than denied or legislated away. Guidelines for their ethical management are addressed. Therapist responsibility for ongoing professional development and personal self-care are discussed as requirements for maintaining competence.

Diagnoses and other constructs of traditional psychotherapy, including traditional ethics codes, are understood as belief systems of a patriarchal culture that serve to perpetuate injustices against women and other oppressed groups. The ethical therapist, from a feminist perspective, challenges the traditional psychotherapy beliefs that are pathologizing and detrimental to her clients.

Criticisms of Feminist Ethics

Their Creation from a Position of Unequal Power

One of the criticisms of feminist ethics is that they are derived from a position of unequal power in a patriarchal culture (Gould, 1988; Hare-Mustin and Marecek, 1990). Women emphasize collegial and mutual processes in relationships out of a one-down position in this society; men emphasize rule-based and individualistic, distant and noncollegial processes in relationships out of a one-up position in this society. The social construction of both positions may be more significant than gender per se. Women, in one-up positions, may function in more one-up ways; men, in one-down positions, may function in more one-down ways. "Typically, those in power advocate rules, discipline, control, and rationality, while those without power espouse relatedness and connection" (Hare-Mustin and Marecek, 1990, p. 39).

If characteristics are perceived as male and female, rather than as human, this linguistic congnitive reference reinforces itself (Lott, 1990). We come to expect certain things from each gender and even tend to observe the same thing differently depending upon the gender of the actor. This limits the full range of humanness for both men and women.

The socially constructed differences in men and women are illustrated in the following steretotypical gender descriptions by Gilligan (1982). Women tend to respond to perceived danger by avoidance of isolation and attempts to prevent aggression. For men, safety is in separation and in rule-bound, competitive achievement situations. Each gender sees as dangerous what the other sees as safe. In addition, healing, for women, has always been seen as part of the relationship. For men, healing takes the form of competition against the disease and, as such, has always had to demonstrate something measurable, concrete, and visible (Ehrenreich and English, 1978).

Both male and female social constructions have interesting relevance to our current ethics codes. The dominant ethical discourse for the mental health professions is, in its rule-based, distant, and concrete approach, clearly more male and the nondominant discourse more female. Each discourse is partial and incomplete. Both mutuality and separation are important aspects of any relationship. Each therapist-client relationship may require a different balance of the two depending on client need, therapist orientation, and the context of meaning in which their relationship occurs. The ethics codes and standards of care, however, follow the male discourse primarily. Practicing from a feminist perspective may not be supported by the administrative or judicial system in the adjudication of complaints.

Women's ways of relating, as described by Gilligan and Ehrenreich and English, still come from a position of unequal power. This is particularly striking when taking into account that more women than men are now entering all of the psychotherapy professions (Philipson, 1993, 1994) and that social work has always been a predominantly female profession.

Privileging of Feminist Values Over Other Values

Another criticism of feminist ethics is its favoring of feminist values over other values (Freedburg, 1993). While mutuality and collegiality are important values of feminist therapists, there are situations in which the therapist must focus more on a clear and differentiated position of herself in relation to the client than on a mutually created therapeutic contract, or she will jeopardize the well-being of both herself and her client. Situations in which clients threaten suicide, pursue the therapist with "relentless entitlement" (Stark, 1995), or threaten the physical safety of either the therapist or others are examples of situations in which action (a male value) may take precedence over collegial talk (a female value). Taking power over oneself, as distinguished from taking power over others, is often as important in maintaining a therapeutic relationship as being collegial.

Support for action as well as talk also challenges the ways in which women have traditionally been encouraged to deal with problems—talking about them rather than taking action to change the underlying social circumstances. Writes Chesler ([1972], 1989, p. 109), "The institutions of therapy and marriage not only mirror each other, they support each other. Therapy encourages women to talk rather than to act."

Although social action is certainly a value of feminist ethics, the one-sided emphasis on collegial and mutual conversation in the therapy relationship may unwittingly bias both the therapist and the client away from action—action that could be construed by the client (or by an audience of peers) as noncollegial and nonmutual, as too patriarchal. Avoidance of action, however, can disempower both the therapist and the client.

Reticence about action and the use of power can also unwittingly support the status quo beliefs that women should not have (and do not need) power. In fact, one of the biggest problems with the feminist ethics model is that it emphasizes the differences between male and female thought and behavior in ways that may only reinforce the norm of male superiority via what Hare-Mustin and Marecek (1990) call "alpha bias." By asserting that women's ways of knowing are more intuitive, expressive, connected, and mutual, the implication is that all other ways of knowing are male. Taken to the extreme, the assertion can lead to the privileging of emotionality over rational thought and to the implication that women are not capable of (or as capable of) rational thought as men. Emphasizing gender differences may also obscure the social construction of such differences and the context of the oppression of women.

Case Examples

Following are two case examples. The first illustrates the usefulness of feminist ethical principles with a client in which mutuality, including appropriate self-disclosure on the part of the therapist, was helpful. The second illustrates the inappropriateness of feminist ethics in case situations in which there is little or no capacity on the part of the client to be mutual and collegial.

Example #1

Susan, a social worker, became immobilized with shame following a licensure board complaint that had been filed against her by the irate ex-husband of one of her clients. The husband held Susan responsible for his wife's decision to leave him. Even though Susan had been exonerated by the licensing board, the event had changed her life. The profession in which she had felt competent, powerful, and safe had, in her experience, become dangerous and disempowering. The complaint had been a kind of reliving of her family-of-origin experiences in which she had felt constantly minimized, her voice never heard. She was deeply shaken.

Susan's therapist, Harry, reassured her that she had done nothing wrong; that no therapist can predict or control when caring might backfire against her; that her shame was partially because of problems in the professional context as well as problems with the client who had complained against her; and that over time she would feel less sad, immobilized, and betrayed.

Susan heard all of his reassurances but was not touched by them. Finally, after much internal debate, Harry shared with her that he, too, had been the subject of a complaint and understood, from a personal as well as a professional point of view, how deeply distressing it can be. Without getting into detail, he conveyed to her how intensely vulnerable he had felt and how painful the whole experience was for him. He also told her that, as a supervisor, therapist, and colleague, he had talked with many professionals who had felt the same vulnerability, and that she was not alone.

This was what made a difference for Susan. Knowing that her vulnerability was shared by others, including her therapist, helped dissolve the shame she felt and offered her hope for healing. Eventually, she joined a support group and no longer needed to come for individual sessions.

Example #2

Jean, an adult survivor, insisted that Sandra, her therapist, consider being her friend outside of the therapy relationship. Sandra clearly explained to Jean all of the reasons she could not engage in friendships with clients, but, in her attempts to be collegial, explored Jean's ideas and feelings about it. Jean responded by escalating her insistence that Sandra should make an exception for her and become her friend. Only by making an exception could Sandra help Jean with her overwhelming blame and self-loathing.

When it became apparent that Jean was not benefitting from Sandra's willingness to discuss her request, Sandra stopped the discussion and simply held the line on her boundaries. She could do this with integrity and compassion because she was in touch with her own needs for protection against the intrusiveness of Jean's demands as well as with Jean's need to face, rather than be protected from, the grief of her early life history.

When Sandra held firm to the limits, Jean protested, escalated, and threatened, continuing to hold fast to her illusion that an all-loving, unconditionally accepting, and totally giving adult in her life would take care of her pain. In her arguments to convince Sandra of her point of view, she used feminist ethical principles to prove that Sandra was being nonmutual (and therefore unethical) in her decision. Sandra eventually terminated with Jean when her behavior escalated into abusive and dangerous threats. It had become evident that Jean had little motivation to work on her own healing; her total energy was invested in changing Sandra.

SOCIAL CONSTRUCTIONIST ETHICS

[E]xcessive loyalty to a specific idea makes the individual who embraces it irresponsible in relation to the moral consequences inherently involved. If some disaster happens it is not the individual who is responsible, but the idea . . . from which the action springs. . . . [I]n the field of psychiatry, a total commitment to the idea that mental disease is of biological origin, or that the problem we face is a result of emotional or environmental deprivation, compels the therapist to become a manager of impossible situations. Then the only "ethical" solution is to become an "expert" and "take charge" of the patient's life. (Cecchin, Lane, and Ray, 1992, p. 8)

Since Chapters 3 through 7 discuss social constructionism and its implications, I refer the reader there for a review of its principles. With specific reference to ethics, social constructionism deconstructs all of our mental health beliefs and our codes of ethics and demonstrates, as with feminist theory, that they are a product of social construction. Adherence to any one idea obscures alternative ideas. When postulated as "truth," any one idea can be dangerous.

The Importance of Context and Nondominant as Well as Dominant Discourses

Social constructionists view pathology through the lens of the social and the political, recognizing that the role of therapist in our society is one of social control agent as well as healer, and understanding that all pathology makes sense in the context of meaning in which it occurs.

Social constructionists, in their attentiveness to the narratives that each client brings to the therapy process, listen carefully to what is *not* said as well as to what is said. They look for nondominant discourses that have become diminished, lost, or overshadowed by the dominant discourse. Nondominant discourses about what constitutes a family, a depression, a normal man or woman, a treatment success or failure, or an ethical behavior are introduced as part of the therapy conversation.

Social constructionists view any attempts to simplify and regulate what *is* and *is not* sayable as an imposition of one point of view on the therapy process at the expense of others. From a social constructionist position, therefore, ethics rules that minimize and attempt to eliminate and control the great variety and complexity of human experience are unethical. The privileging of professional beliefs over other beliefs disempowers clients. It positions the therapist as the expert in his possession of dominant discourse language and knowledge, and the client as the nonexpert. Social constructionists, therefore, approach the client from a position of "not knowing" (Anderson and Goolishian, 1992).

Client Interest as Primary

Social constructionists do not embrace an "anything goes" ethical philosophy. The guiding ethical principle is the client's best interest. Client-therapist sex or insurance fraud would not be condoned by social constructionists. Yet even prohibitions against sexual relationships with clients are not as clear-cut as they might appear. No ethics code permits sexual relationships during therapy, but the codes of both the American Association for Marriage and Family Therapy (1991) and the American Psychological Association (1992) permit sexual relationships (albeit with *lots* of precautions) two years post-therapy.

Sexual relationships posttermination are fraught with questions about how long a client remains a client and about the possible disempowerment and removal of civil liberties from clients that interminable prohibitions might entail. For example, if a client encounters her therapist six years post-therapy termination and freely chooses to engage in sexual intimacies with him, should the *profession* tell her that she is not capable of making such a decision? Or that it is unethical?

The two-year guideline is one example of how, even with the explicit ethics rules that most of us take for granted, there is another perspective—a nondominant discourse that is ever-present. Social constructionists, like feminists, are interested in the unstated as well as the stated discourses. They are particularly interested in the dangers of denying or keeping secret many of the hidden meanings of traditional psychotherapy practices (e.g., the social control aspects of diagnosis, the self-protective aspects of boundaries, the self-interest aspects for the therapist of some long-term treatments).

They are also interested in the benefits to the client of pathologizing some of the dominant societal discourses that disempower and make deviant entire groups of people (Coale, 1994).

The Role of the Therapist

The role of the social constructionist informed therapist is thus as a facilitator of communication that expands possibilities for hope and healing in the client-therapist relationship (Cecchin, 1992; Hoffman, 1990, 1992). Expertise in supporting and guiding this process takes precedence over the expertise implied in any particular brand of theoretical orientation or therapeutic intervention. Honest acknowledgment of one's own professional and personal beliefs as *beliefs* (rather than as *truths*) paves the way for the introduction of multiple beliefs. Awareness of the power of language to privilege some beliefs over others is crucial to ethical functioning.

The ethics of social constructionists thus do not privilege some ways of knowing over others but, rather, facilitate what Hoffman (1992) calls an "ethics of participation," which requires an awareness of the hidden power differentials in the client-therapist relationship and a caution about the espousal of "causes" that privilege some knowledge over others.

The proliferation of ethics rules and the intensified search for ethical perpetrators in today's litigious climate constitute espousal of the kind of causes about which Hoffman warns. The rules serve to reinforce the professions' illusions of power, squelching all but the dominant voice that dictates what is ethical. From a social constructionist position, *this*—our current ethics system—is unethical.

THE ETHICS OF COMMUNAL WELFARE

> To be true to myself, I must be true to other people. I have obligations to them because I am one of them and they are part of me. Working out particular moral decisions—do I attend to my needs or to yours?—is often fraught with difficulty, but there is no inherent contradiction between self-fulfillment and moral responsibility to others. (Doherty, 1995, p. 78)

The following discussion addresses communal ethical obligations at both individual practitioner and institutional levels and analyzes the doublespeak in managed care's use of communal ethics in justifying its practices.

Obligations to Communal Welfare

Increasingly, the emphasis on individualism is being challenged, both in our society and in the mental health professions. Freud's foundational contributions to the field were useful in helping people challenge the tyrannies of a constricting, sexually repressive social atmosphere. The nineteenth-century emphasis on social good at the expense of the individual was indeed debilitating to the individual. A century later, however, the pendulum has swung the other way. Our glorification of the individual at the expense of the community has created massive problems, leading to a breakdown of communal welfare.

Our current ethics codes give lip service to the professional's obligations to community as well as to individual well-being. Social work, unsurprisingly, emphasizes communal obligations more than do the other mental health professions. But even so, the *client* is the individual (or family) and the ethics code is written for the protection of such. Exceptions to this emphasis are *legal* rather than ethical ones, such as the social worker's legal obligation to report child abuse or to notify someone of a client's intent to harm him. The importance of the well-being of nonclients, in other words, has been protected by *legal* requirements which the ethics codes subsequently incorporated.

Family therapists were the first to conceptualize the well-being of the individual as intricately interconnected with the well-being of the family, expanding the concept of client accordingly. Yet, even so, our entire diagnostic system, as discussed in Chapter 5, is based on *individual* pathology and *individual* interest. What originated as a new theoretical orientation that conceptualized relationship systems as the focus of concern was co-opted into the individual model, especially after the DSM bcame *the* diagnostic system in insurance reimbursement and managed care. The concept of client as family was transformed to a treatment modality to cure individuals. The American Association for Marriage and Family Therapy's advocacy on behalf of its members to be included as service providers on managed care panels (which authorize the treatment of *indi-*

viduals) and to achieve licensure, have furthered this process. What was once a relationship-based theoretical orientation has become a mainstreamed *method* to accommodate a mental health market that recognizes only *individual* welfare.

Chapter 2 discusses some of the consequences of our society's emphasis on individual over communal welfare and the resultant crisis of meaning facing our society and the mental health professions. *Individuals* do not fare well in a society that worships the right to climb to the top on the heads of neighbors. *Individuals* need the connection of family and community relationships and a sense of purpose that they are contributing to, as well as taking from, the community. An ethic of communal as well as individual welfare acknowledges the individual's need for such interconnectedness, purpose, and meaning.

Managed Care's Communal Justifications

Some proponents of managed care have utilized the ethic of communal well-being as a justification for the existence of managed care and its control of resource allocation. Carol Shaw Austad's 1996 book, *Is Long-Term Psychotherapy Unethical? Toward a Social Ethic in an Era of Managed Care,* for example, challenges the ethics of long-term psychotherapy for the privileged at the expense of shorter-term mental health benefits for all those who are truly in need. She points to the dangers of traditional fee-for-service arrangements that maximize individual care, inflate the need for care, encourage overuse of services, ignore societal needs, narrow patient choice based on ability to pay, and fail to establish universal standards of care.

Managed care handles these problems in a way which, according to Austad, addresses communal as well as individual good and is, therefore, ethically justified. She acknowledges that profit has been transferred from the provider to the managed care corporations, but justifies this based on the need to put a brake on providers' profit-motivated behaviors which, until the advent of managed care, were rampant drivers of psychotherapy services.

Although Austad calls for a societal ethic of resource allocation in mental health, she does not challenge the profit-driven behaviors of managed care corporations as strongly as she does the profit-driven behaviors of individual practitioners. Nor does she address other ways (besides managed care) to introduce communal as well as individual values into psychotherapy. The practitioner is portrayed as a self-serving, profit-hungry individual, not to be trusted without close supervision and control by managed care reviewers. The dual roles of the managed care companies as guardians of client welfare *and* profit-driven corporate businesses are minimized. So are managed care practices such as capitation, which pass to the provider the total financial (and ethical) risk of providing psychotherapy services while preserving and enhancing profit margins.

True societal ethics take into account the well-being of *all*. This includes the therapist as well as the client, family, and community. Austad's justification of managed care as an institution grounded in societal ethics does not take into account the skew in benefits which privilege managed care corporate profits over both client *and* therapist need.

Communal Ethics at Institutional and Individual Levels

Other writers suggest ways besides managed care to introduce communal as well as individual values into psychotherapy. Michael Lerner (1995, 1996), a prolific speaker and writer on the need for communal ethics, calls for a transformation in the entire sense of meaning in this culture. His emphasis is on changing our society's bottom line from one of profit to one of community—and he challenges psychotherapists to be an integral part of this process. *Any* institution that privileges corporate profits over the needs of people is, from Lerner's point of view, unethical. Ehrenreich and English (1978) called for the same kind of bottom line nearly two decades ago.

At the level of individual practice, William Doherty (1989, 1991, 1993, 1995) calls for therapists to bring communal values into the therapy arena, challenging clients to think about what values guide their decision making. Too often, values are operating but remain implicit—and many of them are derived from individualistic notions of mental health. Our illusion that we can keep values *out* of the therapy arena obscures the fact that the values that guide our actions remain undiscussed. Questions such as "How will your divorce decision affect your son?", "What is in the best interest of your family (as well as yourself)?", "How will your neighborhood and church respond to your divorce?", and "For whose need are you doing this?" open the therapeutic conversation to an exploration of other-oriented as well as individual values.

Both Lerner's and Doherty's suggestions emphasize the interconnectedness of communal and individual welfare. From a social constructionist perspective, if self is only self in relation to others—to a context of meaning and relationships—there is no contradiction, no conflict (theoretically at least) in attending to both self and others in the therapy relationship.

In my own clinical work, I am as attentive to questions about relationship and context as I am to questions about individual concerns. I want to know how my clients are connected to their communities and what values guide their connections (or lack thereof). I attend carefully to openings that invite me to expand and reinforce these connections. I am attentive to the possibility that therapy could become a substitute for other connections, a reinforcer of a client's narcissism, or a destructive element in a family's relationships. Ideally, whatever my client and I do together in our therapeutic relationship should benefit not only my client but also someone else in his family or community.

Benefits to family members are probably an obvious result of successful psychotherapy in the conceptual view of most psychotherapists. Benefits to community are probably not. But contributing to communal welfare can be very healing to clients, as the following case example illustrates.

Susan, a forty-seven-year-old veteran of seven failed marriages and numerous failed therapy experiences, consulted me for depression and a general sense of despair and hopelessness. As I listened to her life story, I noticed that her entire emphasis was on what she had been denied, starting with a childhood history of emotional deprivation and continuing throughout an adulthood of failed relationships. When I asked her what she had done for others in her lifetime, she was at first startled and then enraged. How dare I ask her such a question when she had received so little in her life? Gradually, however, the idea began to intrigue her. She had never thought of herself as *capable* of giving anything to anybody else.

Once she was interested, I suggested that there were hospitalized babies in the AIDS unit of a local hospital that needed holding. I picked this particular volunteer activity because it might provide her with vicarious nurturance, allowing her to give to babies what she had not received as a baby herself. The activity transformed her image of herself from a hopeless, empty taker into a giver of something worthwhile. It also facilitated the necessary grieving that she had defended against by her restless and unfulfilled search for somebody to fill her up emotionally.

Mary Pipher, author of *Reviving Ophelia* (1994) and *Shelter of Each Other* (1996), describes the impossibility of having good mental health in a "lousy community." "Trying to just fix your family is like going first class on the Titanic" (Pipher, in Simon, 1997, p. 28). She challenges all of us to reach out to other people's children as a way of helping our own—an ethic that could be put to good use in psychotherapy offices.

Put another way, " . . . psychology has to recognize community because the psyche *is* a community" (Hillman, in Hillman and Ventura, 1992, p. 84). An ethic of communal welfare is in the interests of both individual and community.

ETHICS BY CHARACTER OF THE THERAPIST

[W]e cannot escape the centrality of the person who is making moral decisions or who is providing health care. Psychotherapy ethics currently is dominated by the rule-oriented approach. . . . These rules establish the outer limits of ethical behavior for therapists but do not touch the character of the therapist and how it affects the clinical relationship and the success of therapy. (Doherty, 1995, p. 116)

Contract Theory

Ethics are theories or systems of moral principles derived from both intuitive thinking and contract theory. Intuitive thinking draws on natural and universal principles such as justice, equality, compassion, truthfulness, liberty, and so forth. Contract theory derives from the specific legal and fiduciary responsibilities inherent in professional relationships because of the unequal power and expertise between the professional and the client and because of the trust the client vests in the professional to provide certain services without causing harm. Current codes of ethics are influenced more by contract theory than by intuitive thinking (Bennett et al., 1990; Levy, 1993; Woody, 1990).

Contract theory, however, does not address all of the nuances of critical thinking necessary in the vast and ambiguous array of situations confronting therapists and their clients. In addition, it does not enhance the public's trust in the professional. If, after all, the professional only behaves ethically because of the *rules* of the contract, what does this say about his trustworthiness?

Intuition and Virtue

Intuitive thinking, based on moral principles, allows for variability in human interactions. It also rests on the assumption that the therapist is capable, without the artificial structure of contracts and rules, of making ethical decisions. The *character* of the therapist and his capacity to utilize basic moral principles for the welfare of his client is central (Jordan and Meara, 1990). Certain qualities of character (what the Greeks called "virtues") predispose the therapist to do what is right or good (as defined by culture). Doherty (1995), a proponent of ethics by character, defines caring, courage, and prudence as the central virtues for ethical therapists. Inger and Inger (1994) combine principles from Martin Buber (1958) and Carol Gilligan (1982) to describe an "ethic of being" for the therapist in which he can truly take the position of the other person into account as well as his own in arriving at an ethical position that makes prominent the relational aspects of psychotherapy.

Who the therapist *is* is the essential component of character ethics:

> The force and spirit of who the therapist is as a human being most dramatically stimulates change. Lock a person, any person, in a room alone with Sigmund Freud, Carl Rogers, Fritz Perls, Albert Ellis, or any other formidable personality, and several hours later he will come out different. It is not what the therapist does that is important—whether she interprets, reflects, confronts, or role plays—but rather who she is. (Kottler, 1993, pp. 3-4)

The therapist with an ethical character uses herself to balance the needs of client, self, family, and community. She is committed to values of justice, fairness, altruism, honesty, compassion, and empowerment. Her actions as well as her thoughts reflect these values. She understands the nuances and variety in human situations and knows that rules cannot be uniformly "applied" to them. The consistent element in the huge variety of dilemmas with which clients present is the therapist's ethical character.

SUMMARY

The alternatives to rule-based ethics, as discussed in this chapter, are more similar than different from one another. All emphasize the importance of social-cultural context in creating meaning, the need to hear nondominant discourses as well as dominant ones, the importance of using power relationally and responsibly, and the interconnectedness of social and individual welfare.

The following chapters suggest an approach which combines the principles of feminist, social constructionist, communal, and character ethics and make recommendations for ethical professional practice, at both the institutional and the individual practitioner levels.

Chapter 12

Toward an Ethic
of Multiplicity and Mutuality

> We are not important.
> Our lives are simply threads
> Pulling along the lasting thoughts
> Which travel through time that way.
>
> —N. Wood, *Many Winters*

An ethic of multiplicity and mutuality combines principles from feminist ethics, social constructionist ethics, and communal and character ethics. The voices of the professional, the client, significant others in the client's life, and the community are all taken into account in the client-therapist relationship. The importance of the well-being of both client *and* therapist and the mutual responsibility of each are emphasized. Suggestions are made that encourage the mental health professions to acknowledge their own interdependence with the social context that created them and to develop more of an ethic of mutuality at an institutional as well as an individual practitioner level.

HONORING ALL VOICES

An ethic of multiplicity honors *all* voices present in the therapy room—the client's, the significant others in the client's life, the therapist's, and the community's. What is good for the client must also take into account how the client's actions touch his family, friends, community, and therapist. In a best-case scenario, what benefits the client also benefits these significant others. In a less optimal scenario, the negative effects of the client's decisions and actions are, at the very least, explored thoroughly with him in the therapy process so that he can be aware of and take responsibility for the results.

The Professional Voice

> [A]ny substance that can promote healing can also induce pathology. (Whitmont, 1993, p. 191)

One of Many

An ethic of multiplicity does not privilege the therapist's voice over the client's. Therapy theories and beliefs are simply that—theories and beliefs—and are presented as such. The fact that there are currently hundreds of brands of therapy theories should, in and of itself, point glaringly to an awareness that the psychotherapy professions have no corner on truth. We have, rather, many "cultures of healing" (Fancher, 1995). Their relevance and usefulness vary according to how they fit both therapist and client; no theory contains within it any superior or inherent truth. In utilizing *any* professional belief, therefore, the therapist should be honest in owning it as a *possibility* for the client to select or reject in achieving the desired treatment objectives.

The establishment of treatment objectives does not honor the therapist's voice over the client's. Both traditional therapy and pop psychology beliefs have within them certain dominant discourses about what constitutes an ideal family, a nonneurotic life, a healthy balance between work and leisure, a "good enough" parent, and so forth. These discourses often get in the way of hearing what the *client* wants for herself. Any temptation to assert the rightness of the professional's voice over the client's should be regarded as a violation of the ethic of multiplicity.

This does not mean that the therapist must adopt an anything-goes philosophy and do whatever the client wants. It simply means that the therapist's voice does not overshadow the client's. If the therapist offers alternatives to the client's way of understanding her own life and the problems which bring her to therapy, she does it in a collegial rather than an expert manner. If the therapist rejects outright the client's view of her situation and suggestions for change, she is honest about *why* and does not retreat behind the voice of professional rightness to justify her rejection. She honestly addresses her own discomfort with or inability to do what the client wants and has no illusions that she has power over the client because of her professional expertise. She only has power over herself and her own decisions and acknowledges this honestly with the client. Even in situations in which the therapist must assert her point of view over the client's, such as with violent behavior or narcissistic entitlement, she asserts her point of view as *hers* and not as *the truth.*

The Therapist's Role

If the therapist abandons the privileged voice of the expert, what then is his role? For what purpose does he receive education, training, and induction into the profession? For what reason do clients seek his assistance?

An ethic of multiplicity moves the therapist from a position of expertise on what is normal or abnormal, healthy or sick, functional or dysfunctional, to a position of expertise in facilitating therapeutic conversations that open up possibilities for clients and, optimally, for their significant others. The therapist, in other words, helps the client search for other voices, themes, and narratives in her life besides the ones that tyrannize, disempower, and create problems for her. In so doing, the therapist is fully aware that his professional voice is just one of many that can offer hope and possibility. He recognizes that his professional voice is often just as liable, when presented as *the* voice, to tyrannize, disempower, and create problems for his client.

An ethic of multiplicity has, for some, been interpreted as totally mutual, collegial, and noninterventive. Techniques and more action-oriented therapeutic tools have been rejected as too instrumental, too expert. Conversation has been privileged above action and technique. In my view, this is contradictory to the whole notion of multiplicity. If a client *wants, expects,* and *will benefit from* a particular action or technique *and* it is introduced by the therapist simply as one possibility and not as *the* solution, then it fits an ethic of multiplicity (Coale, 1992; Held, 1990).

The therapist who functions within an ethic of multiplicity does not, therefore, have to abandon technique or action-oriented interventions in favor of conversation. She must simply use them as ways of introducing other possibilities, other meanings in the therapeutic process. And she must use them in the service of focusing and structuring the therapy process to achieve what the client wants.

> Therapeutic technique provides clinicians with something akin to a magnifying glass that brings together, focuses, and concentrates the forces of change, narrows them to a point in place and time, and causes them to ignite into action. (Miller, Duncan, and Hubble, 1997, p. 184)

Honoring multiplicity requires that the therapist adopt a stance of "not knowing" as well as of "knowing" and a respect for the wisdom of the voices of clients and others in the community and, indeed, the world. What is workable for one client may not be workable for another. The immense variability of both client and therapist perspectives must be respected.

The implications for our current codes of ethics are fairly obvious. What constitutes a healing boundary in one therapist-client relationship may constitute a destructive boundary in another. What is a positive dual role in one relationship may be a damaging dual role in another. *Client* reality and *client* need (as well as *professional* reality and *professional* need) must dictate ethical decisions. Our current ethics codes, from the perspective of an ethic of multiplicity, are unethical in their privileging of professional over client voices.

The Client Voice

> Therapists can see the tragedy, but we also see the courageous struggles and heroic solutions. (Pipher, 1996, p. 133)

The following discussion addresses the importance of client voices and suggests ways of making them more present at both the individual and the institutional level.

Absent but Powerful

Miller, Duncan, and Hubble (1997, pp. 61-62) discuss various research findings that suggest that therapeutic procedures are effective only when they fit client beliefs about problems and the change process. They also discuss the dramatic lack of client voices in professional literature. Conran and Love (1993) describe the professions' relegating client voices to the realm of "unspeakable theories and unknowable experiences." There is a tendency to attribute all change to specific therapeutic theories and interventions and to minimize or ignore all the effects of many extratherapeutic factors on the therapy process, factors such as presession and intersession events that are a part of the client's life.

> [T]herapists are usually cast in the hero/savior role in the stories of successful psychotherapy that either appear in print or circulate among treatment professionals. Whether the therapist is managing resistance, making interpretations, pointing out dysfunctional thoughts, or asking the "miracle question," stories of successful psychotherapy most often emphasize the therapist's contribution over the client's.
>
> These stories not only perpetuate a belief in the magnitude of therapist contribution to change in therapy that is simply not supported by the facts but worse, by continually focusing attention on the therapist's own prowess, may inadvertently lead helping professionals to discount or even ignore the larger contribution to change made by the client. (Miller, Duncan, and Hubble, 1997, pp. 61-62)

The proliferation of therapy theories and the cultlike following of many leaders in the field only compound the tendency of therapists to minimize client voices. Each theory and its founder tend to emphasize the rightness of one professional point of view over others and, in exaggerating its rightness, contribute further to the silencing of client voices. Nowhere is this more apparent than in live interviews staged to demonstrate the virtuosity of therapy gurus before large audiences of therapists. Even when client input is solicited after the interview, it is skewed toward curiosity about what the *therapist* did. There is little, if any, acknowledgment of the *client's* contributions to the session.

The only exception to the discounting of client voices is in complaint procedures. As discussed in Chapters 8 and 9, licensing board investigations are slanted in favor of the client's voice over the therapist's because licensing boards are established for consumer protection. If licensing boards are the only arena in which the profession privileges the client's voice, might we not expect increasing numbers of clients to "balance the scales" via complaint procedures?

Client voices need to be privileged in all professional arenas, not just in complaint procedures. As long as they are muffled in individual therapy *and* in professional literature, training, and practice, we can expect them to surface in some other way. At an individual level, all therapists have experienced the client who, feeling disempowered and misunderstood, balances the unequal power in the therapist-client relationship by terminating treatment, acting out in destructive ways, or "refusing" to heal. Such behavior is almost always a message to the therapist that he has not heard and understood something about the client's perception of the problem and its solution. If the impasse is to be resolved, he must listen in a different way until he truly hears the client's voice.

Case Example

Elsewhere (Coale, in press) I have described a young man who was referred to me by his girlfriend for therapy. Joe had spent his entire adolescence in and out of psychiatric facilities and seemed unable to stay in school or maintain a job as an adult. His treatment history was peppered with failures. I had the hypothesis that failing was one way he gained power, both in his family and in treatment situations. With this in mind, I began the interview with "How have you helped train so many therapists in your life?" The question was a change from what he was used to in initial interviews with therapists. It conveyed the clear message that his therapists, as well as he, had benefitted from their work with him. Joe's guarded and suspicious demeanor changed instantly and he tearfully described to me his lost adolescence.

It became apparent, in hearing his story, that his parents (as well as his therapists) had benefitted greatly from his periodic removals from the home. They had not had to deal with the mess of their marital affairs because of the distractions caused by their son's hospitalizations.

Following the initial session, Joe brought his parents for a family meeting. The parents admitted that their son's frequent hospitalizations had alleviated some of their own distress and owned that their frequent rescue attempts were one way they attempted to salve their guilt for failing Joe as parents. The rescue attempts, even though they further disempowered their son, were all they knew how to do.

I asked Joe what he felt his parents owed him for the sacrifice of his adolescence. Without hesitation, he responded with a monetary figure that the parents instantly agreed was just. The rest of the session was spent in helping the parents negotiate with Joe how the money was to be spent. The sum equalled the cost of an educational program that would equip him for employment. The cycle of failure, rescue, and failure was interrupted and Joe proceeded to function more responsibly in the adult world.

My understanding of what worked in helping this young man and his parents was that Joe's voice was finally heard. Once he was acknowledged for the job he had performed in his family, sacrificing his adolescence in the process, he could move on. As long as he was seen as a psychiatric patient (and a failed psychiatric patient at that), both he and his parents were stuck in a hopeless cycle.

Honoring Client Voices at the Institutional Level

At an institutional level, the profession must begin to incorporate client voices into its research, anecdotal literature, and professional training until the "unsung heroes of psychotherapy" (Miller, Duncan, and Hubble, 1997) get credit for their contributions to the field. What do they think is effective, ethical psychotherapy? What ideas do they have for transforming the mental health professions? What do they want when they need help? Until we listen to their answers to these and other questions, client voices will surface wherever they can.

Ironically, although licensing boards are one of the few arenas that privilege client over therapist voices, they do so under an umbrella of professional, not client, expertise. Clients have little say-so in the formulation of professional ethics codes. The codes simply provide an avenue for being heard but the ambiance is still one of "Father knows best." The board has the ultimate authority to decide whether or not the client voice is accurate. So, although the board is an arena for client voices, it is an unsatisfactory one because the context is still that of professional expertise. The individual therapist about whom the client is complaining may lose her authority and expertise, but the ultimate outcome for both client and therapist is still determined by professionals.

The solutions to increased ethics complaints against therapists have been to legislate more rules, require more ethics continuing education, punish more "perpetrators," and dictate more risk management procedures. All of these solutions only contribute to the problems generated by privileging professional over client voices. Client voices must be heard in *all* therapeutic arenas, including the individual therapist-client relationship, professional literature, professional meetings, and anecdotal discussions of treatment outcomes. *This* is ethical.

The Voices of Significant Others

> To be yourself is to be
> Alone with the wind crying
> When all you ask for is
> The warmth of a human fire
>
> —N. Wood, *Many Winters*

Ethical therapy must listen to the voices of significant others as well as to the voice of the client and the therapist. Whether or not they actually participate in the therapy sessions, their voices can be introduced. How will the client's decisions affect them? What would they say about the client's dilemma if they were present? At whose expense will a client's actions be? How will the client attend to the impact of his actions on others? What is the cost-benefit ratio of a particular change for both the client and others in his life?

In our individualistic bias, the voices of significant others are often ignored. No wonder there has been a backlash. It is not just clients who complain to licensing boards. Significant others also bring complaints against therapists for creating false memories in their clients, not preventing suicides, misdiagnosing, and alienating clients from their families. Our ethics codes and standards of care, which emphasize the protection and care of *individual* clients, do not take into account the interconnectedness of client welfare with the welfare of others.

Even in the context of child welfare, the guiding principle has traditionally been the "best interest of the child," with only token recognition that this is intricately balanced and interconnected with the best interest of the entire family. The child's best interests *cannot* be disconnected from the relationship context any more than the adult client's welfare can be disconnected from family.

There are some ethical guidelines for the therapist when significant others are actually involved in the treatment process, such as in couples and family therapy. There are also both legal and ethical guidelines for the therapist when the client is being harmed by or is about to harm significant others, such as in child abuse reporting laws and *Tarasoff* reporting requirements. But there is little awareness of or attention to the importance of significant others in the client's healing. The voices of significant others, like those of clients, are minimized in favor of the professional's.

An ethic of multiplicity would suggest that, both at an individual practitioner level and at a professional institutional level, the voices of significant others should have more recognition. What do *they* have to say about the effects of the client's therapy on *their* lives? The contributions *they*, as well as the therapist and the client, have made to the client's healing? The difficulties of dealing with the therapist's presence in *their* lives? The long-range consequences of the therapy for *them*?

Until significant others are more included in *all* kinds of therapy, not just family therapy, and in *all* kinds of therapy research and practice, the legal arena will remain one of the contexts in which their voices have power. And, as with client voices, the legal arena still retains the ultimate power, only hearing the voices of significant others through the lens of individualistic professional standards and beliefs.

The Voices of the Community

> [D]oes therapy ever consider the family, the neighbors, the colleagues, and, even more, the furniture, the sea, the effect on the world? See, the therapist isn't supposed to be involved in all that in any way. The basic frame of therapy is to withdraw from all of that, not to have "dual relationships." (Hillman, in Hillman and Ventura, 1992, p. 177)

Problems in Ignoring Community Voices

An ethic of multiplicity hears the voices of the community as well as those of the client and significant others. As already discussed in preceding chapters, all therapy beliefs and practices are socially created and, as such, reflect the values and beliefs of the community in which they occur. In the professional and scientific mantle of the mental health professions, however, the contextual and socially constructed origins of our beliefs are often ignored. Our beliefs become reified, objectified, and disconnected from their context.

One of the problems with this disconnection is the tendency to gird these beliefs in the mantle of truth. Another problem resides in the illusion that the client—individual or family—is also disconnected from context and can thus make changes without being affected by or affecting context. Yet another problem is the lack of credit given to context for the origin of professional beliefs and the bestowing of power on professionals. Professionals only have the power of knowledge and role by virtue of their context. If the context challenges professional knowledge and role, as it is increasingly doing, professional power and the community's trust in it deteriorate.

The Need to Regain the Trust of the Community

The deterioration of professional power has been met with an increased emphasis on the production of new psychotherapy truths through research and "new" theoretical orientations. There has been a proliferation of ethics rules and standards of care. Many of these have been developed in isolation from community input. Instead of becoming more open to the input of others, our boundaries have become more closed.

If the mental health professions are ever to regain power and trust, they must do so with a *community* ethic of multiplicity. We should *acknowledge* rather than hide our contextually created beliefs and open our boundaries to embrace ideas from anthropology, history, literature, the arts, religion, political science, philosophy, and the ideas from other cultures. The latter should be studied, not simply on the basis of a need to be culturally and ethnically sensitive in the application of professional beliefs to the therapy process, but for what they can contribute to the transformation of professional beliefs and practices in psychotherapy in general (Coale, 1994).

Continuing education requirements for licensure and other kinds of professional credentialing should require expanding our knowledge base to include such ideas rather than continuing to perpetuate the myopic tendencies that mandate professional development primarily within the bounds of disciplinary and specialty turf. In fact, the ethics of attending continuing education activities only within such turf should be challenged as should professional theories and treatment modalities developed solely within their confines.

The professions must also increase their understanding of how self and community are inseparable, their welfare intertwined. Current conceptualizations dichotomize self and community, often presenting their interests as antagonistic. Ethics controversies over child-abuse reporting, for example, often pit client welfare against community welfare. One argument for *not* reporting child abuse is that individual client confidentiality and trust in the therapist will be jeopardized at the expense of community values that prohibit the abuse of children (Watson and Levine, 1989). This is a client-versus-community mindset. If the dichotomy is eliminated, the value of treating children nonabusively can be seen as in the best interest of both client *and* community.

The Need for Nondichotomized Points of View

We need much more awareness and sensitivity, at both the individual practitioner and the professional institutional levels, to nondichotomized points of view regarding client and community welfare. In addition to the specific healing aspects of *giving to* as well as *taking from* others (as illustrated in Chapter 11) there is a more generic level of mutuality between client and community welfare. The well-being of each of us contributes to the well-being of community, and vice versa. The psychotherapy professions cannot continue to encourage neutral stands about social and political conditions under the admonition against the risks of imposing such beliefs on individual clients. The personal is political and social—and every position taken, including a so-called neutral one, is a position. The fact that some clinical theories exclude any discussion of ethics (Dean and Rhodes, 1992) does not mean that they are free of ethical values. "To tell a story is inescapably to take a moral stance, even if it is a moral stance against moral stances" (Bruner, 1990, p. 51).

I am not minimizing the political and social stands that the professions as institutions do take on issues of human concern (and that they encourage their members to take). Social work, in particular, has been in the forefront of advocacy for the poor and disenfranchised. What I am challenging is the dichotomy of personal *versus* social that leads the professions to advocate at an institutional level while cautioning the individual therapist to remain neutral in the therapy relationship. And I am suggesting that, in supporting this dichotomy, the professions miss the integral unity of personal and social, not just for the poor and disenfranchised, but for everyone.

Bringing Community Voices into the Therapy Office

An ethic of multiplicity brings contextual voices into the therapy room. How does it affect you to live in a community torn by racism? How do you feel when you pass a homeless person on the street corner? How do you think your anxiety might be connected to having to live with burglar bars and alarm systems? How does it feel when you have to use food stamps at the grocery store? How do you try to contribute to your community to make it better?

The same kinds of questions about self in relation to community can be asked of therapists and should be of concern in professional development and professional ethics. How are you aware of your impact on community and its impact on you? How is it for you to sit in your office knowing that your income is five times more or less than the client you just saw? What's it like to know that your client had more courage than you did to speak out publicly in favor of a controversial zoning law that would allow a hospice in her neighborhood? What are you doing for the betterment of your community? How does your community's welfare impact your life and your family?

Case Example

Dawn, a fifty-year-old wife and mother of three, presented with symptoms of chronic depression exacerbated by an automobile accident that had severely injured one of her daughters. For all of her adult life, she had managed to keep her depression a secret until the crisis with her daughter pushed her over the edge. In the first session, she told me of the legacy of depression affecting women in her family and expressed fear that she had inherited the "disease." She admitted that she felt no hope for getting better and could no longer maintain on her own.

In listening to her descriptions of her mother's, sister's, and grandmother's depressions, as well as her own, I began to understand the causes. Their depressions made complete sense in light of their history of submitting to authoritarian husbands, isolating themselves from other women and suffering in silence, sacrificing their own welfare for the sake of their children, blaming themselves for everything that went wrong in their lives and in the lives of others, and demanding of themselves perfectionistic and impossible accomplishments.

I began asking Dawn questions such as "Do you think your mother might have been happier if she had felt more equal to your father? Do you think it might have jeopardized your father's power and control if your mother had surrounded herself with supportive friends? Do you think it would have made a difference to your sister if she had had equal control of the money in her family? Do you think that your depression would improve if you shared it with your husband and told him what makes you unhappy in the marriage?"

I also asked Dawn more general questions about the social conditions that create depression in women. "Do you think that your depression is similar to or different from the depression that many women experience as they live in a world controlled by men? Do you think that most women would be happier if they occasionally put their own interests first? Do you think that depression would visit you as often if you socialized more with other women?"

As Dawn heard different perspectives about what creates depression in women, she became less depressed. In her second and last session, she told me that she was liberated from self-blame and no longer believed that her depression was genetically inherited. She also told me that she had talked to her husband for the first time about her depression. He had been relieved to know there were things he could change about his own behavior that would help her.

Introducing contextual realities into Dawn's beliefs about her depression gave her new hope—hope she planned to share with other women in her church and community. In addition to the knowledge that her depression had social roots, her eagerness in sharing with others what she had learned represented a significant shift in the isolation she had heretofore experienced as she sat at home alone with her hopeless feelings. Sharing with others was a powerful antidote for her.

MUTUALITY

In intimacy, we are clearly aware that the destruction of either partner in a dyad amounts to the destruction of both. (Malone and Malone, 1987, p. 249)

Empowering the voices of clients, significant others, and community is not enough. We must also acknowledge the mutuality and interdependence of all voices.

The Interdependence of Client, Therapist, and Others

Therapists are interdependent with their clients, their own significant others, and their community. Clients are interdependent with their therapists, their significant others, and their community. Professional institutions are interdependent with their members, the clients served by their members, and the community and cultural contexts in which they exist. Acknowledgment of interdependence is necessary to the development of mutuality.

Instead of closing ranks and dictating more ethics rules, the professions must open ranks and ask hard questions—of clients, of therapists, and of the social context. What do *clients* think is ethical? What do *therapists* need to support their ethical functioning in today's context of litigiousness and distrust? What can the mental health professions do to contribute to the welfare of society as a whole? What are they doing that reduces their credibility in a postmodern world? How are they jeopardizing the well-being of clients, therapists, and society by continuing to search for truths, by sanctioning individual practitioners for things that are essentially social and professional institutional problems, and by developing authoritative rules rather than new ways of thinking about problems?

The Mutuality of Responsibility in the Therapist-Client Relationship

Deconstructing the Beliefs in Unilateral Therapist Responsibility

Acknowledgment of the interdependence of therapists, clients, the professions, and the social context challenges the current codes of ethics, which essentially hold the individual therapist liable for all events in the therapy process. Therapists cannot control what their clients do, what the profession does, or how social and contextual conditions impact the therapy process. They can only control themselves *in relation to clients, the profession, and the sociocultural context.* Even so, there are many events in therapists' lives over which they have no control, such as illness, relocations required for a spouse's career, serendipitous and unpredictable events, and chains of referrals in which other members of their clients' social networks appear for therapy.

To hold the therapist totally responsible for the entire therapy relationship is not only unrealistic, it also disempowers both the therapist *and* the client. If a client continuously challenges and intrudes on the boundaries of the therapist, the therapist can only be accountable for her response to such intrusions. She can continue to negotiate boundaries with the client; introduce other family members into the therapy process to help ease the client's anxiety, fear, entitlement, or other feelings that drive the intrusion; or terminate the therapy. It is not in the best interest of either party for the therapist to continue functioning in a relationship in which boundary intrusions are unworkable. Yet, as discussed in previous chapters, all of the ethics codes mandate boundary setting as essential for the *client's* welfare, ignoring the welfare of the therapist and holding *her* totally accountable.

The potential effects of holding the therapist totally accountable are portrayed in a recent article in *Family Therapy News* (Signore, 1996) titled "Therapist Hurt by Therapy." It describes a client's upset in being terminated by several therapists. The client's role in the terminations is not addressed, only the roles of the therapists. The author recommends that therapists should not be *allowed* to leave a therapeutic relationship without some kind of binding mediation to deal with the dispute.

The author also suggests that "[t]here are few reasons other than sickness which excuse unmitigated ruptured endings" (p. 14). In her description of her therapy experiences, her "unmitigated ruptured endings" consisted of one therapist moving out of town two years post-therapy termination and another terminating with her over an eight-month termination process, beginning during the therapist's pregnancy and ending seven months after the birth.

While this example may be a little extreme, it illustrates the extent to which holding the therapist totally accountable for whatever happens in the therapist-client relationship can go. *Insisting* that the therapist continue with a client—regardless of what the client does or how changed circumstances in the therapist's life might necessitate termination—is not mutual. And more important, it is not in *anyone's* best interest.

Another example of the nonmutuality of one-sided responsibility in the therapist-client relationship comes from my supervisory experience. A client became enraged by her therapist and abruptly terminated the therapy relationship. The ostensible reason for her anger became apparent when she filed an ethics complaint alleging that her therapist (my supervisee) had engaged in a dual role with her. The client's documentation of the dual role consisted of the therapist's sharing some personal anecdotes with her, acknowledging her frustration with the client's constant demands for extra time and other concessions, and rescheduling an appointment or two to accommodate the therapist's family needs.

In the client's belief system, the therapist should never have shared a personal anecdote, acknowledged any feelings, or rescheduled appointments. In her mind, these behaviors all benefitted the therapist, not the client. The underlying dynamic was that the therapist would not provide the extra time and concessions the client wanted. While the therapist was ultimately exonerated, she had to go through a costly investigatory process, which drained her both financially and emotionally. The rationale for hearing the case was based on the client's allegation that the therapist had put *her* own needs ahead of the client's.

Another supervisee had a complaint filed against him because he terminated and referred a client who continually violated a therapeutic contract in which she promised not to harm herself. When the client blatantly continued extremely self-destructive behavior and stated that she had no plans to stop, the therapist arranged for an appropriate referral to the psychiatrist who was already involved with the client for medication supervision. The client filed a complaint based on abandonment. The therapist's right *not* to work with a client who continued overtly self-destructive behavior was challenged in the licensing board complaint. Again, the therapist was exonerated but the complaint process drained him financially, emotionally, and spiritually.

Balancing Client-Therapist Responsibility and Need

An ethic of mutuality would balance the obligations of client and therapist so that *both* are held responsible for what happens in the therapy relationship. The therapist, because of his professional role, has more of the responsibility to make conscientious and ethical decisions about how he conducts himself in the therapy relationship, but the client also has responsibilities. If our ethics codes spelled out their *joint* responsibilities, they would empower clients to fully participate in their own healing, and support therapists in expecting this. As it stands now, clients are not empowered. Instead, they are encouraged to place all responsibility for their healing in the lap of the therapist.

In addition, the current codes, in their lopsided and topsided view of therapist responsibility, support the grandiosity and arrogance of the professional at the expense of the client (*and* the professional). Therapists are not invulnerable. Things do happen in their lives that mean they *cannot* and *should not* continue providing services to some clients. The codes mandate that therapists not work with clients when they do not have the expertise to address the particular problems, when the therapy is no longer beneficial to the client, when dual roles that would negatively affect the client's welfare are discovered, and so forth. However, in their emphasis on therapist responsibility (while ignoring client responsibility), the codes also imply that therapists *should* be able to do more than they can. Unsurprisingly, this implication fuels the rage of certain kinds of clients when the therapist then says "I can't" or "I won't." It gives clients an open invitation to file complaints when their wishes are frustrated by therapist limitations and boundaries. It also makes it more difficult for therapists to acknowledge and own their own limitations and needs in negotiating relationships with clients.

An ethic of mutuality honors both therapist and client need. Denial of therapist need submerges it and makes it a hidden agenda in the therapy relationship. Owning it and responsibly attending to it with clients is inherently more ethical.

The Mutuality and Interdependence of the Mental Health Professions and Their Context

The professions owe their existence to the context in which they were created and are maintained. In the same way that individual practitioners should be free to own and take responsibility for their own needs as well as the needs of clients, the professions themselves must acknowledge their needs and their interdependence with the context in which they exist. They must, for example, admit that a huge part of their agenda in fighting for inclusion in managed care was to protect the economic and career needs of their members, as well as to ensure client access to mental health services. They must own their own confusion and uncertainty in the face of the shifting sands of their knowledge bases. They must discourage professional infighting and competition for which discipline or theoretical orientation has the corner on truth and admit what they do not know. They must acknowledge their ethos of self-interest as well as their commitment to care and healing. They must advertise rather than conceal their uncertainties and imperfections. They must own the privileges that accrue to their members, emotionally, financially, personally, and professionally by virtue of being therapists.

In addition, the mental health professions must acknowledge more openly their interdependence with their social context, giving back to it as well as taking from it. This means providing more pro bono contributions to society and mandating *as an ethical obligation* the provision of pro bono contributions by individual providers. While all of the ethics codes include pro bono work as an important part of being an ethical therapist, none of them *require* it and, to my knowledge, no licensing boards mandate it as grounds for licensure renewal. *Doing good* should certainly be as important as *doing no harm* in our ethical requirements and would go a long way in correcting the tarnished image of the mental health professions.

The professional associations could also integrate an expectation of service to the community into their professional credentialing requirements, association newsletters, and awards. If *every* graduate student were required to take an ethics course that included pro bono work as a part of her induction into the ethics of the profession, then *every* one of them would be socialized into the field with this expectation. If *every* professional newsletter had a column advertising pro bono needs as well as workshops, job opportunities, test materials, therapeutic facilities, and conference announcements, the message of giving as well as getting would be a regular part of all professional communications. If *every* annual meeting honored professionals for their pro bono contributions as well as for their research, teaching, or clinical achievements, then giving and taking would have equal status.

Giving back to the context in which the professions exist would also involve more publicity about what the context gives to them. This might include articles about the joys of being a therapist; public interviews about the uncertainties that affect therapists in their personal and professional functioning (rather than those that tend to magnify the therapist's wisdom and expertise); books about how clients have instructed, edified, and helped heal their therapists; anecdotes about *therapist* as well as *client* vulnerability, imperfection, pathology, and humanity.

SUMMARY

As institutions, the mental health professions must model a more humble, open-minded, flexible, honest, and generous approach for their members, who can then model these qualities for their clients. The authoritative, rule-based, legally supervised, self-protective, and dishonest tenor of our ethics codes does not encourage such an approach. The mental health professions must also encourage, on the part of their members, more acknowledgment of and giving back to the community in which they exist. An ethic of multiplicity and mutuality, in which *all* voices—client, significant others, therapist, and community—are privileged, is a more ethical approach to psychotherapy than the rule-based model we currently use.

Chapter 13

Toward an Ethic of Care, Compassion, and Character

This chapter discusses care, compassion, and character as requirements for ethical functioning and addresses the difficulties in nurturing and sustaining these qualities in the current context of rule-based ethics. Care and compassion are essential for clients, but they are also essential for therapists and colleagues. Character-based ethics, which rely on the therapist's capacity to think and behave morally and ethically, are more conducive to ethical functioning than are rule-based ethics.

CARE AND COMPASSION IN A 1990s CONTEXT

Care and compassion are probably viewed by most therapists as an obvious part of their work. If we did not care about people, why did we become therapists in the first place? Yet somehow, in the competitive, litigious market of psychotherapy today, care seems to have become secondary. Other concerns overshadow the ethics of care and compassion—succeeding financially, keeping abreast of paperwork required by managed care, staying educated for licensure renewal, learning risk management strategies, and dealing with our own crises of meaning in a social context in which therapists have lost public confidence and trust. There are new complexities facing us in daily decision making that often require us to think of ethical and legal rules before we think of care and compassion.

Sometimes Threatening, Sometimes Dangerous

Care and compassion sometimes backfire. One example is in the treatment of severely traumatized, often character-disordered clients who confuse the therapist with past perpetrators and threaten her physical, emotional, and/or legal safety. Prior to the evolution of licensing boards in every state and the increase in complaints and lawsuits against practitioners, the therapist could extend herself with such a client out of an ethic of care and compassion. She could do so with some sense of security that she would be supported contextually if the client escalated his transference issues with her by triangulating other people into the therapy relationship. In today's more litigious climate, she cannot count on such contextual support. In fact, she can often count on the opposite.

Anxiety about vulnerability makes it difficult for therapists who continue to work with fragile clients to relate to them primarily out of an ethic of care and compassion. In fact, there is some indication that acting primarily out of this ethic often precedes a complaint process. Therapists who go the extra mile with a client for whom the therapy is his first viable relationship with another human being are often surprised when the client turns against them (Hedges, 1996).

I once had a client who cried profusely about the heroic family role he had had to play in his childhood and his tendency to repeat (at his own expense) the learned patterns of overresponsibility and self-denial in his adult relationships. His story touched me and I was empathic and supportive of his pain. I felt great care and compassion for him. At the end of the session, he looked at me and brusquely pointed out a problematic legal technicality in my intake form (he was a lawyer). Sharing his pain made him feel very vulnerable and his comment about my intake form seemed to help him pull himself back together. I thanked him courteously for his free legal advice. I have never forgotten the lesson I learned in that session. Care and compassion can be threatening to some clients, even though they may desperately need them.

In another situation, I extended care and compassion to a family dealing with a complicated school refusal problem with one of the adolescent sons. The parents had been at war with each other for many years and had squared off the troops, with one son on each side. Previous therapists had not involved the entire family in the treatment. The mother and "her" son were upset that I extended care to *everyone* in the family, even though the family sessions did help the parents unite enough to get the boy back to school.

Many years later, the mother and "her" son wrote me an angry letter, threatening to sue me because I had seen the entire family in treatment. (In a recent therapy experience, the son had been diagnosed as an agoraphobic. The current therapist had told the mother and son that individual therapy was the treatment of choice and that the previous family therapy experience had been a therapeutic error based on misdiagnosis.) The core issue, as I understood it, however, was that I had upset the status quo in the family's organization and beliefs by extending care to *everyone* rather than taking sides in their internal war.

In this case, I later discovered that the mother and son had, in fact, attempted to sue me but were foiled by the expiration of the statute of limitations. In today's litigious context, their claim of misdiagnosis might be more serious than it would have been in the social and professional context of the 1970s when the family first came to my office.

Sometimes, extending care and compassion can not only upset the internecine warfare of a family or threaten a client's vulnerability; it can be dangerous to the therapist. But it is dangerous primarily because of the current social and professional context. If the family described above had filed a suit against me in the 1970s, they would probably not have been successful. They might not even have been able to find a lawyer who would assist them.

The 1990s are another matter entirely. Looking back, there is nothing that I would have done differently with this family. I led with an ethical principle of care and compassion for the entire family, used appropriate family therapy interventions, was successful in helping them accomplish the treatment goals they established, and sought the consultation of experienced colleagues. If the same family approached me today for services, I would probably do exactly the same thing. The only difference would be that I would have more awareness of the risks.

Care and Compassion in a Litigious Context

Hedges (1996) describes the unpredictability of complaints and the hazards of today's psychotherapy marketplace, which render *all* therapists vulnerable: "No one knows how to predict the nature and course of an emergent psychotic reaction and no one can say with certainty that he or she will not be its target" (p. 2).

For those therapists who have been the target of complaints based on honest clinical mistakes and/or client transference problems or psychotic processes, operating from an ethic of care and compassion can become more difficult. Such an ethic requires that we have contextual support for the inevitable complications encountered not only with fragile clients, but potentially with *all* clients. It also means that care and compassion for ourselves and our colleagues, as well as for our clients and our community, must be valued. The following sections discuss the importance of care and compassion for clients, therapist, and colleagues.

CARE AND COMPASSION: ESSENTIAL COMPONENTS IN THE CLIENT-THERAPIST RELATIONSHIP

Miller, Duncan, and Hubble (1997), in a comprehensive review of the literature, demonstrate that the *relationship* between therapist and client is one of the highest predictors of successful psychotherapy outcome. Therapist warmth, acceptance, positive regard, and humanity are more important than *any* specific theoretical orientations or treatment modalities. Many clients, in fact, view the therapist's struggle to understand them (whether he actually does or not) as evidence of an empathic connection. The importance of the therapist's care and compassion permeates *all* successful psychotherapy experiences and is used as one factor in the authors' plea for a unifying language for psychotherapy. Instead of continuing to develop more brands of theory and technique, they argue, we should be looking for the *commonalities* of successful psychotherapy.

In the profiles researchers have gathered on therapists who sexually exploit their clients, empathy, care, and compassion were consistently absent, particularly with repeat offenders. Empathy, care, and compassion are part of what keeps therapists appropriately focused on client need.

Jean Shinoda Bolen (1996, p. 93) describes an experience in her psychiatric residency in which she worked with a patient from a neutral psychoanalytic perspective. Years later, when she saw this same patient in her private practice, he told her that what made a difference to him in his previous relationship with her was that she had smiled at him as he was leaving, no matter what he had said in the session. "Your smile," he said, "told me that I was alright." Bolen understood his comment to mean that her smile was the only nonneutral communication he had experienced with her and the one that most communicated her optimism and care for him.

Years ago, when I was directing a community mental health program, I had a client who faithfully and regularly kept her appointments. She was the mother of thirteen children and a consumer of services in just about every social service agency in town. I wondered what I was doing that she found helpful. I felt overwhelmed by the grinding poverty and seeming hopelessness of her life. One day I asked her why she continued to see me. Her response was "Because you are the only one [of all her various service providers] who really cares." I shall never forget her face when she told me this and the lesson she taught me.

Care and compassion from the therapist are essential ingredients for psychotherapy clients. Their presence in the relationship can go a long way toward buffering an occasional clinical mistake and facilitating healing regardless of theoretical orientation or treatment technique. They can also create anxiety in clients who feel vulnerable, fearful of abandonment, and confused between present and past abuse experiences.

CARE AND COMPASSION:
THE SELF OF THE THERAPIST

As discussed in Chapter 12, the one-sided emphasis on client welfare minimizes the importance of the therapist's care of self and aggravates conditions in which her own self-interest is denied. In order for the therapist to be therapeutic, she must also have care and compassion for herself.

The Need for Personal as Well as Professional Self-Care

Only the *Feminist Therapy Code of Ethics* (Feminist Therapy Institute, 1987) and feminist writers (e.g., Faunce, 1994; Porter,

1995) specifically refer to self-care as an ethical *requirement*. The other codes emphasize professional competence and development, the importance of getting consultation in difficult cases, the need to terminate or refer when the client is not benefitting from treatment or is in need of services beyond the scope of the therapist, and the need for continuing education and training. Nowhere do the other codes suggest the need for routine *personal*, as well as *professional* self-care except when the therapist is impaired.

This absence is particularly glaring because personal as well as professional self-care appear repeatedly in the literature as a prophylactic against burnout and as a necessary part of surviving and remaining therapeutic (Edelwich and Brodsky, 1980; Farber, 1983a,b; Farber and Heifatz, 1981, 1982; Grosch and Olsen, 1994; Guy, 1987; Guy and Liaboe, 1985; Guy, Poelstra, and Stark, 1989; Kottler, 1993; Kottler, Sexton, and Whiston 1994). Personal psychotherapy, hobbies and interests, friendships with nontherapists, extended vacations and sabbaticals, time with family and friends, physical wellness programs, spiritual nourishment, and a good balance between work and play are all part of personal care. So are consultation and supervision, ongoing training programs, interdisciplinary contacts, professional association activities, open discussions of *all* feelings with colleagues and supervisors, reasonable scheduling, and the balance of clinical activities with supervision, consultation, teaching, research, or even another career.

Bolen (1996) talks about the need for *kairos* time as well as *kronos* time for self-care. *Kairos* is soul-nourishing time in which a person becomes oblivious to *kronos*, or measured time, by getting lost in whatever activity (or nonactivity) grabs her. Gardening, surfing, walking in the woods, meditating, sewing, reading novels—whatever removes her from the responsibilities of scheduling and from the "time is money" mentality that controls so much of her professional life.

In addition to the kinds of personal and professional activities described above, an ethic of compassion and care of self for the therapist requires that she stay focused on her own needs, feelings, and points of view as well as on those of her clients during every therapy encounter. Too much empathy can lead to a lack of awareness of self and a merger with the client in ways that can be nonproductive and even harmful in the therapeutic relationship. Too little empathy can lead to a disconnection from the client that can also be nonproductive and harmful.

Honesty About Self-Interest

Staying in touch with their own needs helps therapists be honest about *why* they are doing what they are doing, and when their actions are protective of themselves as well as their clients. Beliefs, for example, that chronic lateness to appointments is a communication about ambivalence or resistance to psychotherapy, suggest therapeutic interpretations that deal with such lateness in the service of the client's needs to heal. Another perspective, however, is that, for most therapists, a client's lateness is irritating because it shortens the session time and makes the work harder, creates empty time which cannot be used to run to the bank or make telephone calls, and may convey (in our culture, anyway) that the client is discourteous and does not value the therapist's time. Owning that lateness is difficult for the *therapist,* in some way models the honesty and clear communication that clients need.

Therapist need is also met through payments for services. While they clearly benefit the therapist, payments for services are often discussed as if they are primarily in the client's best interest. The benfits of paying are believed to enhance the value (and the work) of the therapy. It is the rare therapist who says "*I* need you to pay session by session because *I* do not like the hassles of monthly billing."

My point is that honesty about self-interest is essential to sustaining a positive therapeutic relationship. I once had a client who had trouble with projectile vomiting. She tended to lose control and vomit primarily in public contexts and usually in the presence of family and friends. While there were clear psychological as well as physiological components to the symptom, I was clear from the time of my first contact with this client that I wanted no demonstration of the symptom in my office. I told her that vomiting was not something my stomach could handle and, if she felt a need to do so, she must leave the office. I told her that my difficulty being in the presence of vomiting was so great that even my children rarely vomited when they were growing up. The client had no problem with my stating my needs clearly and even learned something about the control she *did* have over what had heretofore felt like an uncontrollable symptom. She also learned to trust that I would always tell her the truth. After a lifetime of abuse in the name of love, this was essential for her healing.

With suicidal clients, I often talk about *my* needs to have a suicide contract with them so that *I* do not have to worry constantly about them between sessions. The contract is clearly to help *them* stay alive, which they generally want to do or they would not be in therapy in the first place; but, once I have entered into a relationship with them and *care* about them, the contract is also for my needs. I have been struck with how readily most clients will agree to such a contract when I am honest about my need for it as well as theirs. When I first started practice, I generally framed suicide contracts more one-sidedly and got less compliance.

I have also let clients know, from time to time, that their violent or illegal behavior is intolerable to *me*. Not just that it is not in their therapeutic best interests or is in violation of the law, but that it goes beyond the bounds of *my* tolerance.

Case Example

Honesty about one's practice context, the profession, third-party payers, legal and ethical issues, and any other factor that affects the therapist-client relationship is also important, as the following case example illustrates.

Suzanne was referred to me from a colleague in another state when she and her husband were transferred to Atlanta by his employer. When I first saw her, her lifelong chronic depression was aggravated by the total disruption of all of her supportive relationships during the move. Her depression had reached vegetative proportions and she found herself unable to get up in the morning or perform even the simplest of tasks. She was disheveled and inattentive to personal hygiene, disinterested in any activity in which her husband and children tried to engage her, was sleeping twelve to fifteen hours a day and was withdrawn, guarded, and shell-like in all conversations with me.

Gradually, as Suzanne became more communicative and started to feel better, she began to express her fears of becoming too dependent on me and losing me as she had her previous therapist. Simultaneously, her case manager expressed his concerns about the same thing. I had already had this concern myself and was attentive to allowing just enough dependency to keep Suzanne moving in her healing process without fostering the kind of dependency that might interfere with her growth.

I felt I was monitoring this well based on her marked improvement in functioning, both at home and in her neighborhood and community, and also based on her infrequent complaints that I was not giving her enough and or meeting her wishes for more connection with me. I took the latter as evidence that her dependency needs were being both satisfied and frustrated sufficiently to keep her moving in the direction of her own healing. I carefully stayed empathic but unhooked when she periodically escalated symptoms as a way of (unconsciously) trying to commandeer more attention from me. I also helped her husband and children in family sessions to revise their stuck patterns of interaction around Suzanne's symptoms, gradually replacing attention to symptoms with other, more positive, activities and connections in the family.

As Suzanne felt stronger, she began to question the ongoing use of medication and talked with the managed care-referred psychiatrist about tapering off. He was supportive of this but the case manager said that ongoing medication would be required in order to authorize additional psychotherapy sessions for Suzanne with me. Just as Suzanne was ready to take a major step toward independence by tapering off her medication, the case manager was requiring that she either stay on it or terminate all supports. As Suzanne's therapist, I was unsuccessful in advocating for a more gradual move toward termination because of the managed care company's official requirement that medication as well as psychotherapy be used to treat severe depression.

Because of her refusal to continue on medication, the case manager sent Suzanne an official notice that her psychotherapy sessions were limited to one more month. Suzanne's response was to make a suicide attempt. This necessitated a revision in the managed care company's allocation of sessions. By insisting on an all-or-nothing approach, the managed care company had unwittingly fostered Suzanne's regression to old patterns, at her own and her family's expense.

Shortly thereafter, I had a conversation with Suzanne in which I presented all of the dilemmas in our relationship from my perspective. I laid out my ethical concerns in adhering to the managed care company's dictates about medication. I likened her feelings about the company's withdrawal of services to her mother's withdrawal from her. I told her that, although I had tried to advocate for her with the case manager, I had failed and felt impotent, powerless, and unsure of what to do next—and that this was uncomfortable and frustrating for me. I agreed with her that she was not yet finished with the healing process and made it clear in as calm and nonjudgmental a way as possible that the managed care company had a divided agenda—her care and company profits—and that its decision was about its profit margin as well as her treatment needs. I spelled out that requirements about medication in the treatment of depression was a belief used to justify the company's position—and not a "truth."

As I talked, Suzanne's face and body relaxed and she blurted out with apparent relief, "*You* feel powerless, too? I thought it was only me." And, in my response to making explicit the managed care company's dual agenda, she expressed relief that its decision was not her fault. She had expected that I would be angry with her for her suicide attempt and blame her for the "failure" of the therapy. Hearing me admit to the limitations of my power and the vulnerability and helplessness I felt in the face of the managed care company's unmoveable position about medication, Suzanne felt connected with and understood in some very powerful ways. She even empathized with me about how torn I felt ethically.

This conversation led to other discussions about ethical issues. Once she and I had decided how to use the remaining sessions allocated to her, stretching them out over three months, she then asked me, for example, why the psychotherapy professions did not allow for post-therapy friendships between therapist and client. She had hammered this issue out with her previous therapist, who had gently but firmly closed the door on Suzanne's request for a post-therapy friendship without ever really discussing it thoroughly with her.

In hearing Suzanne's question, I understood it as one of her many ways of talking about her dependency needs, her fears about the termination of the therapy relationship with me, the trauma of her mother's frequent emotional abandonments, and her constant questioning about her "loveability." I also heard it as a legitimate ethical question in and of itself. Initially, I started to respond with all of the "protection of the client" rationales promulgated by the various ethical codes, e.g., persistence of power imbalances post-therapy, risks of client exploitation, interference with potential future therapy needs, and so forth. Then, as I watched Suzanne's face and realized that she was less engaged and connected in the conversation than when she had initially raised the question, I knew that I had to respond to her out of my needs as well as hers. She knew at some level that I was only presenting half of the picture. She had had a lifetime of experience in being on the receiving end of a one-sided story with her mother, who always framed her needs as in Suzanne's best interest. She did not need the same lopsided approach from me.

I carefully began to explore with her the unstated "secrets" of the profession, e.g., that ethics rules are often to protect the professional as well as the client. That, while under other circumstances I might be friends with her and with other clients, the demands of trying to maintain friendship connections with so many people would probably eventually burn me out. And that I also might have trouble trying to "hold" confidential information outside of the protection of the therapy sanctum. I shared with her some of my pain in liking my clients and having constantly to say good-bye to them. I also (with a little humor) talked about the therapist's need to be sure that she did not convert all of her clients to friends or she would lose her source of income.

This conversation and several others like it were extremely empowering for Suzanne. Having me make explicit my own (and the profession's and the managed care company's) self-interest agendas was very freeing. By the time we reached the end of the allocated number of sessions, Suzanne was still resisting the termination but was accepting it and, most importantly, was reasonably functional.

The Right to Say No

There are more ways to exploit clients than by taking advantage of them sexually or financially. Emotional exploitation can occur when the therapist is out of touch with his own needs. Ethical principles that address practicing beyond the scope of one's competence should therefore address *emotional* as well as technical competence and the need for personal as well as professional development. Included in these requirements should be some support for the right to say no.

When I was in my graduate training, I was studying and simultaneously trying to deal with the impending death of a very close friend. For my first field placement, I requested a nonmedical setting because I was on emotional overload with my friend's complicated medical needs. I was promptly placed in a pediatric unit of my city's large public hospital. When I queried my advisor regarding the basis of her decision, she informed me that the thing that I was most afraid of was the thing I needed to conquer and that social workers had to learn to set aside their personal needs for the benefit of their clients. I learned to work with the families of dying children but had to distance from my friend somewhat in order to bear the emotional strain. I did well in the field placement but always felt that it was at some expense to my personal life.

The Wounded Healer: Confusions in Definitions of Therapist Impairment

Since my graduate school experience, I have been very tuned in to the importance of personal as well as professional need and have tried to pace my work with clients who touch my vulnerable spots. I feel comfortable in relating to clients who suffer from chronic pain, for example, now that there is some scar tissue over my own experience with it. Over time, my experience has become a gift I can offer my clients. If I had forced myself to do this before I was able, it would have been at both my and my clients' expense. The wounded healer would have been still too wounded to be useful.

All of us, if we live long enough, have difficult situations to face in our own lives—situations that cause trauma, pain, anxiety, fear, and shame. The categorical thinking of current ethics codes does not allow for much vulnerability or imperfection on the part of the therapist. She is either competent or impaired without clear standards to describe either. Where is there acknowledgment for how impairment, if dealt with appropriately and sufficiently, can facilitate client healing? Where is there room for therapists not to rise to the challenge (as my graduate school advisor believed was necessary), if doing so would rub salt into open wounds? Where is there permission to say "I can't?"

If we valued personal self-care as an ethical principle for the benefit of our clients as well as ourselves, these and other questions could be more openly addressed. As it stands now, most therapists are fearful of admitting their vulnerabilities to clients, colleagues, and often, even to family and friends, out of their need to preserve their image as competent and unimpaired.

I once had a client who became upset with me because I would not yield to her demands for between-session time and other special treatment. She accused me of functioning while impaired, referring to my back problems. For awhile, I pondered her accusation. Should I cease practicing psychotherapy until my back sufficiently healed so as to not bother me? Would this ever happen? Was I impaired because I occasionally had to lie on the floor during sessions in order to be comfortable? Should I examine more closely the ways in which I dealt with my physical and emotional pain? Was I, in fact, impaired?

I then thought of colleagues who continued to practice with diagnoses of cancer or in the context of the personal pains created by divorces, deaths of family members, or other life crises. I sought consultation and personal therapy to assist me in my self-examination. I observed the benefits to many clients derived from the ways in which I shared some of the pain of my health crisis with them. I regained perspective.

The literature is beginning to address the complexities and variations of what constitutes impairment and of ways to use and deal with the vagaries and imperfections of therapists in their own life cycles for the benefit of clients (Munn, 1995; Rabinor, 1995; Shub, 1995; Smith, 1995). The ethics codes, however, simply address competence and impairment with no acknowledgment that impairment can be managed therapeutically and can serve as well as harm the client. Dealing with impairment constructively requires more self-disclosure on the part of the therapist, first because the impairment is often obvious and impossible to hide. Second, if denied, it can create confusion in the client-therapist relationship regarding who is responsible for taking care of the therapist.

Self-Disclosure

Self-disclosure is a controversial topic in the psychotherapy professions today and yet it is necessary for adequate care of self in the psychotherapy relationship and for honesty in relating to clients. Self-disclosure starts with being honest with the therapist's self—an awareness of her own feelings and thoughts. What is then disclosed to the client may be minimal and probably will focus primarily on the here and now or on useful anecdotes from the therapist's experience that relate to a particular clinical dilemma.

The more fragile the client and the more her tendency to personalize everything, the more necessary for the therapist to self-disclose. I routinely tell both fragile and not-so-fragile clients that my squirming in my chair is because I am trying to find a comfortable position for my back, and not because I am bored with or inattentive to them. When my mother died, I selectively let clients know that my sad affect was related to my own grieving and not because of anything they were doing or not doing.

Care and compassion for self are essential to doing good work.

CARE AND COMPASSION FOR COLLEAGUES

If we exercise care and compassion for ourselves, we are more able to do so in relation to colleagues. Accepting our own humanity helps us accept the humanity of others. Open discussion of feelings, therapeutic dilemmas with clients, fears, anxieties, sexual attractions, fantasies, and doubts are necessary to competent and ethical professional functioning. Yet open discussions are becoming more and more difficult in a context in which clinical mistakes can become escalated to full-blown ethical violation charges. Professionals are either fearful of complaints or have their heads in the sands of denial, believing that complaints only happen to bad therapists.

When Colleagues Are Accused of Ethical Violations

All of the codes have provisions directing therapists to treat their colleagues with respect. The American Psychological Association *Ethical Principles of Psychologists and Code of Conduct* (1992) and The National Association of Social Workers *Code of Ethics* (1996) both suggest consulting with a colleague suspected of an ethics violation. They encourage attempting to assist the professional in getting help and in correcting the problematic behavior prior to filing an arbitrary, and perhaps unfounded, report. As discussed in Chapter 8, both codes also acknowledge the existence of unfair or frivolous complaints and the importance of not participating in them.

The fact that some therapists support clients in the filing of complaints, without any attempts to talk with the alleged ethics violator, is more than alarming. It is also in direct contradiction, not only with the ethics codes, but also with the systemic knowledge bases that currently guide our work. In the arenas of child custody and child sexual abuse work, for example, we know that it is important for an evaluator to have access to all relevant parties before coming to any conclusive recommendations for the guardian ad litem or the court. Otherwise, the recommendations can be incomplete and skewed. Is it not appropriate to establish similar principles in the evaluation of alleged therapist violators?

As discussed in Chapter 9, I think that no case should be heard by a licensing board or professional association ethics committee that does not have full and complete information from all relevant parties in adjudicating complaints. Full information would include releases to talk with other therapists who have treated the client as well as to the accused therapist, when information from previous therapists is relevant to the accusation. For example, if a client accuses a therapist of incorrect treatment but has also had five previous failed therapy experiences, the prior treatment history is probably relevant to the accusation. If the accusing client refuses to give a release to the investigatory body to obtain such information, the allegation should be discarded.

If a therapist is solicited by a client attempting to get his support for filing a complaint against the client's previous therapist, he should ask for a release to speak to the accused therapist before going willy nilly into the support of a legal complaint process. If not, then the current therapist's behavior should be considered ethically questionable.

Once a complaint has been filed against a therapist, colleagues tend to scatter and gossip and often assume that she is guilty. Even if she is vindicated, she is often seen (and may see herself) as guilty and tainted. An ethical response to such rumor mill contagion is to refuse to participate in it, saying "Any situation has multiple perspectives and I cannot discuss this with you without having access to *all* of them."

If, after a full assessment, the therapist *is* guilty, then she needs compassion, support, and professional services to help in her rehabilitation. With some exceptions, such services are difficult to find. If the therapist is not guilty, then she needs compassion, support, and professional services to help in healing from the trauma of false allegations. Either way, it seems to me that our professional duty should be to connect, not disconnect, from colleagues, regardless of their guilt or innocence. "There but for the grace of God go I." More of us need to get involved in extending a helping hand.

The Role of Ethics Committees in Promoting Care and Compassionate Treatment of Colleagues: Some Recommendations

Support

Ethics committees should be more supportive of therapists. What about saying "good job" to therapists who are vindicated in an ethics investigation rather than just "no violation found?" What about publishing articles in professional association newsletters about competent and ethical functioning in the trenches, not just about therapists' ethical mistakes? What about case anecdotes that describe therapist errors and their rectification?

Acknowledgment of Therapist Vulnerability

In addition, we need to pay more attention to the context of dangerousness and vulnerability with more humble accountings of how therapists can be targeted for complaints regardless of what risk management strategies they use. The current emphasis on rules and risk management implies that, with proper procedures and careful planning, no therapist should be vulnerable. This is grandiosity at its worst and encourages the tendency of therapists to separate from rather than support accused colleagues.

Awareness of False Complaints

We should also pay more attention to the kinds of clients who are likely to file false complaints against therapists so that not only the members of regulatory bodies but also the average practitioner in the field is aware of the possibility of false complaints as part and parcel of practice in the 1990s. This awareness should facilitate a just and compassionate response to colleagues who become targeted.

Peer Consultation Groups as an Ethical Requirement

Perhaps an ethical requirement for therapists should be ongoing participation in peer consultation and support groups in which honest and full disclosure of feelings, uncertainties, and frustrations could be aired. This not only would assist each therapist in dealing with difficult cases but would also provide a ready-made support group to assist him in the event of a complaint. It would also keep others aware of their own vulnerability. Workshops and ongoing training experiences do not foster the necessary trust that such continuing support groups can provide.

Therapist as Well as Client Protection

As discussed in Chapter 8, we also need more support for taking care of both self and colleagues when working with dangerous clients. Just as we have clear mandates for some of the most basic kinds of therapist behavior (e.g., no sexual exploitation), we need clear mandates that protect the therapist from client behavior in extreme situations. A useful frame for such a mandate might be a legal one. Just as child abuse or threats to harm others become a legal, rather than a therapeutic issue, so should violence toward the therapist. It should be grounds for immediate termination with no requirements for facilitating a referral requiring ongoing participation. The therapist's civil rights should not take a backseat to his fiduciary responsibility to clients.

Following this idea, perhaps an exception to confidentiality should be the duty to warn another therapist of a client's dangerousness. How many so-called "dump" referrals are currently made as a way of getting rid of a client? If a client refuses to provide a release for full disclosure to the new therapist, the referring therapist should be allowed to disclose information about dangerousness anyway, without being at risk for a charge of breaching confidentiality. Such a regulation honors an ethic of caring and compassionate concern for colleagues and is ultimately in the client's best interests.

Supervisees in agency settings also need the right to refuse to see clients who present serious risk to their safety. They should be invited to discuss with their supervisors the conditions under which they would feel safe. There is often little or no protection for therapists who must work under agency administrative and supervisory mandates.

I recently spent hours on the telephone with one such supervisee, for example, who had been traumatized by a riot in the inpatient facility in which she worked. The patients had severely injured three staff members. This young woman was feeling relieved that she had not been hurt but guilty that others had been. She was questioning the wisdom of continuing her employment in the facility. When I asked her how the administrator had dealt with the riot, she described a rather laissez faire response that basically minimized the extent of the trauma to staff members and made it clear that they were expected to continue functioning with no changes in the understaffing problem that had fueled the riot in the first place. I advised her to quit based on the lack of any semblance of care and compassion displayed for staff in his attitude. If supervisors do not care for their supervisees, how can supervisees care for their clients? Care and compassion should guide supervision as well as clinical work.

THE CHARACTER OF THE THERAPIST

Care and compassion for self, client, significant others, and community emanate from the *character* of the therapist—her capacity to balance all needs in an ethical, just, fair, and respectful manner; her clarity about the morality of her choices; and her willingness and commitment to act on them. Strength of character is required for true caring and compassion to occur. It is the authentic *person* of the therapist that is the cornerstone of effective psychotherapy (Aponte, 1982; Kaslow, Cooper, and Linsenberg, 1979; Malone and Malone, 1987).

The development of therapist character cannot occur in a vacuum. In addition to all of the personal factors that foster character development, the professions themselves must do more to support and reinforce *the ethical being* of therapists. The professions could, for example, operate more out of the presumption that therapists are (for the most part) honest, caring, and well-motivated professionals who can be trusted not to harm their clients. In socializing new therapists into the professions, the *expectation of morality and character* could be emphasized in intensive discussions of clinical situations that put morality and character to the test.

Professional newsletters, conferences, and journals could highlight the *good* things that therapists are doing to use their character in balanced attention to client, self, significant others, and community. Mentoring relationships could be nurtured and encouraged by the professional associations, even to the point of an expectation that all therapists spend some of their time on a pro bono basis mentoring younger therapists. Client voices reporting the helpful and healing things that their therapists did with them might be given more press. Currently, most professional association newsletters focus more on what therapists have done *wrong* than on what they have done *right* and on education for avoiding mistakes rather than for taking proactive positions.

Fostering *therapist* character also would involve a transformation in the character of the *professions* themselves. As organizations, they must clean up their own moral acts. Individual therapists with strong character cannot function effectively in contexts where immorality— whether it is adaptation to managed care, privileging of destructive beliefs, or blatant self-interest—threatens their functioning.

SUMMARY

Care and compassion are not only essential to the client-therapist relationship, they are also essential in the therapist's approach to himself and to his colleagues. Care and compassion emanate from the character of the therapist—his capacity to be just and fair, clear about the morality of his choices, and committed to acting on them. There are many ways in which the mental health professions could support care, compassion, and character, all based on a presumption of therapist *goodness* as the norm and therapist *badness* as the exception and on the premise that therapist goodness must be nurtured, supported, and developed.

Chapter 14

Toward Transformation

[M]eaning, depending on its context, symbolic nature, and origin, can inspire or oppress.

—Saleebey,
"Culture, Theory, and Narrative:
The Intersection of Meanings in Practice"

True lostness is when you have forgotten the spiritual center of your life, when your values have gotten so warped with time that you do not remember what is truly important.

—T. Brown,
The Tracker

Psychology has no self-help manual for its own affliction.

—J. Hillman,
The Soul's Code: In Search of Character and Caring

PROBLEMS IN OUR CURRENT APPROACH TO ETHICS

In this book, I have described the crisis of meaning in society in general and in the mental health professions in particular. I have discussed the ways in which the professions' attempts to solve the problems engendered by such a crisis in meaning compound the problem. These include attempts to develop more and more scientific knowledge bases, competition among the more than 400 schools of psychotherapy theories, expansion of turf into every possible social institution and every normal aspect of living, increased pathologization of everything, and the development of rule-based ethics codes that distance rather than connect therapists with their clients. These and other trends only thinly disguise the professions' self-interest and self-protection and make them less, rather than more, trustworthy in the eyes of consumers.

The fact that *all* of our beliefs—scientific and otherwise—are socially constructed has tremendous implications for the future of the psychotherapy professions. Unless we begin deconstructing some of our traditional beliefs and acknowledging that they are simply *beliefs* rather than *truths*, we increasingly put ourselves out on a limb that is bound to fall. The wedding of managed care and DSM diagnoses (socially and politically constructed but presented as scientific certainties) has magnified the fragility of the professions' claims; so has a consumer market more skeptical than ever about both our competence and our motivation.

Complaints against therapists are bound to multiply in such a context. Instead of examining the contextual reasons for this, however, the professions' response has been to develop ever-more rule-based ethical standards and ever-more stringent risk management strategies. This jeopardizes the individual practioner and subjects her to more rather than less risk. It dishonestly frames such increased standards and strategies as serving client interest without owning the powerful agenda of institutional self-preservation and self-interest. It also constrains ethical action on the part of therapists, dictating rules that do not lend themselves to the complexities and unique needs of varying human dilemmas and circumstances.

ALTERNATIVE ETHICAL MODELS

I have discussed alternative ethical principles derived from feminism, social constructionism, communal welfare, and therapist character, with an emphasis on the ethics of multiplicity, mutuality, care, compassion, and character—not only for clients, but for ourselves, our colleagues, and our communities. Multiplicity privileges *all* voices, not just the traditionally powerful voices of professionals. Mutuality acknowledges the interconnectedness of client, therapist, significant others, and the community. The ethics of care, compassion, and character *assume* that the therapist can lead from the heart and from strength of character (rather than from rules) and can therefore be trusted to balance the needs of client, self, and others in the treatment relationship.

THE ETHICAL THERAPIST

Awareness of Social Construction and Interdependence

The ethical therapist is aware of the socially constructed meanings that create problems in the lives of clients and works to deconstruct them in the individual therapy arena and to challenge them on the broader playing field of social advocacy. She is sensitized to how self and community are not separate, isolated entities and works to promote healing that benefits the welfare of the client, significant others in the client's life, and the community. She role models the interdependence of individuals with others in her own connections with family and community.

Honoring of Client Voices

The ethical therapist approaches each client from a "not knowing" position and is truly curious about the *client's* as well as *her own* meaning in any situation. She does not lose herself in the client's meaning, but rather works to create a space in which both her meaning and the client's can be heard and respected.

Clarity About Moral Values

The ethical therapist appreciates that the therapeutic relationship must be *mutually* beneficial. She is tuned in to her own feelings, doubts, fantasies, and ideas as well as to the client's. She does not hide her discomfort with violent, immoral, illegal, or other disturbing behaviors behind a veil of neutral acceptance, hoping that they will disappear. Rather, she uses her own moral ideas, presented as *ideas* rather than *truths*, in the client-therapist relationship. She challenges the client to think about the effects of his behavior on others, including the therapist. She takes clear stands about what she will and will not, can and cannot, do in her role as therapist.

Honesty About Self

The ethical therapist is honest about his own self-interest and does not frame everything in terms of client welfare. He is in touch with the benefits, joys, and privileges of being a therapist and keeps these ever present in his work. He is aware of his own human frailties and vulnerabilities and seeks to use them, when appropriate, for both his own and the client's needs, in the service of the therapeutic relationship. He is open to acknowledging and discussing his own mistakes, uncertainties, vulnerabilities, and ethical dilemmas with clients when this would be beneficial to them.

TOWARD AN ETHICAL PERSPECTIVE AT THE INSTITUTIONAL LEVEL

In order to support the ethical functioning of therapists, our professional associations and institutions must change.

From Truth to "Cultures of Healing"

The professions must move from a position of certainty about professional and scientific knowledge to a position that owns that most of what we do constitutes different "cultures of healing" (Fancher, 1995). Each culture is useful with different kinds of clients and therapists and treatment situations. No one culture is true.

The Client-Therapist Relationship as Core

The professions must also work to emphasize the similarities among the various psychotherapy cultures and stop encouraging the emphasis on difference. Since most effective psychotherapy depends more on the *relationship* between client and therapist than on any specific theoretical orientation or treatment technique, it is the *relationship* that should be the primary focus.

Open Boundaries with Other Disciplines

They must support the opening of psychotherapy's boundaries to include knowledge from a wide variety of fields—literature, religion, anthropology, history, and linguistics. Opening boundaries is an antidote to the myopia which has constrained our thinking up to this point.

Acknowledgment of Psychotherapy's Interdependence with Its Context

The professions must acknowledge their interdependence with the sociocultural context and work harder for community as well as individual well-being, not only in advocacy efforts on behalf of large groups of people, but in the support given to individual practitioners for community service work.

Empowering Client Voices

They must start admitting what they don't know and actively listen to the voices of clients and others (including those from different cultures) for ideas about mental health, family functioning, and communal well-being.

Admitting Ordinariness and Imperfection

They must admit their own ordinariness and human imperfections so that they can support the ordinariness and human imperfections of the therapists within their ranks. One of the best places to start would be with the current ethics codes and complaint processes. Changing from a rule-based system of ethics to one that relies on multiplicity, mutuality, care, compassion, therapist character, and the importance of the client-therapist relationship might be a start in acknowledging that therapy is inexact, variable, and imperfect. Because of this, some mistakes are unavoidable.

Assuming a Leadership Role in Addressing Society's Crisis in Meaning

They must stop responding to the crisis of meaning in this society and within themselves by legislating fear-based rules and standards, most of which are more appropriate for attorneys than for therapists. A better way to use their resources would be to take a leadership role in working to change the dispiritedness and hopelessness of our society's current frame of mind. As long as we have an over-emphasis on individualism, profit, survivalism, victimhood, and disregard for the future, individuals (both clients and their therapists) are vulnerable. As long as the professions mirror these traits in their own efforts to stay afloat in today's crisis of meaning, they are rendering both their members *and* clients more, not less, vulnerable. A significant step in changing their own bottom line from profit to people would be a soul-searching examination of their participation in the managed care machine.

Michael Lerner's (1995, 1996) work to create national Summits on Ethics and Meaning and small discussion groups across the country to bring people together to discuss an ethic of *people* rather than of *profit* is one example of how to use our energy. *The Family Therapy Networker,* a magazine and conference sponsor, has joined this effort, encouraging its readers and conference attendees to participate. What if the American Psychiatric Association, the American Psychological Association, the National Association of Marriage and Family Therapists, the American Association for Marriage and Family Therapy, and all of the other mental health professional associations joined in the effort? Couldn't this make a difference in the crisis of meaning?

Supporting Self in Relation to Community

Perhaps the psychotherapy professions have outlived their usefulness. Perhaps transformation is not possible. If it *is*, it will only be in the understanding that the dichotomy between self and other, self and community is artificial. The only true healing of our world will occur when the distinctions disappear. Work at *any* level—individual, family, community, nation—affects all levels and must be attentive of and respectful to all levels.

Nurturing and Supporting Ethical Functioning

Transformation requires that we search for what is *right* about psychotherapy as well as what is *wrong* with it and that we continuously work to expand the possibilities for hope and healing, at both institutional and individual practitioner levels. Miller, Duncan, and Hubble remind us that

> . . . therapists are more likely to facilitate hope and expectation
> in their clients when they stop trying to figure out what is

wrong with them and how to fix it and focus instead on what is possible and how their clients can obtain it. (1997, p. 128)

If we followed this guideline for the professions, it might be instructive. It would shift our energy from making rules and searching out bad therapists (except for extreme cases) to creating the kinds of situations in which good therapists—those who expand possibilities for hope and expectation—can function ethically.

Orienting Toward the Future

Transformation also requires an understanding of how, in the present, we are creating a future. There is a connection between us and the generations yet to come. If we thought more about the future than about our immediate survival, we would reexamine our participation in managed care, risk management strategies, professional infighting and turf-guarding, preservation of boundaried theories created in isolation, and pathologizing of whole populations.

These things might take on a different perspective if we asked ourselves what historians will be saying 100 years from now about the psychotherapy professions. Will they say we were helpful in creating a better tomorrow for the generations yet to come? Will they say we were able to rise above self-interest and survivalism to contribute to a better community? Will they say we contributed to a restoration of hope in our society? "We are fast losing the sense of historical continuity, the sense of belonging to a succession of generations originating in the past and stretching into the future" (Lasch 1979, p. 5). Psychotherapy must play a lead role in thinking about the future.

Role-Modeling Change

Perhaps the magnitude of these questions and the anxiety they evoke make us more comfortable in scurrying around in the managed care cage to maintain our economic solvency—formulating rules, punishing perpetrators, and hunkering down in our disciplinary corners firing potshots at each other—than in addressing the big questions of our times, questions that challenge our existence, usefulness, and trustworthiness. Like the parents whose solution to their symptomatic child is to escalate their disciplinary measures (rather than to question the meaning of the child's symptomatic communication in the family system), the mental health professions are focusing on behaviors—both real and imagined—of therapists. They are doing so without an examination of the meanings of such behaviors in the overall professional and societal context. Focusing on rules and consequences is a detour from the larger problem. We, of all people, should know better. *How can we help clients change if we ourselves do not?*

I recently saw a family in which the adolescent son and his father had come to physical blows with each other after years of mutually exchanged verbal abuse and hostility. The parents had tried unsuccessfully to set rules for the son and were at their wit's end. In the first session, the son cursed, yelled, told his parents they "owed" him because they had brought him into the world, demanded all kinds of material things, and was generally obnoxious and hostile. The father sat on his hands, forcing himself with great effort not to react. The mother cried quietly.

After listening to the son berate his parents, I started asking them questions like "What are the things you as parents most admire about your son? What does your son do well? How does he contribute to the family—just by being who he is? What are your hopes and dreams for him in the future? What kind of a relationship do you want with him? How is he a good person?"

As the parents responded to these questions, the son gradually quieted down and began to listen intently. He literally changed his physical position, moving closer to his parents. The parents' demeanor of hopelessness and depletion changed almost immediately to energetic and passionate renditions of the things they loved about their son and their hopes for him. This, and other conversations like it, created new, more benevolent and hopeful meanings in the family. The son began to cooperate with some of his parents' rules and, with a little coaching in the family sessions, to negotiate new rules and privileges for himself. The parents were able to validate their son's goodness and his contributions to the family. Hope was restored.

This case—and many like it in my office and yours—illustrate the importance of introducing new meaning to clients. New meaning paves the way for all kinds of possibilities for change in ways that rules do not. Writes Bruner (1986, p. 53), " . . . [T]he object of understanding human events is to sense the alternativeness of human possibility." This is the challenge for the mental health professions today. We must challenge *all* of our traditional meanings. Nowhere is this more urgent than in the current beliefs and practices in our professional ethics and standards of care.

We must also understand our interdependence with the world around us and the urgent need to make our world a better place for both the present and the future.

> [W]hen a housefly flaps his wings, a breeze goes round the world; when a speck of dust falls to the ground, the entire planet weighs a little more; and when you stamp your foot, the earth moves slightly off its course. Whenever you laugh, gladness spreads like the ripples in a pond; and whenever you're sad, no one anywhere can be really happy. And it's much the same thing with knowledge, for whenever you learn something new, the whole world becomes that much richer. (Juster, 1961, pp. 233-234)

References

Abramovitz, M. (1991). Putting an end to double speak about race, gender, and poverty: An annotated glossary for social workers. *Social Work 36*(5): 380-384.

Adler, G. (1985). *Borderline psychopathology and its treatment*. Northvale, NJ: Jason Aronson.

Ahrons, C. R., and R. H. Rodgers. (1987). *Divorced families: A multidisciplinary developmental view.* New York: W. W. Norton.

American Association for Marriage and Family Therapy (AAMFT). (1991). *AAMFT code of ethical principles for marriage and family therapists.* Washington, DC: American Association for Marriage and Family Therapy.

American Association of State Social Work Boards. (1997). *Summary of disciplinary actions taken as of January 7, 1997.* Culpepper, VA: American Association of State Social Work Boards.

American Psychiatric Association. (1952). *Diagnostic and statistical manual of mental disorders first edition.* Washington, DC: American Psychiatric Association.

_____. (1966). *Diagnostic and statistical manual of mental disorders, second edition.* Washington, DC: American Psychiatric Association.

_____. (1980). *Diagnostic and statistical manual of mental disorders, third edition.* Washington, DC: American Psychiatric Association.

_____. (1987). *Diagnostic and statistical manual of mental disorders, third edition, revised.* Washington, DC: American Psychiatric Association.

_____. (1994). *Diagnostic and statistical manual of mental disorders, fourth edition.* Washington, DC: American Psychiatric Association.

American Psychological Association (APA). Committee on Professional Standards and Board of Professional Affairs. (1987). *General guidelines for providers of psychological services.* Washington, DC: American Psychological Association.

_____. (1992). *Ethical principles of psychologists and code of conduct.* Washington, DC: American Psychological Association.

_____. (1994). *Guidelines for child custody evaluations in divorce proceedings.* Washington, DC: American Psychological Association. Reprinted in *American Psychologist* (July): 677-680.

_____. (1996). Report of the ethics committee, 1995. *American Psychologist*, December: 1279-1286.

Andersen, M. L. (1994). The many and varied social constructions of intelligence. In *Constructing the social*, ed. T. R. Sarbin and J. I. Kitsuse, pp. 119-138. London: Sage.

Andersen, T. (1992). Reflections on reflecting with families. In *Therapy as social construction*, ed. S. McNamee and K. J. Gergen, pp. 54-68. London: Sage.

Anderson, C. M., and D. P. Holder. (1989). Women and serious mental disorders. In *Women in families: A framework for family therapy,* ed. M. McGoldrick, C. M. Anderson, and F. Walsh, pp. 381-405. New York: W. W. Norton.

Anderson, H., and H. Goolishian. (1992). The client is the expert: A not-knowing approach to therapy. In *Therapy as social construction,* ed. S. McNamee and K. J. Gergen, pp. 25-39. London: Sage.

Anderson, H., H. A. Goolishian, and L. Windermand. (1986). Problem determined systems: Towards a transformation in family therapy. *Journal of Strategic and Systemic Therapies* 5(4): 1-12.

Anderson, S. C. (1994). A critical analysis of the concept of codependency. *Social Work* 39(6): 677-685.

Ansel, L. V. (1996). Bad medicine. *Tikkun* 2(1): 25-28.

Aponte, H. J. (1982). The person of the therapist: The cornerstone of therapy. *Family Therapy Networker* (March-April): 19-22.

Appelbaum, P. S. (1993). Legal liability and managed care. *American Psychologist 48*: 251-257.

Association of State and Provincial Psychology Boards. (1997). *Reported disciplinary actions for psychologists, August, 1983-January, 1997.* Montgomery, AL: Association of State and Provincial Psychology Boards.

Austad, C. S. (1996). *Is long-term therapy unethical? Toward a social ethic in an era of managed care.* San Francisco: Jossey-Bass.

Avis, J. M. (1991). Power politics in therapy with women. In *Women and power,* ed. T. J. Goodrich, pp. 183-200. New York: W. W. Norton.

Ballou, M. (1990). Clients' rights, values, and contexts. In *Feminist ethics in psychotherapy,* ed. H. Lerman and N. Porter, pp. 239-247. New York: Springer.

Barasch, R. (1996). APA false memory group sharply split. *The National Psychologist* 5(4): 1-2.

Barker, R. L. (1992). *Social work in private practice, second edition.* Washington, DC: National Association of Social Workers Press.

Barnett, B., and L. Morris. (1996). The new California administrative procedure act: A step towards due process. *PAN Observer* 2(2): 1,3.

Bateson, M. C. (1989). *Composing a life.* New York: Atlantic Monthly Press.

Bayes, M. (1981). The prevalence of gender-role bias in mental health services. In *Women and mental health,* ed. E. Howell and M. Bayes, pp. 83-85. New York: Basic Books.

Beal, E. W. (1980). Separation, divorce, and single-parent families. In *The family life cycle: A framework for family therapy,* ed. E. A. Carter and M. McGoldrick, pp. 241-264. New York: Gardner.

Bellah, R. N., R. Madsen, W. M. Sullivan, A. Swidler, and S. M. Tipton. (1985). *Habits of the heart: Individualism and commitment in American life.* New York: Harper and Row.

Bennett, B. E., B. K. Bryant, G. R. VandenBos, and A. Greenwood. (1990). *Professional liability and risk management.* Washington, DC: American Psychological Association.

Bentley, K. J. (1993). Points and Viewpoints. The right of psychiatric patients to refuse medication: Where should social workers stand? *Social Work 38*(1): 101-106.

Bergantino, L. (1996). For the defense: Psychotherapy and the law. *Voices* (fall): 29-33.

Berger, P. L., and T. Luckman. (1966). *The social construction of reality: A treatise in the sociology of knowledge.* New York: Doubleday, Anchor Books.

Berliner, A. K. (1989). Misconduct in social work practice. *Social Work* (January): 69-72.

Bernstein, H. (1981). Surveys of threats and assaults directed toward psychotherapists. *American Journal of Psychiatry 35*: 542-549.

Bersoff, D. N. (1975). Professional ethics and legal responsibilities: On the horns of a dilemma. *Journal of School Psychology 13*: 359-376.

Bersoff, D. N. ed. (1995). *Ethical conflicts in psychology.* Washington, DC: American Psychological Association.

Bersoff, D. N., and P. M. Koeppl. (1993). The relation between ethical codes and moral principles. *Ethics and Behavior 3*: 345-357.

Besharov, D. J., and S. H. Besharov. (1987). Teaching about liability. *Social Work* (November-December): 517-522.

Biaggio, M., and B. Greene. (1995). Overlapping/dual relationships. In *Ethical decision making in therapy: Feminist perspectives*, ed. E. J. Rave and C. C. Larsen, pp. 88-123. New York: Guilford.

Bograd, M. (1992). The duel over dual relationships. *Family Therapy Networker* (November/December): 33-37.

Bolen, J. S. (1996). *Close to the bone: Life-threatening illness and the search for meaning.* New York: Scribner.

Borys, D. S., and K. S. Pope. (1989). Dual relationships between therapist and client: A national study of psychologists, psychiatrists, and social workers. *Professional Psychology: Research and Practice 20*: 283-293.

Boscolo, L., G. Cecchin, L. Hoffman, and P. Penn. (1987). *Milan systemic family therapy.* New York: Basic Books.

Boston Women's Health Collective. (1984). *Our bodies, ourselves.* New York: Simon and Schuster.

Bowen, M. (1978). *Family therapy in clinical practice.* New York: Jason Aronson.

Bouhoutsos, J., J. Holroyd, H. Lerman, B. Forer, and M. Greenberg. (1983). Sexual intimacy between psychotherapists and patients. *Professional Psychology: Research and Practice 14*: 185-196.

Boyle, M. (1994). Gender, science and sexual dysfunction. In *Constructing the social*, ed. T. R. Sarbin and J. I. Kitsuse, pp. 101-118. London: Sage.

Breggin, P. R. (1991). *Toxic psychiatry.* New York: St. Martin's Press.

Bridges, N. A. (1995). Psychotherapy with therapists: Countertransference dilemmas. In *A perilous calling: The hazards of psychotherapy practice*, ed. M. B.

Sussman, pp. 175-187. New York: John Wiley and Sons. Revision of paper published in 1993. *American Journal of Orthopsychiatry 63*(1): 34-44.

Brieland, D. (1990). The Hull-House tradition and the contemporary social worker: Was Jane Adams really a social worker? *Social Work* (March): 134-138.

Briere, J. (1989). *Therapy for adult survivors molested as children: Beyond survival.* New York: Springer.

Brock, G. W., and J. Coufal. (1994). A national survey of the ethical practices and attitudes of marriage and family therapists. In *Ethics casebook,* ed. G. W. Brock, pp. 27-48. Washington, DC: American Association for Marriage and Family Therapy.

Brodsky, A. M., and J. Holroyd. (1981). Report of the task force on sex bias and sex-role stereotyping in psychotherapeutic practice. In *Women and mental health*, ed. E. Howell and M. Bayes, pp. 98-112. Study authorized by the Board of Professional Affairs of the American Psychological Association, 1974. New York: Basic Books.

Broverman, I. I., and D. M. Broverman, F. E. Clarkson, P. S. Rosenkrantz, and S. R. Vogel. (1970). Sex-role stereotypes and clinical judgments of mental health. *Journal of Consulting and Clinical Psychology, 34*: 1-7.

Brown, L. S. (1994). *Subversive dialogues: Theory in feminist therapy.* New York: HarperCollins, Basic Books.

Brown, T. Jr. (1982). *The tracker.* New York: Berkley Books.

Bruner, J. (1986). *Actual minds, possible worlds.* Cambridge: Harvard University Press.

_____. (1990). *Acts of meaning.* Cambridge: Harvard University Press.

Buber, M. (1958). *I and thou.* New York: Charles Scribner's Sons.

Butler, K. (1994). Surviving the revolution. *Family Therapy Networker* (March-April): 28-29.

_____. (1995). Caught in the crossfire. *Family Therapy Networker* (March-April): 28-29.

Calof, D. (1993). Facing the truth about false memory. *Family Therapy Networker* (September-October): 39-45.

Caudill, B. (1991). Administrative injustice: How therapists are denied due process before the licensing boards. *Association for the Advancement of Psychology Newsletter* (summer): 11, 15.

Cecchin, G. (1992). Constructing therapeutic possibilities. In *Therapy as social construction*, ed. S. McNamee and K. J. Gergen, pp. 86-95. London: Sage.

Cecchin, G., G. Lane, and W. Ray. (1992). *Irreverence: A strategy for therapists' survival.* London: Karnac Books.

Charles, S. C., and E. Kennedy. (1985). *Defendant: A psychiatrist on trial for medical malpractice.* New York: The Free Press.

Chesler, P. [1972], (1989). *Women and madness.* New York: Harcourt Brace, Harvest.

Coale, H. W. (1989a). A family systems approach to child abuse: The mental health professional. In *Child abuse and neglect: An interdisciplinary method of treatment*, ed. N. Barker, pp. 101-116. Dubuque, IA: Kendall Hunt.

_____. (1989b). Common dilemmas in relationships. *Journal of Strategic and Systemic Therapies*, 8(1): 10-15.

_____. (1992). The constructivist emphasis on language: A critical conversation. *Journal of Strategic and Systemic Therapies 11*(1): 12-26.

_____. (1994). Using cultural and contextual frames to expand possibilities. *Journal of Systemic Therapies 13*(2): 5-23.

_____. In press. Therapeutic rituals and rites of passage: Helping parentified children and their families. In *Parentified children: Theory, research and treatment*, ed. N. Chase. Thousand Oaks, CA: Sage.

Comstock, C., and D. Vickery. (1992). The therapist as victim: A preliminary discussion. *Dissociation 5*(3): 155-158.

Conran, T., and J. Love. (1993). Client voices: Unspeakable theories and unknowable experience. *Journal of Systemic Therapies 12*(2): 1-19.

Cooperstock, R. (1981). A review of women's psychotropic drug use. In *Women and mental health*, ed. E. Howell and M. Bayes, pp. 131-140. New York: Basic Books.

Courtois, C. (1988). *Healing the incest wound: Adult survivors in therapy.* New York: W. W. Norton.

Craig, T. J. (1982). An epidemiologic study of problems associated with violence among psychiatric inpatients. *American Journal of Psychiatry 139*: 1262-1266.

Cummings, M., and S. Sobel. (1985). Malpractice insurance: Update on sex claims. *Psychotherapy 22*: 186-188.

Davis, J. W. (1981). Counselor licensure: Overkill? *Personnel and Guidance Journal 60*(2): 83-85.

Dawes, R. M. (1994). *House of cards: Psychology and psychotherapy built on myth.* New York: The Free Press.

Dean, R. G., and M. L. Rhodes. (1992). Ethical-clinical tensions in clinical practice. *Social Work 37*(2): 128-132.

Dell, P. F. (1983). Is pathology normal? From pathology to ethics. *Family Therapy Networker 7*(6): 29-31, 64.

Denton, W. (1989). DSM III-R and the family therapist: Ethical considerations. *Journal of Marital and Family Therapy 15*(4): 367-378.

Dillard, A. (1974). *Pilgrim at Tinker Creek.* New York: Harper Perennial.

Doherty, W. J. (1989). Unmasking family therapy. *Family Therapy Networker* (March-April): 34-39.

_____. (1991). Virtue ethics: The person of the therapist. *American Family Therapy Academy Newsletter* (winter): 6-9.

_____. (1993). I'm OK, you're OK, but what about the kids? *Family Therapy Networker* (September-October): 46-53.

_____. (1995). *Soul searching: Why psychotherapy must promote moral responsibility.* New York: HarperCollins, Basic Books.

DuMez, E., manager, Office of Ethics and Adjudication, National Association of Social Workers. (1997). Telephone conversation with author. January 14.

Dumont, M. P. (1990). Editorial. In bed together at the market: Psychiatry and the pharmaceutical industry. *American Journal of Orthopsychiatry 60*(4): 484-485.

Dutton, M. A., and F. L. Rubenstein. (1995). Working with people with PTSD: Research implications. In *Compassion fatigue: Coping with secondary traumatic stress disorder in those who treat the traumatized*, ed. C. R. Figley, pp. 82-100. New York: Brunner/Mazel.

Edelwich, J., and A. Brodsky. (1980). *Burn-out: Stages of disillusion in the helping professions*. New York: Human Sciences Press.

Efran, J. S. and L. E. Clarfield. (1992). Constructionist therapy: Sense and nonsense. In *Therapy as social construction*, ed. S. McNamee and K. J. Gergen, pp. 200-217. London: Sage.

Efran, J. S., M. D. Lukens, and R. J. Lukens. (1990). *Language, structure and change: Framewords of meaning in psychotherapy*. New York: W. W. Norton.

Ehrenberg, M. F., and M. F. Elterman. (1995). Evaluating allegations of sexual abuse in the context of divorce, child custody, and access disputes. In *True and false allegations of child sexual abuse*, ed. T. Ney, pp. 209-230. New York: Brunner/Mazel.

Ehrenreich, B. (1989). *Fear of falling: The inner life of the middle class*. New York: HarperCollins, HarperPerennial.

Ehrenreich, B., and D. English. (1978). *For her own good: 150 years of the experts' advice to women*. New York: Doubleday, Anchor Books.

English, O. S. (1976). The emotional stress of psychotherapy practice. *Journal of the American Academy of Psychoanalysis 4*: 191-201.

Epstein, E. K. and V. E. Loos. (1989). Some current thoughts on the limits of family therapy: Toward a language-based explanation of human systems. *Journal of Family Psychology 2*: 405-421.

Epston, D. and M. White. (1992). *Experience, contradiction, narrative, and imagination*. Adelaide, South Australia: Dulwich Centre Publications.

Erikson, E. H. (1950). *Childhood and society*. New York: W. W. Norton.

Estés, C. P. (1992). *Women who run with the wolves*. New York: Ballantine.

Everson, M. D. and B. W. Boat. (1989). False allegations of sexual abuse by children and adolescents. *Journal of the American Academy of Child and Adolescent Psychiatry 28*(2): 230-235.

Faludi, S. (1991). *Backlash: The undeclared war against American women*. New York: Doubleday, Anchor Books.

Family Therapy News. (1997). Legal issues surrounding false memories (February): 16, 25.

Fancher, R. T. (1995). *Cultures of healing: Correcting the image of American mental health care*. New York: W. H. Freeman.

Farber, B. A. (1983a). Dysfunctional aspects of the psychotherapeutic role. In *Stress and burn-out in the human service professions*, ed. B. A. Farber, pp. 97-118. New York: Pergamon.

———. (1983b). The effects of psychotherapeutic practice upon psychotherapists. *Psychotherapy Theory, Research and Practice 20*(2): 174-182.

Farber, B. A., and L. J. Heifetz. (1981). The satisfactions and stresses of psychotherapeutic work: A factor analytic study. *Professional Psychology 12*: 621-630.

_____. (1982). The process and dimensions of burnout in psychotherapists. *Professional psychology 13*(2): 293-301.

Faunce, P. S. (1994). The self-care and wellness of feminist therapists. In *Feminist ethics in psychotherapy*, ed. H. Lerman and N. Porter, pp. 123-130. New York: Springer.

Fausto-Sterling, A. (1985). *Myths of gender: Biological theories about women and men.* New York: Basic Books.

Feldman-Summers, S., and G. Jones. (1984). Psychological impacts of sexual contact between therapists or other health care professionals and their clients. *Journal of Consulting and Clinical Psychology, 52*: 1054-1061.

Feminist Therapy Institute, Inc. (1987). *Feminist therapy code of ethics.* Denver: Feminist Therapy Institute, Inc. Reprinted in *Ethical decision making in therapy: Feminist perspectives*, ed. E. J. Rave and C. C. Larsen, pp. 38-41. New York: Guilford.

Figley, C. R. (1995a). Compassion fatigue as secondary traumatic stress disorder: An overview. In *Compassion fatigue: Coping with secondary traumatic stress disorder in those who treat the traumatized*, ed. C. R. Figley, pp. 1-20. New York: Brunner/Mazel.

Figley, C. R., ed. (1995b). *Compassion fatigue: Coping with secondary traumatic stress disorder in those who treat the traumatized.* New York: Brunner/Mazel.

Fish, V. (1993). Poststructuralism in family therapy: Interrogating the narrative/conversational mode. *Journal of Marital and Family Therapy 19*(3): 221-232.

Fisher, K. (1985). Charges catch clinicians in cycle of shame, slipups. *APA Monitor 16*(5): 6-7.

Fleischer, J. A. and A. Wissler. (1985). The therapist as patient: Special problems and considerations. *Psychotherapy 22*(3): 587-594.

Foucault, M. (1972). *The archaeology of knowledge and the discourse on language.* New York: Pantheon Books.

Frankl, V. E. ([1959], 1984). *Man's search for meaning.* New York: Washington Square Press, Pocket Books.

Freedberg, S. (1993). The feminine ethic of care and the professionalization of social work. *Social Work 38*(5): 535-540.

Freudenberger, H. J. (1983). Burnout: Contemporary issues, trends, and concerns. In *Stress and burnout in the human service professions*, ed. B. A. Farber, pp. 23-28. New York: Pergamon.

Friedan, B. (1963). *The feminine mystique.* New York: Dell.

Friedman, E. H. (1985). *Generation to generation: Family process in church and synagogue.* New York: Guilford.

Fruggeri, L. (1992). Therapeutic process as the social construction of change. In *Therapy as social construction*, ed. S. McNamee and K. J. Gergen, pp. 40-53. London: Sage.

Gabbard, G. O. (1995). Psychotherapists who transgress sexual boundaries with patients. In *Breach of trust: Sexual exploitation by health care professionals and clergy*, ed. J. C. Gonsiorek, pp. 133-144. Thousand Oaks, CA: Sage.

Gabbard, G. O. and S. M. Wilkinson. (1994). *Management of countertransference with borderline patients.* Washington, DC: American Psychiatric Press.

Gabel, P., T. Rosenbaum, and N. Schorr. (1996). Meaning matters. Politics of meaning draft platform, plant on law. Drafted at The National Summit on Ethics and Meaning and printed in *Tikkun 11*(5): 31-35.

Ganaway, G. K. (1989). Historical versus narrative truth: Clarifying the role of exogenous trauma in the etiology of MPD and its variants. *Dissociation 2*: 205-220.

Gardner, R. A. (1987). *The parental alienation syndrome and the differentiation between fabricated and genuine child sex abuse.* Cresskill, NJ: Creative Therapeutics.

Gergen, K. J. (1991). *The saturated self: Dilemmas of identity in contemporary life.* New York: HarperCollins, Basic Books.

_____. (1994). *Realities and relationships.* Cambridge: Harvard University Press.

Gilligan, C. (1982). *In a different voice: Psychological theory and women's development.* Cambridge: Harvard University Press.

Goldner, V. (1985). Feminism and family therapy. *Family Process 14*: 31-47.

_____. (1988). Generation and gender: Normative covert hierarchies. *Family Process 27*: 17-31.

Gonsiorek, J. C. (1995). Assessment for rehabilitation of exploitive health care professionals and clergy. In *Breach of trust: Sexual exploitation by health care professionals and clergy,* ed. J. C. Gonsiorek, pp. 145-162. Thousand Oaks, CA: Sage.

Good, M. D., and B. J. Good. (1989). Disabling practitioners: Hazards of learning to be a doctor in American medical education. *American Journal of Orthopsychiatry 59*(2): 303-309.

Goodman, M., C. J. Stewart, and F. Gilbert. (1977). Patterns of menopause: A study of certain medical and physiological variables among Caucasian and Japanese women living in Hawaii. *Journal of Gerontology 32*: 297. Cited in A. Fausto-Sterling (1985), *Myths of gender: Biological theories about women and men.* New York: Basic Books.

Goodrich, T. J. (1991). Women, power, and family therapy: What's wrong with this picture? In *Women and power,* ed. T. J. Goodrich, pp. 33-35. New York: W. W. Norton.

Goolishian, H. A., and H. Anderson. (1988). Human systems as linguistic systems: Preliminary and evolving ideas about the implications for clinical theory. *Family Process 27*: 317-394.

Gottlieb, A. (1997). Crisis of consciousness: Therapy's split personality: Quick fixes versus soulcraft. *Utne Reader* (January-February): 44-48, 106-109.

Gottlieb, M. C. (1993). Avoiding exploitive dual relations: A decision-making model. *Psychotherapy 40*: 41-47.

Gould, K. H. (1988). Old wine in new bottles: Feminist perspective on Gilligan's theory. *Social Work* (September-October): 411-415.

Gove, W. R. (1972). The relationship between sex roles, marital status, and mental illness. *Social Focus 51*: 34-44.

Greenburg, S. L., and J. H. Greenburg. (1988). Malpractice litigation: Fears and facts. In *Psychotherapy in private practice 6*(1), 47-62.

Greenleaf, B. (1978). *Children through the ages: A history of childhood.* New York: McGraw-Hill.

Greenspan, M. (1995). Out of bounds. *Common Boundary* (July-August): 51-56.

Griffin, S. (1992). *A chorus of stones: The private life of war.* New York: W. W. Norton.

Grosch, W. N., and D. C. Olsen. (1994). *When helping starts to hurt: A new look at burnout among psychotherapists.* New York: W. W. Norton.

Grotstein, J. S. (1981). *Splitting and projective identification.* New York: Jason Aronson.

Group for the Advancement of Psychiatry Committee on the Family. (1996). Global assessment of relational functioning scale (GARF): 1. Background and rationale. *Family Process 35*: 155-172.

Gutheil, T. G., and G. O. Gabbard. (1995). The concept of boundaries in clinical practice: Theoretical and risk-management dimensions. In *Ethical Conflicts in Psychology*, ed. D. N. Bersoff, pp. 218-223. Washington, DC: American Psychological Association. Reprinted from *American Journal of Psychiatry 150*: 188-196.

Guy, J. D. (1987). *The personal life of the psychotherapist.* New York: John Wiley and Sons.

Guy, J. D., and G. P. Liaboe. (1985). The impact of conducing psychotherapy on psychotherapists' interpersonal functioning. *Professional Psychology: Research and Practice 17*(2): 111-114.

Guy, J. D., P. L. Poelstra, and M. J. Stark. (1989). Personal distress and therapeutic effectiveness: National survey of psychologists practicing psychotherapy. *Professional Psychology: Research and Practice 20*(1): 48-50.

Haas, L. J., and N. A. Cummings. (1995). Managed outpatient mental health plans: Clinical, ethical, and practical guidelines for participation. *Professional Psychology: Research and Practice 22* (1991): 45-51. Reprinted in *Ethical conflicts in psychology*, ed. D. N. Bersoff, pp. 506-511. Washington, DC: American Psychological Association.

Haas, L. J., J. L. Malouf, and N. H. Mayerson. (1986). Ethical dilemmas in psychological practice: Results of a national survey. *Professional Psychology: Research and Practice 17*: 316-321.

Haley, J. (1981). *Leaving Home.* New York: McGraw Hill.

Hare-Mustin, R. T. (1989). The problem of gender in family therapy theory. In *Women in families: A framework for family therapy*, ed. M. McGoldrick, C. M. Anderson, and F. Walsh, pp. 61-77. New York: W. W. Norton. Revised from *Family Process* (1987) *26*: 15-33.

_____. (1991). Sex, lies, and headaches: The problem is power. In *Women and Power*, ed. T. J. Goodrich, pp. 63-85. New York: W. W. Norton.

Hare-Mustin, R. T., and J. Marecek. (1990). Gender and the meaning of difference: Postmodernism and psychology. In *Making a difference: Psychology and the construction of gender*, ed. R. T. Hare-Mustin and J. Marecek, pp. 22-64. New Haven: Yale University Press.

Hare-Mustin, R., J. Marecek, A. G. Kaplan, and N. Liss-Levinson. (1995). Rights of clients, responsibilities of therapists. *American Psychologist 34* (1979): 3-16. Reprinted in *Ethical conflicts in psychology,* ed. D. N. Bersoff, pp. 305-310. Washington, DC: American Psychological Association.

Harrington, M. (1962). *The other America: Poverty in the United States.* New York: Macmillan.

Harris, E. A. (1995). The importance of risk management in a managed care environment. In *A perilous calling: The hazards of psychotherapy practice*, ed. M. B. Sussman, pp. 247-258. New York: John Wiley and Sons.

Hatti, S., W. R. Dubin, and K. J. Weiss. (1982). A study of circumstances surrounding patient assaults on psychiatrists. *Hospital and Community Psychiatry 33*: 660-661.

Haug, I. (1994). Notes from the ethics committee. *Family Therapy News* (February): 27.

Hedges, L. E. (1993a). In praise of the dual relationship, part 1. *The California Therapist* (May-June): 46-50.

_____. (1993b). In praise of the dual relationship, part 2. *The California Therapist* (July-August): 42-46.

_____. (1993c). In praise of the dual relationship, part 3. *The California Therapist* (September-October): 36-41.

_____. (1996). False accusations against therapists: Where are they coming from, why are they escalating, when will they stop? *PAN Observer 2*(1): 1-2, 4-5.

Held, B. (1990). What's in a name? Some confusions and concerns about constructivism. *Journal of Marital and Family Therapy 16*(2): 179-186.

Herman, J. L. (1992). *Trauma and recovery.* New York: HarperCollins, Basic Books.

Hillman, J. (1996). *The soul's code: In search of character and caring.* New York: Random House.

_____. (1997). Waking up with the house on fire: An interview with James Hillman. By S. Perry. *Utne Reader* (January-February): 53-55.

Hillman, J., and M. Ventura. (1992). *We've had a hundred years of psychotherapy and the world's getting worse.* New York: HarperCollins, HarperSanFrancisco.

Hiratsuka, J. (1988). Attacks by clients threaten social workers. *NASW News* (September): 3.

Hoffman, L. (1985). Beyond power and control: Toward a second order family systems therapy. *Family Systems Medicine 3*(4), 381-396.

_____. (1990). Constructing realities: An art of lenses. *Family Process 29*(1): 13-28.

_____. (1992). A reflexive stance for family therapy. In *Therapy as social construction*, ed. S. McNamee and K. J. Gergen, pp. 7-24. London: Sage.

Hogan, D. B. (1983). The effectiveness of licensing: History, evidence, and recommendations. *Law and Human Behavior 7*(2-3): 117-138.

Holder, D. P., and C. M. Anderson. (1989). Women and serious mental disorders. In *Women in families: A framework for family therapy*, ed. M. McGoldrick, C. M. Anderson, and F. Walsh, pp. 381-405. New York: W. W. Norton.

Holstein, J. A., and J. F. Gubrium. (1994). Constructing family: Descriptive practice and domestic order. In *Constructing the social*, ed. T. R. Sarbin and J. I. Kitsuse, pp. 232-250. London: Sage.

Houston-Vega, M. K., and E. M. Nuehring, with E. R. Daguio. (1997). *Prudent practice: A guide for managing malpractice risk.* Washington, DC: National Association of Social Workers Press.

Howell, E. (1981). The influence of gender on diagnosis and psychopathology. In *Women and mental health*, ed. E. Howell and M. Bayes, pp. 153-159. New York: Basic Books.

Imbert, P. T., executive vice-president, American Professional Agency. (April 1, 1992). Personal communication cited in F. G. Reamer. (1995). Malpractice claims against social workers: First facts. *Social Work 40*(5): 595-601.

Inger, I., and J. Inger, (1994). *Creating an ethical position in family therapy.* London: Karnac Books.

Jacobson, N. (1995). The overselling of therapy. *Family Therapy Networker* (March-April): 40-47.

Jayaratne, S., and W. A. Chess. (1983). Job satisfaction and burnout in social work. In *Stress and burnout in the human service professions*, ed. B. A. Farber, pp. 129-141. New York: Pergamon.

Jayaratne, S., T. Croxton, and D. Mattison. (1997). Social work professional standards: An exploratory study. *Social work 42*(2): 187-199.

Jobes, D. A., and J. T. Maltsberger. (1995). The hazards of treating suicidal patients. In *A perilous calling: The hazards of psychotherapy practice*, ed. M. B. Sussman, pp. 200-216. New York: John Wiley and Sons.

Johnson, D. A., and D. Huff. (1987). Licensing exams: How valid are they? *Social Work*: 75-77.

Jones, D. P. H., and J. M. McGraw. (1987). Reliable and fictitious accounts of sexual abuse to children. *Journal of Interpersonal Violence 2*(1): 27-45.

Jordan, A.E., and N. M. Meara. (1990). Ethics and the professional practice of psychologists. *Professional Psychology: Research and Practice 21*: 107-114.

Juster, N. (1964). *The phantom tollbooth.* New York: Random House, Windward.

Kagle, J. D., and P. N. Giebelhausen. (1994). Dual relationships and professional boundaries. *Social Work 39*(2): 213-220.

Kaslow, F. W. (1984). Divorce: An evolutionary process of change in the family system. *Journal of Divorce 7*: 21-39.

——. (1993). Relational diagnosis: An idea whose time has come? *Family Process 32*: 255-259.

Kaslow, F., B. Cooper, and M. Linsenberg. (1979). Family therapist authenticity as a key factor in outcome. *International Journal of Family Therapy 1*(2): 184-199.

Keeney, B. P. (1983). *Aesthetics of change.* New York: Guilford.

Keeney, B. P., and J. M. Ross. (1985). *Mind in therapy: Constructing systemic family therapies.* New York: Basic Books.

Kelly, G. A. (1955). *The psychology of personal constructs, volumes 1 and 2.* New York: W. W. Norton.

Kernberg, O. ([1975] 1985). *Borderline conditions and pathological narcissism.* New York: Jason Aronson.

Kipper, W. (1986). Violence and the social worker. *New Society* (26 September): 7-8.

Kirk, S. A., and H. Kutchins. (1992). *The selling of DSM: The rhetoric of science in psychiatry.* New York: Aldine de Gruyter.

Kluft, R. (1994). Countertransference in the treatment of multiple personality disorder. In *Countertransference in the treatment of PTSD,* ed. J. P. Wilson and J. D. Lindy, pp. 122-150. New York: Guilford.

Knudson-Martin, C., and A. R. Mahoney. (1996). Gender dilemmas and myth in the construction of marital bargains: Issues for marital therapy. *Family Process* 35: 137-152.

Kottler, J. A. (1993). *On being a therapist, revised edition.* San Francisco: Jossey-Bass.

Kottler, J. A., T. L. Sexton, and S. C. Whiston. (1994). *The heart of healing: Relationships in therapy.* San Francisco: Jossey-Bass.

Kübler-Ross, E. (1969). *On death and dying.* New York: Macmillan.

Kutchins, H., and S. A. Kirk. (1988). The business of diagnosis: DSM-III and clinical social work. *Social Work* (May-June): 215-220.

Lakoff, G. (1987). *Women, fire, and dangerous things.* Chicago: University of Chicago Press.

Lakoff, G., and M. Johnson. (1980). *Metaphors we live by.* Chicago: University of Chicago Press.

Lakoff, R. (1975). *Language and women's place.* New York: Harper and Row, Harper Colophon Books.

_____. (1990). *Talking power: The politics of language.* (New York): Harper-Collins, Basic Books.

Lambert, D. A., and T. G. McGuire. (1991). Determinants of stringency of psychologist licensure. *International Journal of Law and Psychiatry* 14(4): 315-329.

LaSala, M. A. (1994). Due process is long overdue. *PAN Observer* 1(1): 1, 6.

Lasch, C. (1979). *The culture of narcissism: American life in an age of diminishing expectations.* New York: W. W. Norton.

_____. (1984). *The minimal self: Psychic survival in troubled times.* New York: W. W. Norton.

Lerman, H., and D. N. Rigby. (1994). Boundary violations: Misuse of the power of the therapist. In *Feminist ethics in psychotherapy,* ed. H. Lerman and N. Porter, pp. 51-59. New York: Springer.

Lerner, M. (1995). The assault on psychotherapy. *Family Therapy Networker* (September-October): 44-52.

_____. (1996). *The politics of meaning: Restoring hope and possibility in an age of cynicism.* New York: Addison-Wesley.

Levy, C. S. (1993). *Social work ethics on the line.* Binghamton, NY: The Haworth Press.

Lewis, H. C. (1981). What's in a word? *Stepfamily Bulletin* (3): 4-6.

_____. (1983). Teaching therapists to use their right brains. *Journal of Systemic and Strategic Therapies* 4(1): 13-23.

_____. (1985). Family therapy with stepfamilies. *Journal of Strategic and Systemic Therapies* 4(1): 13-23.

Lewis, J. L., and D. R. Stokes. (1996). Obligated clinician self-disclosure: One therapist's interventions following a family member's publicized murder. *Journal of Marital and Family Therapy* 22(1): 41-52.

Lexchin, J. (1988). The medical profession and the pharmaceutical industry: An unhealthy alliance. *International Journal of Health Services* 18(4): 603.

Lidz, C. W., A. Meisel, E. Zerubavel, M. Carter, R. M. Sestak, and L. H. Roth. (1984). *Informed consent: A study of decision making in psychiatry.* New York: Guilford.

Lion, J. R., and W. H. Reid, eds. (1983). *Assaults within psychiatric facilities.* New York: Grune and Stratton.

Lipchik, E. (1991). Spouse abuse: Challenging the party line. *Family Therapy Networker* (May-June): 59-63.

Littlechild, B. (1995). Violence against social workers. *Journal of Interpersonal Violence* 10(1): 123-130.

Loftus, E., and K. Ketcham. (1994). *The myth of repressed memory: False memories and ligations of sex abuse.* New York: St. Martin's.

Loftus, E. F., and M. D. Yapko. (1995). Psychotherapy and the recovery of repressed memories. In *True and false allegations of child sexual abuse*, ed. T. Ney, pp. 176-191. New York: Bruner/Mazel.

Lott, B. (1990). Dual natures or learned behavior: The challenge to feminist psychology. In *Making a difference: Psychology and the construction of gender*, ed. R. T. Hare-Mustin and J. Marecek, pp. 65-101. New Haven: Yale University Press.

Maccoby, E. E. (1988). Gender as a social category. *Developmental Psychology* 24: 755-765.

MacNab, S. S. (1995). Listening to your patients, yelling at your kids: The interface between psychotherapy and motherhood. In *A perilous calling: The hazards of psychotherapy practice*, ed. M. B. Sussman, pp. 37-44. New York: John Wiley and Sons.

Madanes, C. (1984). *Behind the one way mirror.* San Francisco: Jossey-Bass.

Madden, D., J. F. Lion, and M. W. Penna. (1976). Assaults on psychiatrists by patients. *American Journal of Psychiatry* 133: 422-425.

Malone, T. P., and P. T. Malone. (1987). *The art of intimacy.* New York: Simon and Schuster, Fireside.

Maltsberger, J. T. (1993). A career plundered. *Suicide and Life-Threatening Behavior* 23: 285-291.

Marine, E., vice-president, American Professional Agency. (1997). Telephone conversations with author. January 15 and March 25.

Marmor, J. (1983). The feeling of superiority: An occupational hazard in the practice of psychotherapy. *American Journal of Psychiatry 110*: 370-376.

Marziali, E., and L. Alexander. (1991). The power of the therapeutic relationship. *American Journal of Orthopsychiatry, 61*(3): 383-391.

Maser, J. D., C. Kaelber, and R. E. Weise. (1991). International use and attitudes toward DSM-III and DSM-III-R: Growing consensus in psychiatric classification. *Journal of Abnormal Psychology 100*: 171-179.

Maslach, C. (1976). Burned-out. *Human Behavior 5*: 16-22.

Masson, J. M. (1984). *The assault on truth: Freud's suppression of the seduction theory.* New York: Farrar, Straus and Giroux.

_____. (1986). *A dark science: Women, sexuality, and psychiatry in the nineteenth century.* New York: Farrar, Straus and Giroux.

McCann, I. L., and L. A. Pearlman. (1990). Vicarious traumatization: A framework for understanding the psychological effects of working with victims. *Journal of Traumatic Stress 3*(1): 131-149.

McGoldrick, M. (1989). Women through the family life cycle. In *Women in families: A framework for family therapy*, ed. M. McGoldrick, C. M. Anderson, and F. Walsh, pp. 200-226. New York: W. W. Norton.

McGoldrick, M., C. M. Anderson, and F. Walsh. (1989). Women in families and family therapy. In *Women in families: A framework for family therapy*, ed. M. McGoldrick, C. M. Anderson, and F. Walsh, pp. 3-15. New York: W. W. Norton.

McGoldrick, M., and E. A. Carter. (1980). Forming a remarried family. In *The family life cycle: A framework for family therapy*, ed. M. McGoldrick and E. A. Carter, pp. 165-194. New York: Gardner Press.

Meyrowitz, J. (1985). *No sense of place.* New York: Oxford University Press.

Middleton, D., and D. Edwards, eds. (1990). *Collective remembering.* London: Sage.

Miller, J. B. (1991). Women and power reflections ten years later. In *Women and power*, ed. T. J. Goodrich, pp. 36-47. New York: W. W. Norton. Reprinted from Work in Progress Series from the Stone Center for Developmental Services and Studies. (1982). Wellesley, MA: Wellesley College.

Miller, S. D., B. L. Duncan, and M. A. Hubble. (1997). *Escape from Babel: Toward a unifying language for psychotherapy practice.* New York: W. W. Norton.

Minuchin, S. (1982). Reflections on boundaries. *American Journal of Orthopsychiatry 552*(4): 655-663.

_____. (1991). The seductions of constructivism. *Family Therapy Networker* (September-October): 47-50.

Morawski, J. G. (1990). Toward the unimagined: Feminism and epistemology in psychology. In *Making a difference: Psychology and the construction of gender*, ed. R. T. Hare-Mustin and J. Marecek, pp. 150-183. New Haven: Yale University Press.

Munn, K. T. (1995). Making room for illness in the practice of psychotherapy. In *A perilous calling: The hazards of psychotherapy practice*, ed. M. B. Sussman, pp. 100-114. New York: John Wiley and Sons.

National Association of Social Workers. (1989). *NASW standards for the practice of clinical social work (revised edition)*. Washington, DC: National Association of Social Workers.

_____. Council on the Practice of Clinical Social Work. (1991). *NASW guidelines for the private practice of clinical social work*. Silver Spring, MD: National Association of Social Workers.

_____. (1995). *Overview of a decade of adjudication*. Washington, DC: National Association of Social Workers.

_____. (1996). *Code of Ethics*. Washington, DC: National Association of Social Workers.

_____. National Council on the Practice of Clinical Social Work, Office of Policy and Practice. (1996). *Social work practice update: Evaluation and treatment of adults with the possibility of recovered memories of childhood sexual abuse*. Washington, DC: National Association of Social Workers.

_____. The Massachusetts Chapter. (n.d.) Committee for the study of violence against social workers. Brochure from the Committee for the Study and Prevention of Violence Against Social Workers. Boston, MA: National Association of Social Workers.

National Association of Social Workers Insurance Trust and The American Professional Agency. Professional Liability Insurance Program. (1997). *Claims experience, individual policies, 1969-1996*. Washington, DC: NASW Insurance Trust.

NASW News. (1995). Lawsuits: No more immunity. Washington, DC: National Association of Social Workers (January): 7.

_____. (1995). Study cites most-reported ethics breaches. Washington, DC: National Association of Social Workers (April): 4.

_____. (1997). Board's restriction of privacy opposed. (March): 14.

Newhill, C. E. (1995). Client violence toward social workers: A practice and policy concern for the 1990s. *Social Work 40*(5): 631-636.

Newman, R., and P. M. Bricklin. (1991). Parameters of managed mental health care: Legal, ethical, and professional guidelines. *Professional Psychology: Research and Practice 22*: 26-35.

Newman, F., and K. J. Gergen. (1995). Diagnosis: The human cost of the rage to order. Paper presented at the 103rd annual convention of the American Psychological Association. New York.

Newmark, M., and C. Beels. (1994). The misuse of science in family therapy. *Family Process 33*: 3-17.

Ney, T. (1995). Assessing allegations in child sexual abuse: An overview. In *True and false allegations of child sexual abuse*, ed. T. Ney, pp. 3-20. New York: Brunner/Mazel.

Nolan, J. O., and E. C. Marine. (1997). Malpractice claims management: An insurance perspective. Unpublished paper presented at the Illinois Psychiatric Society Meeting, Oakbrook, IL. March 1.

Norris, D. (1990). *Violence against social workers: The implications for practice.* London: Kingsley.

Ofshe, R., and E. Watters. (1994). *Making monsters: False memories, psychotherapy, and sexual hysteria.* New York: Charles Scribner's Sons.

Otto, R. K., and W. C. Schmidt. (1991). Malpractice in verbal psychotherapy: Problems and potential solutions. *Forensic Reports 4*(3): 309-336.

PAN Observer. (1994) 1(1).

Passoth, R. (1995). Letter to Editor. *Family Therapy News* (February): 5-6.

Pearlman, L. A., and K. W. Saakvitne. (1995). *Trauma and the therapist: Countertransference and vicarious traumatization in psychotherapy with incest survivors.* New York: W. W. Norton.

Peck, M. S. (1983). *People of the lie: The hope for healing human evil.* New York: Simon and Schuster, Touchstone.

Peele, S. (1989). *The diseasing of America: Addiction treatment out of control.* Lexington, MA: Lexington Books.

Peterson, J. (1997). Apology and clarification. Letter to the editor, *Family Therapy Networker* (January-February): 7.

Peterson, M. R. (1992). *At personal risk: Boundary violations in professional-client relationships.* New York: W. W. Norton.

Philipson, I. (1993). *On the shoulders of women: The feminization of psychotherapy.* New York: Guilford.

_____. (1994). Following the money: Why fewer and fewer men are becoming therapists. *Family Therapy Networker* (March-April): 40-44.

Pipher, M. (1994). *Reviving Ophelia: Saving the selves of adolescent girls.* New York: Ballantine Books.

_____. (1996). *Shelter of each other: Rebuilding our families.* New York: G. P. Putnam's Sons, Grosset/Putnam.

_____. (1997). The family. Interview with R. Simon, ed. *Family Therapy Networker* (January-February): 25-33.

Pittman, F. (1992). It's not my fault. *Family Therapy Networker* (January-February: 56-63.

Pope, K. S. (1986). New trends in malpractice cases and changes in APA liability coverage. *The Independent Practitioner 6*(4): 979-981.

_____. (1991). Dual relationships in psychotherapy. *Ethics and Behavior 1*: 22-34.

_____. (1988). How clients are harmed by sexual contact with mental health professionals: The syndrome and its prevalence. *Journal of Counseling and Development 67*: 222-226.

_____. (1994). *Sexual involvement with therapists: Patient assessment, subsequent therapy, forensics.* Washington, DC: American Psychological Association.

Pope, K. S., J. L. Sonne, and J. Holroyd. (1993). *Sexual feelings in psychotherapy: Explorations for therapists and therapists-in-training.* Washington, DC: American Psychological Association.

Porter, N. (1995). Therapist self-care: A proactive ethical approach. In *Ethical decision making in therapy: Feminist perspectives,* ed. E. J. Rave and C. C. Larsen, pp. 247-266. New York: Guilford.

Postman, N. (1982). *The disappearance of childhood.* New York: Vintage.

Professional Advocacy Network. (n.d.) Membership brochure. Los Angeles, CA: Professional Advocacy Network.

Rabinor, J. K. (1995). Overcoming body shame: My client, myself. In *A perilous calling: The hazards of psychotherapy practice,* ed. M. B. Sussman, pp. 89-99. New York: John Wiley and Sons.

Reamer, F. G. (1995). Malpractice claims against social workers: First facts. *Social Work 40*(5): 595-601.

Rimpoche, S. (1992). *The Tibetan book of living and dying.* San Francisco: HarperCollins, HarperSanFrancisco.

Rosenbaum, R., and J. Dyckman. (1995). Integrating self and system: An empty intersection? *Family Process 34*: 21-44.

Rothman, C. G. (1984). Philanthropists, therapists, and activists. Cambridge, MA: Schenkman Publishing Company.

Rowett, C. (1986). *Violence in social work.* Cambridge, England: Institute of Criminology.

Saleebey, D. (1994). Culture, theory, and narrative: The intersection of meanings in practice. *Social Work 39*(4): 351-359.

Sarbin, T. R. (1964). Anxiety: Reification of a metaphor. *Archives of General Psychiatry 10*: 630-638. Cited in R. S. Hallam. (1994). Some constructionist observations on "anxiety" and its history. In *Constructing the social,* ed. T. R. Sarbin and J. I. Kitsuse, pp. 139-156. London: Sage.

———. (1968). Ontology recapitulates philology: The mythic nature of anxiety. *American Psychologist 23*: 411-418. Cited in R. S. Hallam. (1994). Some constructionist observations on "anxiety" and its history. In *Constructing the social,* ed. T. R. Sarbin and J. I. Kitsuse, pp. 139-156. London: Sage.

Schoener, G. R. (1989a). A look at the literature. In *Psychotherapists' sexual involvement with clients: Intervention and prevention,* ed. G. R. Schoener, J. H. Milgrom, J. C. Gonsiorek, E. T. Luepker, and R. M. Conroe, pp. 11-50. Minneapolis, MN: Walk-in Counseling Center.

———. (1989b). Sexual involvement of therapists with clients after therapy ends: Some observations. In *Psychotherapists' sexual involvement with clients: Intervention and prevention,* ed. G. R. Schoener, J. H. Milgrom, J. C. Gonsiorek, E. T. Luepker, and R. M. Conroe, pp. 265-287. Minneapolis, MN: Walk-in Counseling Center.

Schoener, G. R., and J. H. Milgrom. (1989). False or misleading complaints. In *Psychotherapists' sexual involvement with clients: Intervention and prevention,* ed. G. R. Schoener, J. H. Milgrom, J. C. Gonsiorek, E. T. Luepker, and R. M. Conroe, pp. 147-155. Minneapolis, MN: Walk-in Counseling Center.

Schultz, L. (1987). The social worker as a victim of violence. *Social Casework* *68*: 240-244.

_____. (1989). The victimization of social workers. *Journal of Independent Social Work 3*: 51-63.

Seattle Times. (1993). Psychologist wins apology and $100,000. December 29.

Sheehy, G. (1976). *Passages: Predictable crises of adult life.* New York: Bantam Books.

Sherven, J. (1994). Guilty until proven innocent. *The Independent Practitioner* (spring): pp. 48-50. Washington, DC: American Psychological Association, Division 42.

Shields, C. G., L. C. Wynne, S. H. McDaniel, and B. A. Gawinski. (1994). The marginalization of family therapy: A historical and continuing problem. *Journal of Marital and Family Therapy 20*(1): 117-138.

Shotter, J. (1990). The social construction of remembering and forgetting. In *Collective remembering,* ed. D. Middleton and D. Edwards, pp. 120-138. London: Sage.

_____. (1993). *Conversational realities: Constructing life through language.* London: Sage.

Shub, N. F. (1995). The journey of the characterologic therapist. In *A perilous calling: The hazards of psychotherapy practice,* ed. M. B. Sussman, pp. 61-80. New York: John Wiley and Sons.

Signore, C. (1996). Therapist hurt by therapy. *Family Therapy News* (August): 2,14.

Singer, M. T., and J. Lalich. (1996). *Crazy therapies: What are they? Do they work?* San Francisco: Jossey-Bass.

Sluzki, C. (1992). Transformations: A blueprint for narrative changes in therapy. *Family Process 31*: 217-230.

Smith, E. W. L. (1995). On the pathologization of life: Psychotherapist's disease. In *A perilous calling: The hazards of psychotherapy practice,* pp. 81-89. New York: John Wiley and Sons.

Smith, R. C. (1978). Psychology and the courts: Some implications for recent judicial decisions for state licensing boards. *Professional Psychology* (August): 489-497.

Smith-Rosenberg, C. (1973). Puberty to menopause: The cycle of femininity in 19th century America. *Feminist Studies 1.* Cited in A. Fausto-Sterling. (1985). *Myths of gender: Biological theories about women and men.* New York: Basic Books.

Specht, H., and M. Courtney. (1994). *Unfaithful angels: How social work has abandoned its mission.* New York: Macmillan, The Free Press.

Spence, D. (1984). *Narrative truth and historical truth: Meaning and interpretation in psychoanalysis.* New York: W. W. Norton.

Spiegel, D. (1994). Dissociated or fabricated: Psychiatric aspects of repressed memory in criminal and civil cases. *International Journal of Clinical and Experimental Hypnosis 17*(4): 411-432.

Stanley, L., ethics case manager, American Association for Marriage and Family Therapy. (1997a). Telephone conversation with author. January 6.

_____. (1997b). Letter describing Ethics Committee's findings in cases deliberated from 1994-1996. Washington, DC: American Association for Marriage and Family Therapy. February 14.

Star, B. (1984). Patient violence/therapist safety. *Social Work 29*: 225-230.

Stark, M. (1995). The therapist as recipient of the patient's relentless entitlement. In *A perilous calling: The hazards of psychotherapy practice*, ed. M. B. Sussman, pp. 188-199. New York: John Wiley and Sons.

Steinberg, L., executive director, Professional Advocacy Network. (1997). Telephone conversation with author. January 14.

Stephenson, P. S., and G. A. Walker. (1979). The psychiatrist-woman patient relationship. *Canadian Journal of Psychiatry 24*: 5-16.

Stern, L. (1990). The future of private practice: Weathering the uncertain times ahead. *Family Therapy Networker* (November-December): 54-57, 65.

Stone, L. G. (1980). A study of the relationships among anxious attachment, ego functioning, and female patients' vulnerability to sexual involvement with their male psychotherapists. Unpublished doctoral dissertation. Los Angeles: California School of Professional Psychology.

Strasburger, L. H., L. Jorgenson, and R. Randles. (1991). Criminalization of psychotherapist-patient sex. *American Journal of Psychiatry 148*: 859-863.

Strong, T. (1993). DSM-IV and describing problems in family therapy. *Family Process 32*: 249-253.

Sturkie, K., past president, Association of Marital and Family Therapy Regulatory Boards. (1997). Telephone conversation with author. January 28.

Sullivan, W. M. (1996). Experts and citizens: Rethinking professionalism. *Tikkun 11*(1): 15-18.

Sussman, M. B., ed. (1995). *A perilous calling: The hazards of psychotherapy practice*. New York: John Wiley and Sons.

Taggart, M. (1989). Epistemological equality as the fulfillment of family therapy. In *Women and families: A framework for family therapy*, ed. M. McGoldrick, C. M. Anderson, and F. Walsh, pp. 97-116. New York: W. W. Norton.

Tavris, C. (1990). The politics of codependency. *Family Therapy Networker* (January-February): 43.

_____. (1992). *Mismeasure of woman*. New York: Simon and Schuster, Touchstone.

Terr, L. (1994). *Unchained memories: True stories of traumatic memories, lost and found*. New York: Simon and Schuster.

Tick, E. (1995). Therapist in the combat zone. In *A perilous calling: The hazards of psychotherapy practice,* ed. M. B. Sussman, pp. 24-36. New York: John Wiley and Sons.

Tomm, K. (1991). The ethics of dual relationships. *The Calgary Participator* (winter): 11-15.

Tomm, K., C. Storm, S. Engelberg, N. Ratcliff. (1993). Dual relationships: sex, power, and exploitation. Panel discussion at the 50th annual meeting of the

American Association for Marriage and Family Therapy Annual Meeting. Annaheim, CA.

Visher, E. B., and J. S. Visher. (1979). *Step-families: A guide to working with step-parents and step-children.* New York: Brunner/Mazel.

———. (1982). *How to win as a step-family.* Chicago: Contemporary Books.

Vygotsky, L. (1962). *Thought and language.* Cambridge: M. I. T. Press. Cited in J. Bruner. (1986). *Actual minds, possible worlds.* Cambridge: Harvard University Press.

———. (1978). *Mind in society: The development of higher psychological processes,* ed. M. Cole, S. Scribner, V. John-Steiner, and E. Souderman. Cambridge: Harvard University Press. Cited in J. Bruner. (1986). *Actual minds, possible worlds.* Cambridge; Harvard University Press.

Waites, E. A. (1993). *Trauma and survival: Post-traumatic and dissociative disorders in women.* New York: W. W. Norton.

Walsh, F., and M. Scheinkman. (1989). (Fe)male: The hidden gender dimension in models of family therapy. In *Women in families: A framework for family therapy,* ed. M. McGoldrick, C. M. Anderson, and F. Walsh, pp. 16-41. New York: W. W. Norton.

Walters, M. (1990). The codependent Cinderella who loves too much . . . fights back. *Family Therapy Networker* (July-August): 552-557.

Walters, M., B. Carter, P. Papp, and O. Silverstein. (1988). *The invisible web: gender patterns in family relationships.* New York: Guilford.

Watkins, S. A., and J. C. Watkins. (1989). Negligent endangerment: Malpractice in the clinical context. *Journal of Independent Social Work* 3(3): 35-50.

Watson, H., and M. Levine. (1989). Psychotherapy and mandated reporting of child abuse. *American Journal of Orthopsychiatry* 59(2): 246-256.

Watts, P. (1996). Are we becoming a profession without a soul? *National Psychologist* (July-August): 18.

Weiner, M., and D. Marcus. (1994). A sociocultural construction of "depressions." In *Constructing the social,* ed. T. R. Sarbin and J. R. Kitsuse, pp. 213-231. London: Sage.

Weiner-Davis, M. (1995). *How to fire your shrink: Do it yourself strategies for change.* New York: Simon and Schuster.

Weissman, M. M., and G. L. Klerman. (1981). Sex differences in the epidemiology of depression. *Archives of General Psychiatry* 34: 98-111.

White, M. (1984). Pseudoencopresis: From avalanche to victory, from vicious to virtuous cycles. *Journal of Family Systems Medicine* 2(2).

———. (1995). *Re-authoring lives: Interviews and essays.* Adelaide, South Australia: Dulwich Centre Publications.

White, M., and D. Epston. (1990). *Narrative means to therapeutic ends.* New York: W. W. Norton.

White, W. L. (1995). A systems perspective on sexual exploitation by clients of professional helpers. In *Breach of trust: Sexual exploitation by health care professionals and clergy,* ed. J. C. Gonsiorek, pp. 176-192. Thousand Oaks, CA: Sage.

Whiteside, M. (1982). Remarriage: A family developmental process. *Journal of Marital and Family Therapy 89*(1): 49-68.

Whitman, R. M., B. B. Armao, and O. B. Dent. (1976). Assault on the therapist. *American Journal of Psychiatry 133*: 426-429.

Whitmont, E. W. (1993). *The alchemy of healing: Psyche and soma.* Berkely, CA: North Atlantic Books.

Wilson, J. P., and J. D. Lindy. (1994a). Empathic strain and countertransference. In *Countertransference in the treatment of PTSD,* ed. J. P. Wilson and J. D. Lindy, pp. 5-30. New York: Guilford.

_____. (1994b). *Countertransference in the treatment of PTSD.* New York: Guilford.

Wood, N. (1974). *Many winters.* Garden City, New York: Doubleday.

Woody, J. D. (1990). Resolving ethical concerns in clinical practice: Toward a pragmatic model. *Journal of Marital and Family Therapy 16*(2): 135-150.

Wright, R. H. (1981). Psychologists and professional liability (malpractice) insurance. *American Psychologist 36*: 1485-1493.

Wylie, M. S. (1989). Looking for the fence posts. *Family Therapy Networker* (March-April): 23-33.

_____. (1994). Endangered species: Is private practice becoming an oxymoron? *Family Therapy Networker* (March-April): 30-33.

_____. (1995). DSM and the medical model. *Family Therapy Networker* (May-June): 27.

Yapko, M. (1994). *Suggestions of abuse: True and false memories of childhood sexual trauma.* New York: Simon and Schuster.

Yuille, J. C., M. Tymofievich, and D. Marxsen. (1995). The nature of allegations of child sexual abuse. In *True and false allegations of child sexual abuse,* ed. T. Ney, pp. 21-46. New York: Brunner/Mazel.

Index

OTHER RECENTLY PUBLISHED BOOKS FROM
HAWORTH PSYCHOTHERAPY/MENTAL HEALTH

A FEMINIST CLINICIAN'S GUIDE
TO THE MEMORY DEBATE
**Edited by Susan Contratto, EdD,
and M. Janice Gutfreund, PhD**
Makes proactive statements of what constitutes ethical,
healing treatment for the profoundly deforming
experience of child sexual abuse.
(A monograph published simultaneously as
Women & Therapy, Vol. 19, No. 1.)
$29.95 hard. ISBN: 1-56024-822-X.
$14.95 soft. ISBN: 1-56023-085-1. 1996. 140 pp.

THE RELATIONAL SYSTEMS MODEL
FOR FAMILY THERAPY
Living in the Four Realities
Donald R. Bardill, PhD, MSW

Over **250** Pages!

Teaches the therapist important self-differentiating
capacities that set the tone for creating a powerful
therapeutic atmosphere.
$49.95 hard. ISBN: 0-7890-0074-1.
$24.95 soft. ISBN: 0-7890-0183-7.
1996. 278 pp. with Index.

ELABORATE SELVES
Edited by Anthony Molino, NCPsyA

Over **200** Pages!

Explores the life work and thought of a diverse
group of therapists who have played key roles
in furthering postmodern perspectives on self experience.
(A monograph published simultaneously as
The Psychotherapy Patient, Vol. 10, Nos. 1/2.)
$34.95 hard. ISBN: 0-7890-0011-3.
Text price (5+ copies): $19.95. 1996. 225 pp.

CALL OUR TOLL-FREE NUMBER: 1–800–HAWORTH
US & Canada only / 8am–5pm ET; Monday–Friday
Outside US/Canada: + 607–722–5857
FAX YOUR ORDER TO US: 1–800–895–0582
Outside US/Canada: + 607–771–0012

E-MAIL YOUR ORDER TO US: getinfo@haworth.com

VISIT OUR WEB SITE AT: http://www.haworth.com

Visit our online catalog and search for
publications of interest to you by title,
author, keyword, or subject! You'll find
descriptions, reviews, and complete tables
of contents of books and journals
http://www.haworth.com

TAKE 20% OFF EACH BOOK! Special Sale!

Order Today and Save!

TITLE	ISBN	REGULAR PRICE	20%–OFF PRICE

- Discount good only in US, Canada, and Mexico and not good
  in conjunction with any other offer.
- Discount not good outside US, Canada, and Mexico.
- Individual orders outside US, Canada, and Mexico must be prepaid
  by check, credit card, or money order.

Please complete the information below or tape your business card in this area.

NAME _____

ADDRESS _____

_____

CITY_____

STATE_____ZIP_____

COUNTRY_____

COUNTY (NY residents only)_____

TEL _____ FAX _____

E-MAIL_____
May we use your e-mail address for confirmations and other types of
information? ( ) Yes ( ) No. We appreciate receiving your e-mail address
and fax number. Haworth would like to e-mail or fax special discount offers to
you, as a preferred customer. We will never **share, rent, or exchange** your
e-mail address or fax number. We regard such actions as an invasion of your
privacy.

- Postage & handling: US: $3.00 for first book & $1.25 for each additional
  book; Outside US: $4.75 for first book & $1.75 for each additional book.
- In Canada: Add 7% for GST after postage & handling.
- Outside USA, Canada, and Mexico: Add 20%
- MN, NY, and OH residents: Add appropriate local sales tax.
- If paying in Canadian funds, please use the current
  exchange rate to convert total to Canadian dollars.
- Payment in UNESCO coupons welcome.
- Please allow 3–4 weeks for delivery after publication.
- Prices and discounts subject to change without notice.

❑ **BILL ME LATER** ($5 service charge will be added).
(Bill-me option available on US/Canadian/Mexican orders only. Not good for
subscription agencies. Service charge is waived for booksellers/wholesalers/jobbers.)

Signature _____

❑ PAYMENT ENCLOSED_____
(Payment must be in US or Canadian dollars by check or money order drawn on a US or Canadian bank.)

❑ PLEASE CHARGE TO MY CREDIT CARD:

❑ VISA ❑ MASTERCARD ❑ AMEX ❑ DISCOVER ❑ DINERS CLUB

Account #_____ Exp Date _____

Signature _____
May we open a confidential credit card account for you for possible future
purchases? ( ) Yes ( ) No

The Haworth Press, Inc. (14) 02/98 BBC98
10 Alice Street, Binghamton, New York 13904–1580 USA